Galatians
Pentecostal Commentary

Pentecostal Commentary Series

Editor

John Christopher Thomas

Deo Publishing

GALATIANS

Pentecostal Commentary

Gordon D. Fee

BLANDFORD FORUM

Pentecostal Commentary Series

Published by Deo Publishing
P.O. Box 6284, Blandford Forum, Dorset DT11 1AQ, UK

Reprinted by Henry Ling Ltd, at the Dorset Press, Dorchester, DT1 1HD, UK

The Odyssea Greek font used in the publication of this work is available from Linguist's Software, Inc., www.linguistsoftware.com, PO Box 580, Edmonds, WA 98020-0580 USA, tel. (425) 775-1130.

British Library Cataloguing-in-Publication data
A catalogue record for this book is available from the British Library

ISBN 978-1-905679-02-7

Contents

Editor's Preface

The purpose of this commentary series is to provide reasonably priced commentaries written from a distinctively Pentecostal perspective primarily for pastors, lay persons, and Bible students. Therefore, while the works are based upon the best of scholarship, they are written in popular language. The aim is to communicate the meaning of the text, with minimal technical distractions.

In order to explain the need for such an attempt to read the biblical text, it is necessary to understand something of the ethos of Pentecostalism.

Pentecostalism is a relatively recent phenomenon in comparison to its Christian siblings, given that its formal origins go back about a hundred years. By any means of calculation it continues to grow very rapidly in many places around the globe and accounts for a not insignificant percentage of the world's Christians. Current estimates of those who would identify themselves as part of the Pentecostal-Charismatic movements range from 380,000,000 to 600,000,000. According to David Barrett, the global profile of Pentecostalism is as follows:

> Some 29 percent of all members worldwide are white, 71 percent are nonwhite. Members are more urban than rural, more female than male, more children (under eighteen years) than adults, more third-world (66 per cent) than western world (32 per cent), more living in poverty (87 per cent) than affluence (13 per cent), more family-related than individualist.[1]

Yet, despite its demographic significance, Pentecostalism continues to be largely misunderstood by many outside the movement. For example, there are those who '... see Pentecostalism as essentially fundamentalist Christianity with a doctrine of Spirit baptism and gifts added on' and others who view it '... as an experience which fits equally well in any spirituality or theological system – perhaps adding some needed zest or interest.'[2] Yet, those who know the tradition well are aware

---

[1] D. Barrett, 'Statistics, Global', *Dictionary of the Pentecostal and Charismatic Movements* (S.M. Burgess and G.B. McGee, eds.; Grand Rapids: Zondervan, 1988), p. 811.

[2] Steven J. Land, *Pentecostal Spirituality: A Passion for the Kingdom* (JPTS 1; Sheffield:

how far from the truth such assessments are. As Donald W. Dayton[3] and Steven J. Land[4] have demonstrated, standing at the theological heart of Pentecostalism is the message of the five-fold gospel: Jesus is Savior, Sanctifier, Holy Spirit Baptizer, Healer, and Coming King. This paradigm not only identifies the theological heart of the tradition, but also immediately reveals the ways in which Pentecostalism as a movement is both similar to and dissimilar from others within Christendom. When the five-fold gospel paradigm is used as the main point of reference Pentecostalism's near kinship to the holiness tradition is obvious, as is the fundamental difference with many of those within the more reformed evangelical tradition. It also reveals the surprising similarities between Pentecostalism and the Roman Catholic and Orthodox traditions.

Therefore, the production of a Pentecostal Commentary Series representative of the tradition's ethos requires more than simply selecting contributors who have had a glossolalic experience. Rather, the process of composition as well as the physical format of the commentary should be in keeping with the ethos and spirituality of the tradition.

In the attempt to insure a writing process representative of the tradition, each contributor has been urged to incorporate the following disciplines in the writing of the commentary on a particular biblical book.

Writers have been encouraged to engage in prayer for this project, both as individuals and as members of a community of believers. Specifically, the guidance of the Holy Spirit has been sought in these times of prayer, for the leadership of the Spirit in interpretation is essential. Specific times of prayer where the body intercedes on the writer's behalf and seeks to hear from the Lord have been encouraged.

Given the Pentecostal commitment to body ministry, where various members of the body have specific calls and responsibilities, writers have been asked to explore ways in which their scholarship might be contextualized within their own local church body and thereby be strengthened by the dynamic interaction between the Holy Spirit, the body of Christ, and the Word of God. Writers were encouraged to covenant with their churches concerning this writing project in order to seek out their spiritual support. Where possible, writers were asked to explore the possibility of leading a group Bible study on the given biblical book. Ideally, such groups included representatives from each group of the target readership.

Sheffield Academic Press, 1993), p. 29.

[3] Donald W. Dayton, *The Theological Roots of Pentecostalism* (Peabody, MA: Hendrickson, 1991).

[4] Land, *Pentecostal Spirituality*.

Writers were also encouraged to seek out the advice and critique of gifted colleagues who would join with them in this project so as not to work in isolation. This endeavor was conceived as too difficult and far reaching to go alone. Rather it is conceived of as part of the ministry of the body of Christ, for the glory of God.

The commentary attempts to be in keeping with the ethos and spirituality of the tradition in its physical format as well. Specifically, the commentaries seek to reflect the dialogical way in which the tradition tends to approach the biblical text. Thus, each commentary begins with a series of questions designed to lift up corporate and individual issues that are illuminated in the biblical book under examination. This section identifies those key issues that are taken up in the commentary which follows. As a hermeneutical task, this section invites the reader to interpret his/her life context in a confessional-critical manner, revealing the need(s) to be addressed by the text. Such an opening serves to contextualize the commentary in the life of the church from the very beginning and serves to teach the reader how the Bible can legitimately be used in contemporary life.

Flowing out of this initial section, the introduction proper seeks to inform the reader as to the need, process, purpose, time, and place of composition. As a trajectory of the initial section, the introduction proper seeks be a necessity for the reader, and seeks to avoid the strange and irrelevant discussions that introductions often pursue. The introductions normally include topics of special interest to Pentecostals along with the normal introductory matters of authorship, place of composition, destination, audience, date, and theological emphases. A rather detailed discussion of the genre and structure of the book forms the basis of organization for the exposition that follows. In addition, a section devoted to the book's teaching about the Holy Spirit is included in the introduction.

The commentary proper provides a running exposition on the text, provides extended comments on texts of special significance for Pentecostals, and acknowledges and interacts with major options in interpreting individual passages. It also provides periodic opportunities for reflection upon and personal response to the biblical text. The reflection and response components normally occur at the end of a major section of the book. Here, a theme prominent in a specific passage is summarized in the light of the reading offered in the commentary. Next, the readers encounter a series of questions designed to lead them in corporate and personal reflection about this dimension of the text. Finally, the readers are encouraged to respond to the biblical text in specific ways. Such reflection and response is consistent with the tradition's practice of not simply hearing the words of Scripture but responding to them in concrete ways. It is the literary equivalent to the altar call.

In the attempt not to overtax the popular reader footnotes have been used *carefully and sparingly*. However, when additional, more technical discussions are deemed necessary, they are placed in the footnotes. In addition, Greek and Hebrew words are ordinarily found only within parentheses or in the footnotes.

Every attempt has been made to insure that the constituency of the movement are represented in some way among the contributors. It is my hope and prayer that the work of these women and men, from a variety of continents, races, and communities, will aid the Pentecostal community (and other interested individuals and communities) in hearing the biblical text in new and authentic ways.

The General Editor

Author's Preface

When I was first asked to write this commentary, I admit to having had considerable doubts about the veracity of such a series. After all, I had spent my entire academic life trying to be a legitimate New Testament scholar, who at the same time happened to be a lifelong committed member of the Pentecostal tradition. Indeed, when I received my Ph.D. in New Testament studies in 1966, it turned out that I was only the second Pentecostal to earn such a degree. But I did not pursue the degree for that reason; rather, I wanted to pursue God's calling to be a teacher, and by that time I needed the degree in order to teach Scripture even within my own historic denomination (the American Assemblies of God). But three years later, when I began my teaching career in an evangelical college, I was considered as something of a walking oxymoron: a Pentecostal New Testament scholar. I must admit to cringing at this combination, as though a New Testament scholar who was Pentecostal was something different from being one who was Baptist or Presbyterian. Should not any legitimate New Testament scholar pursue the meaning of the biblical text, and let the chips fall where they may?

In any case, it did not take long for me to recognize that as a member of this tradition, which for a lot of reasons was considered suspect by other evangelicals, I did indeed have something to contribute to the academy, where the Holy Spirit was believed in, but held at arm's length, lest he get too close for comfort. And although it was not the first priority of my academic career, this concern eventually led to my exegetical-theological study of all the passages in Paul where he mentions the Holy Spirit, published as *God's Empowering Presence: The Holy Spirit in the Letters of Paul* (Hendrickson, 1994). So even though I have spent most of my academic career teaching New Testament in evangelical institutions (Wheaton College; Gordon-Conwell Theological Seminary; Regent College, Vancouver), I have done so as an openly confessing and practicing Pentecostal. But I have also done so with an intentionally fine difference: a New Testament scholar, who happened also to be Pentecostal, as over against being a Pentecostal New Testament scholar, as though the latter were a different breed from others. So one can perhaps understand my reluctance to write a commentary for a series that was (originally) entitled, *The* Pentecostal Commentary on....

All of this to say, that I do not consider what follows to be *the* decisive commentary on Galatians from within this tradition. It is simply *A* Pentecostal commentary on this letter, written by a committed Pentecostal for others within my tradition, but one whose first intent is to understand Paul's letter on its own terms, not in terms of a special agenda.

But having made that proper disclaimer, let me herewith thank the editor John Christopher Thomas for the invitation to write this commentary – and also for helping me with some of the items in the "response" section at the end of each major section of text. Actually, when Chris approached me to contribute to the series, the invitation was rather wide open; so the choice of writing the Galatians commentary in the series was my own. The sheer joy of this experience has been unmatched in my academic career. Here, at last, was the opportunity simply to expound this great letter, without having to cover my tracks with copious footnotes, interacting with scholarship at almost every point. I have indeed been well aware of what others have written on this letter; but here was an opportunity just to write about the text as I had come to understand it after teaching it periodically for nearly forty years. To be sure, my understanding has grown over all those years, so this finished product looks very little like the course I taught during summer school at Southern California College in 1967. So, Chris, thank you for the joy this exercise has afforded me. I confess to all that I love the Apostle with deeply Pentecostal passion; and despite the sometimes strident Paul one meets in Galatians, I also love this letter with equal passion – although I fall considerably short of Luther's love for it, who regarded Galatians as his "wife."

Maudine is still my first love, and she has read every word of this commentary, catching my many (probably unworkable) idioms, making suggestions of all kinds for improvement, and trying her best to calm my ardor at many points. Any reader who is helped by this commentary should thank her for her contribution as well. And thanks also are due to my pastor son, Mark, who read significant portions of it from a pastor's point of view, and helped (hopefully) to make it more user friendly for the pastors for whom it is ultimately intended.

May God the Holy Spirit use this commentary for his own purposes in the church, as it pleases him.

Abbreviations

AB	The Anchor Bible
BCE	Before the Christian era
BDAG	Bauer-Danker-Arndt-Gingrich, eds., *A Greek-English Lexicon of the New Testament and Other Early Christian Literature* (^{3}2000)
CE	Christian era
ESV	English Standard Version
ET	English translation
GEP	G.D. Fee, *God's Empowering Presence*
GNB	Good News Bible (= TEV)
ICC	International Critical Commentary
IVPNTC	InterVarsity Press New Testament Commentary
JB	The Jerusalem Bible
KJV	King James Version (Authorized Version)
LXX	The Septuagint
MSS	manuscripts
NA^{27}	Nestle-Aland Greek New Testament, 27th edition
NAB	New American Bible
NASB	New American Standard Bible
NASU	New American Standard Bible, Updated Version (1995)
NEB	New English Bible
NETB	New English Translation Bible
NICNT	New International Commentary on the New Testament
NIGNT	New International Greek New Testament Commentary
NIV	New International Version
NJB	New Jerusalem Bible
NLT	New Living Translation
NRSV	New Revised Standard Version
NT	New Testament
OT	Old Testament
REB	Revised English Bible
RSV	Revised Standard Version
SNTSMS	Society for New Testament Studies Monograph Series
SP	Sacra Pagina
TDNT	*Theological Dictionary of the New Testament*
TNIV	Today's New International Version
UBS^4	United Bible Societies Greek New Testament (4th edition)
WBC	Word Biblical Commentary
WUNT	Wissenschaftliche Untersuchungen zum Neuen Testament

Introduction

Writing a commentary on Paul's letter to the Galatians can be a daunting task. On the one hand, most people who will use a commentary like this will usually also assume a great deal of prior knowledge about the letter, and will therefore tend to dip into the commentary "to see what Fee has to say" on this or that point. In so doing, they may very well miss a major concern of the commentary itself – namely, to help people read Galatians as if the Reformation had never happened. For as important as Galatians was for that crucial turning point in church history, it is also true that both Luther and Calvin read the letter through the eyes of their struggle with Roman Catholicism; and therefore they tended to read the letter as having primarily to do with justification by works or by faith. But that is decidedly *not* the matter that called forth this letter, which is stated most clearly in one of the opening sentences of the argument proper: "Having *begun* by the Spirit, are you now trying to *finish* by means of the flesh?" (3:3), where "flesh" is a play on words, referring to literal circumcision of the flesh as the primary issue regarding their "keeping" the law. At issue throughout the letter is not the question, "How are people saved?" (to use contemporary language) but whether people who are already "saved" also need to practice specific aspects of the Jewish law. The concern, then, is not how one *begins* life in Christ, but whether, once begun, one must also add these aspects of the law to be *completed* in one's faith in Christ.

Furthermore, since I have taught Galatians over many years from the point of view here presented, and without spending much time on issues of historical criticism, I have chosen to maintain that practice in the commentary itself. The reason for this is simple: Galatians is one of the most thoroughly ad hoc documents in the New Testament; thus the level of understanding between author and readers is at the very highest level. This further means that Paul often assumes more than he explains, which leaves us with very little data with which to "reconstruct" the various matters that make up questions of "Introduction." Hence these matters (author, recipients, occasion, date, place of writing, the opposition) will be given short shrift here, in part because the

only one on which there is universal agreement is the question of authorship, while there is also a generally high degree of unanimity as to
what occasioned the letter. So while the commentary assumes a very
decided point of view on all these other matters, I have almost no concern to convince anyone about my point of view; nonetheless I do
have an obligation briefly to set forth the various reasons for my
choices.

Authorship

As just noted, there is universal agreement on the question of authorship. The letter in its entirety is from the Apostle Paul, who dictated all
the way through 6:10, and then took the pen in hand to "sign off" the
letter as a way of authenticating its authorship.

Nonetheless there is much that one can learn about the Apostle
from this letter. Indeed, the Paul we meet in this letter is so unlike the
one we meet, for example, in 1 Thessalonians or Philippians (although
he partially reappears in the latter in ch. 3), that some observations
about this matter are in order. First, it should be noted that Paul has
had his share of detractors over the past two centuries. What is striking
is that every one of these people uses this letter as their primary source
for understanding Paul and thus for disliking him – sometimes intensely so. Even though Paul's tone changes in his major appeal to the
Galatians with regard to their former relationship (4:12-20), this gets
drowned out by the blistering attacks on his opponents in 1:6-9 and
6:7-12. But what Paul recognized far more clearly than do his detractors is not simply that the gospel itself was at stake here, but especially
the future of the church as embracing Gentiles without putting them
through the hoops of also becoming good Jews.

It is true, of course, that these two issues – the gospel itself and the
full and free inclusion of Gentiles apart from doing the Jewish law – are
so thoroughly woven together in the Apostle's worldview that one can
scarcely talk about one without also talking about the other. But in this
letter it is the latter, the full inclusion of Gentiles apart from the law,
that drives the argument from beginning to end. For Paul, of course,
that also means a careful spelling out of the essential features of the
gospel. Hence, this letter would not have worked at all, nor would the
future of the gospel itself ever have been the same, if the Apostle Paul
had not been so passionately Paul in writing as he does.

Who Were the Galatians?

The thoroughly ad hoc nature of this letter is perhaps best demonstrated by the fact that we learn so little from the letter itself about the recipients. Paul mentions them by name only twice: first, in the salutation proper (1:2) he writes "to the churches in Galatia," which turns out to be the shortest of all the salutations in the Pauline corpus; second, in 3:1 he addresses them with a measure of exasperation, "You foolish Galatians!" Finding out who they are, therefore, should be quite simple; but in fact it is not so. The name itself derives from their origins in ancient Gaul (modern France), when in the third century BCE a large number of Gauls emigrated to north central Asia Minor (modern Turkey) and settled in a hilly region there in the area near present-day Ankara, the capital of Turkey. Thus locating the recipients of this letter would ordinarily have been an easy matter, except for the fact that the Roman Empire chose to give their name to a province they established in the first century BCE in central Asia Minor that included the Galatians in the north and the Lycaonians and some Pisidians in the south. Thus Paul's mention of "the churches of Galatia" and remonstrance "You foolish Galatians!" could refer either to the people group itself (in north central Asia Minor) or the province (and thus include non-Galatian people in south central Asia Minor). So from Paul's letter itself, that is the best we can do.

Historically, however, the resolution to this matter has tended to be determined from Luke's account of Paul's "missionary journeys" to these areas recounted in Acts 13-14 (the southern part of the province) and his returning through this area in Acts 16:1-5, followed by his traveling further "throughout the region of Phrygia and Galatia" in 16:6. Since "Galatia" is here mentioned specifically at the beginning of a new narrative in v. 6, after he had gone through the towns in the southern part of the province in the preceding narrative, the most natural way to read this mention of Galatia is to assume that he and his companions had gone to the northern part of the province at this point. But while that would seem to be the natural reading of the passage, there is nothing here that borders on certainty.

To complicate matters further, in our letter Paul mentions his first visit to these "Galatians" as occasioned by an "illness," apparently related to his eyes (4:13-15). None of this is easily placed within Luke's account; but that can be explained in terms of Luke's purpose, which did not include all the reasons for every twist and turn in the narrative.

The net result, therefore, is that we simply do not know who these Galatians were, either where they lived or whether they were "Galatians" as a people group (northern Galatia) or as inhabitants of the province of Galatia, which could put them in the southern part of the province. Perhaps what seems most to favor "provincial Galatia" over against "ethnic Galatia" is Paul's mentioning Barnabas twice (2:1 and 13), as someone known to the "Galatians." And since Barnabas was not in Paul's company when he apparently went through territorial Galatia, this would seem to favor our letter as having been written to the "Galatians" of the province, and thus the southern part of the province. At the end of the day, however, the resolution of this question does not affect our understanding of the letter as such, except at the points where the Galatians themselves are mentioned by name. But what is sometimes affected by this question is the issue of date, which we look at next.

Date and Place of Writing

Although it is currently unpopular for an evangelical scholar to do so, I think one can best make sense of Galatians within the Pauline corpus by placing it between 2 Corinthians and Romans, and thus as the fifth letter in the Pauline canon (after 1 & 2 Thessalonians and 1 & 2 Corinthians). This would date it roughly between 55 and 57 CE, give or take a year or two on either side. This is another instance where, if one were reading Galatians on its own without trying to reconcile it with outside data (in this case from the book of Acts), this would probably be the universal point of view. After all, it is a matter of simple math that there were seventeen years between Paul's conversion and his significant visit to Jerusalem narrated in 2:1-10, where he specifically says that the reason for the visit was "to set before them the gospel that I preach among the Gentiles."

What has complicated this matter of "simple math," is the fact that Luke in Acts 11:27-30 narrates a visit to Jerusalem by Paul for famine relief, which would have happened around the year 48 CE. At issue is whether this visit can be easily factored into Paul's chronology, so that his conversion would appear to be much earlier than the data either Acts or Galatians would seem to allow. After all, by the time of his conversion he had already had a considerable history of trying "to lay waste the church" and was on his way to Antioch for this very purpose. While it is possible to do the math so as to make this work for an early dating of Galatians, it seems most improbable to me that such is the case.

But in the end my reason for dating Galatians in the mid-50's of the first Christian century is its linguistic and stylistic relationship to 1 & 2 Corinthians and Romans, on the one hand, and its almost total non-relationship to 1 & 2 Thessalonians, on the other. While there is obviously a degree of subjectivity to this judgment, there are many small features in the latter two letters that suggest the Paul of the later letters had not yet emerged, features having to do both with theological content and stylistic matters. Hence I have for years believed the scholars of earlier generations had the right instincts in believing that 1 & 2 Thessalonians are the earliest letters in the Pauline corpus, and that Galatians fits best after 2 Corinthians and before Romans.

As to the place of writing itself we are even more in the dark, and this is so no matter what view one takes as to the recipients. There is not a hint of any kind within our letter that might give one some clues, so that everything said on this issue is a matter of (calculated) speculation. One may assume that someone who cared about what was happening in Galatia knew where Paul was and got word to him; but there is no mention of such a person in the letter itself, nor is there a clue of any kind as to where he was or who was with him. So this is another matter which lies in the area of total mystery, and does not affect one's understanding of the letter in the least.

Occasion/Purpose and Opponents

Here is the one area where we may have some degree of confidence about things in general, even if we lack specific details. Some men had come among the Galatian believers, churches that had been founded by Paul, and were insisting that these Gentiles also adhere to some basic elements of the Jewish law. But the issue is not with law-keeping as such. Paul's immediate concerns, specifically mentioned in this letter, have to do with Gentiles' adhering to the three aspects of the Mosaic Law that in the Diaspora distinguished the Jewish community from Gentiles: circumcision (see 2:3; 5:2-3), Sabbath (and other holy days; see 4:10), and food laws (see 2:11-14). For these reasons, rather than use the word "law" or "law-keeping," I will regularly refer to this primary issue in terms of the Jewish Torah; this is not only a less loaded term but also one which will keep the issue of "law" within the boundaries of this letter, rather than in the larger theological arena of "doing the law" as a means of justification.

One may guess, therefore, that for the agitators the gift of the Spirit probably signaled the need to be "completed" by adhering to Torah. This, after all, was common Jewish expectation, derived from Jer 31:31-34 and Ezek 11:19-20 and 36:26-27, namely that the gift of the eschatological Spirit would lead people to obey the law. Thus, to use the language of E.P. Sanders,[1] but not his conclusions in this case, at stake in this letter are not *entrance* requirements (i.e., how people get "saved"), but *maintenance* requirements (that for full membership into

---

[1] See E.P. Sanders, *Paul, the Law, and the Jewish People* (Philadelphia: Fortress, 1983).

God's covenant people Gentiles must become Abraham's true children by means of circumcision).

Throughout this commentary I will regularly refer to these men as "the agitators," which is my translation of Paul's own language for them in 5:11, where he speaks of "those who are upsetting you," language, interestingly enough, used by Luke in Acts 17:6 regarding the accusation against Paul and his companions in Thessalonica (!). The more traditional term, "Judaizers," was historically created from the two words in Paul's speech in 2:14, "live like a Jew," which in turn became a verb in English, "to Judaize," meaning to force people to accept certain aspects of the Jewish law. It is hardly a useful term anymore because it has now had a long history in English as carrying overtones of being legalistic rather than living by grace. While one can understandably argue that such is the ultimate theological issue involved in Galatians, this now misleading word misses the more ethnic dimension of the problem, the passion of Paul's life and calling: Jew and Gentile as one people of God thus fulfilling the biblical promises that included the Gentiles in the eschatological people of God, a theme that originates in the Abrahamic promise itself.

That leads to a final question on this matter. Had the Galatians already capitulated by the time this letter was written. On the issue of the Jewish calendar, 4:10 suggests apparently so; and if so, one might assume they were also being persuaded regarding food – although that is altogether a guess on my part. But the matter of circumcision seems to be more ambiguous. Most likely, Paul has got wind of the fact that they were contemplating doing so, and thus he dashed off this letter to stop them from such (from his perspective) disastrous action.

Galatians as a Letter

Only because of the events of recent years would one need to have a section of an Introduction to a commentary on Galatians that deals with the issue of "Galatians as a Letter." But all of this changed with the publication of Hans Dieter Betz's commentary on this letter in the *Hermeneia* series, in which he argued that one can best understand Galatians in light of classical rhetoric, and thus dubbed Galatians as "an example of the 'apologetic letter' genre" (p. 14) – even though he offered no hard evidence for the so-called genre as such. Nonetheless, Betz's influence has been considerable, so that he was followed by several others who have tried to impose rhetorical categories on this letter – although seldom in agreement with each other.

While some of these studies have had a measure of usefulness for understanding Galatians, two things make one properly hesitant about applying classical rhetorical categories to Paul in any of his letters, espe-

cially so in this one. First, and whatever else, Galatians was in fact written as a letter – a letter that was intended to be read aloud in the
churches of Galatia, and probably to a people who would have had
very little interest or knowledge of the fine workings of classical rhetoric.[2] This does not mean, of course, that Paul could not have used such
rhetorical patterns; but it is not clear whether our finding such patterns
will help us sit among the Galatians, as it were, and hear Paul any better. But second, and this seems to be the crucial matter, those who
insist on reading Paul through the lens of ancient rhetoric have had
considerable difficulty agreeing on how that is to be done. Indeed,
they have as many disagreements among themselves as to how the
argument of Galatians works as do those who read it primarily as a
letter of persuasion.

At the end of the day, my greatest difficulty with applying rhetorical
categories to this letter in particular is that it tends to mislead the reader
as to how Galatians "works" *as a letter*, and especially fails to recognize
the various aspects of the argument itself. This is especially true regarding the pattern of argument that emerges in the letter, where, after the
opening recital of his (basically non-)relationship with Jerusalem (chs.
1-2), Paul works from a pattern of "argument from Scripture, application, and appeal." And since this is what Paul actually does, by
whatever name it is called, I have chosen to follow these patterns as
they emerge in Paul's extended "argument" with his converts. Thus
the final item in this Introduction is a presentation of the outline of
Galatians, as I see it, which in turn will guide the presentation in the
commentary itself. But first some words are in order, highlighting the
special interests of this commentary series.

The Holy Spirit in Galatians[3]

Because of the major role the Spirit plays in the argument of this letter,
both by explicit statements and by the implications lying behind much
of what he says, Paul here opens the windows to give a rather full-
orbed view of life in the Spirit in his experience and understanding.
Christian life, individually and corporately, begins, is carried on, and
comes to eschatological conclusion by means of God's empowering
presence, the Holy Spirit. This includes several features that are especially pronounced in this letter.

---

[2] For a definitive critique of this perspective on Galatians, and thus for the rest of
Paul's letters as well, see Philip H. Kern, *Rhetoric and Galatians: Assessing an Approach to
Paul's Epistle* (SNTSMS 101; Cambridge: Cambridge University Press, 1998).

[3] With permission from the publisher I here reproduce the conclusions to the chapter on the Holy Spirit in Galatians in *God's Empowering Presence* (Peabody, MA:
Hendrickson, 1994), 469-70.

1. As in Paul's earlier letters, the Spirit is absolutely the *sine qua non* of a person's becoming a believer in Christ. Here is the verification that one belongs to Christ; the Spirit has now replaced Torah as the new "identity marker" of God's people. At the time of the Galatians' conversion, God marked them as his children by sending the Spirit into their hearts, who enabled them to cry out *"Abba"* to God – the personal language of Jesus, God's Son, and therefore the evidence of their "sonship" (4:6-7).

2. At the same time, it is equally transparent that the coming of the Spirit was a dynamic, experienced reality – so much so that Paul can appeal without fear of contradiction to their reception of the Spirit as the impeccable proof that righteousness is predicated on faith in Christ and has absolutely nothing to do with Torah observance. The Galatians' own experience of the Spirit preceded the coming of Torah by way of the agitators; for Paul this is evidence enough that the time of Torah is over (3:3-5). Thus those who are led by the Spirit are not under Torah at all (5:18).

3. The heart of the argument, however, has less to do with Christian beginnings and more to do with "coming to completion," that is, with the ongoing life of the believer and the believing community. Here again the Spirit as God's empowering presence is the key to everything. At the heart of things in this letter, related to the controversy that triggered it, is the question of righteousness apart from Torah. For Paul the life of the Spirit – being led by the Spirit so as to walk in the ways of the Lord – means the end of Torah observance. Those who live by the Spirit will thus bear the fruit of the Spirit, and for such a life Torah as obligation is absolutely no help and thus has no significance at all.

4. But Paul's primary concern is not with the individual believer, but with the life of the Spirit as it works its way out in the community of faith. Hence this letter provides ample expression of this dimension of Spirit life as well. Included in this larger arena of life together by the Spirit is both their ethical life – their relationships with one another as evidencing the presence of the Spirit (5:16-26) – and their corporate life of worship, since Paul can appeal to the ongoing presence of the miraculous in their midst as further evidence that righteousness is by the hearing of faith, not by Torah observance (3:4-5).

5. Absolutely presuppositional to the Pauline understanding is the Spirit as the main eschatological reality, the certain evidence

that the future has begun and the guarantee of its consummation. Although this note is sounded less here than in other letters, it is so foundational for Paul that it can scarcely stay silenced. Hence in 5:5, besides everything else, the Spirit supersedes Torah precisely because his presence guarantees our hope that Christ's righteousness has afforded. But even more so, as in 2 Corinthians 3, Paul understands the Spirit himself as the fulfillment of God's promise, in this case, including the promise made to Abraham that included his blessing on the Gentiles (3:13-14).

6. Finally, it is noteworthy that the Spirit as God's *personal* presence is also presuppositional throughout. By his Spirit, Christ lives within the believer (4:6); and the Spirit leads his people into the fulfilling of the righteousness the law called for but could not produce (5:18, 22-25).

As everywhere else in the apostle, the Spirit is not the central matter; that place is taken by Christ alone. But for the ongoing life that Christ has afforded through his death and resurrection, the Spirit is the key to everything: conversion, ethics, community life, miracles, revelation, eschatology. Without the Spirit there simply is no genuinely Christian life.

An Outline of Galatians

In keeping with the foregoing analysis of Galatians as a genuine letter, more than an example of Greek rhetoric in the guise of a letter, the following outline seems to capture the ebb and flow of the argument. In any case, it will be the framework within which the following discussion takes place.

1:1-9   **Introductory Matters**
  1:1-5   Salutation
  1:6-9   A Curse on Paul's Opponents

1:10–2:21   **Paul Defends Himself and his Gospel**
  1:10-12   The True Source of Paul's Gospel
  1:13-21   Paul's Lack of Relationship with Jerusalem
  2:1-10   Jerusalem Affirms Paul's Gospel
  2:11-14a   Jerusalem Reneges on Paul's Gospel
  2:14b-21   Paul's Speech Introduces His Gospel

3:1–4:20   **The First Argument from Scripture**
  3:1–4:7   The Argument from Scripture

I gladly dedicate this work to my colleagues (since 1990) on the Committee for Bible Translation, which produced the NIV in 1978 (rev. 1984) and more recently the TNIV. Not surprisingly, the latter serves as the biblical text for the commentary that follows.

Galatians 1:1-9

The Text

Introductory Matters

Almost all letters from the Greco-Roman period[1] begin with a threefold salutation: The Writer, to the Addressee, Greetings.[2] Very often the next item would be a wish or prayer for the health or well-being of the addressee. Paul's letters, which generally follow this standard form, also include a thanksgiving (twice in the form of "blessing God"). Since Galatians is a letter written to Gentile believers who became converts through Paul's own personal ministry, the news about what has recently been happening in these churches calls forth some unique features regarding these matters. Indeed, so remarkably different is this salutation from all the others that it offers us our first clues as to Paul's urgencies. Even though the Galatians themselves would not have been privy to Paul's other correspondence, and thus would not be aware of these unique features, we do have some of that correspondence and such a comparison throws considerable light on what is going on in the churches in Galatia. What emerges is that Paul uses the standard salutation to introduce in an indirect way the two primary concerns of this letter: his own divinely appointed apostleship (v. 1) and the fact that salvation is by grace alone, the direct result of divine activity willed by God and effected by Christ (vv. 4-5).

Furthermore, what immediately follows is not a thanksgiving or "blessing of God" as in 1 & 2 Corinthians, but a double curse on those who have been upsetting things in these churches.

That this double curse stands where one finds a thanksgiving in most of his letters indicates that Paul's first concern with the Galatian communities is to put their present "teachers" into *divine* perspective. They come not from Christ himself, as Paul does, but from human beings with a merely "human" gospel. Indeed, theirs is not a gospel ("good news") at all and its purveyors therefore stand under God's curse, not his blessing. It is the strong nature of the curse that follows

---

[1] For helpful studies of letter writing in the Greco-Roman period, see S.K. Stowers, *Letter Writing in Greco-Roman Antiquity* (Philadelphia: Westminster, 1986).

[2] All the true "letters" in the NT follow this pattern (including the letter from James in Acts 15:23–29), except for 3 John, which lacks the standard greeting.

in vv. 8 and 9 that in turn helps us go back and read the salutation with a bit more insight.

Galatians 1:1-5 – Salutation

> [1]*Paul, an apostle – sent not with a human commission nor by human authority, but by Jesus Christ and God the Father, who raised him from the dead –* [2]*and all the brothers and sisters with me,*
> *To the churches in Galatia:*
> [3]*Grace and peace to you from God our Father and the Lord Jesus Christ,* [4]*who gave himself for our sins to rescue us from the present evil age, according to the will of our God and Father,* [5]*to whom be glory for ever and ever. Amen.*

When one compares this salutation with those of the other letters, three things stand out. First, regarding the *writer*. In Paul's earliest letters (1 & 2 Thessalonians[3]) there is no elaboration of any kind; but beginning with 1 Corinthians, where his own authority is being called into question, Paul identifies himself in terms of "called to be an apostle of Christ Jesus through the will of God," an identification which is found in some form in all his subsequent letters except for Philemon ("prisoner of Christ Jesus") and Philippians ("servants of Christ Jesus").

Second, regarding the *recipients*. In all his other letters Paul adds some form of an identifying feature. This begins in 1 & 2 Thessalonians ("the church of the Thessalonians in God our Father and the Lord Jesus Christ") and carries through in some form in all the remaining letters, except this one.

Third, regarding the *greeting*. The form of the greeting itself (v. 3) is basically the same in all the letters, except for the addition of "mercy" in 1 & 2 Timothy. Beginning with 2 Thessalonians and consistently thereafter (including our letter), Paul adds the source of the grace and peace – usually as "from God our Father and the Lord Jesus Christ." Only in this letter does this part of the salutation receive an extended elaboration.

While one should probably not make too much of the second item (about the recipients), the elaborations regarding the sender and the greeting proper give us several clues as to how we are to understand the content of the letter that follows.

---

[3] For this historical judgment, see the Introduction, pp. 4-5.

Verses 1-2a – The Writer(s)

That the writer of this letter is the Apostle Paul himself is agreed on by all New Testament scholars. In fact it is difficult to imagine the circumstances under which a letter with this much passion and personal data, with its singular concern over whether Gentile believers must also keep Torah,[4] could have been written by someone else under Paul's name. However, what is sometimes not noted by the reader is that, after the considerable "interruption" whereby Paul identifies the source of his apostleship, he has also included "all the brothers" (v. 2a) as co-authors of the letter. Even so, a merely casual reading of Galatians indicates that the actual author is Paul himself, and that it has not been *written* by him and others – although one of them may very well have penned the letter at Paul's dictation, which Paul then signs off at the end (6:11). The inclusion of his companions in this case is very likely for two reasons. First, it is his way of reinforcing the urgency of what he is setting out to write, that it is not simply his own personal opinion against his detractors, but that what he writes is held in common by those who presently accompany him – and perhaps in this case a larger group of fellow believers in his present location.[5] Second, some of these "brothers" were almost certainly in his company when he had come to Galatia and there proclaimed the good news about Christ, since solitary travel by an itinerant teacher was seldom ever done. Thus in the next paragraph when Paul speaks of the gospel "we" preached to you, some of the brothers mentioned here were almost certainly in Paul's company when he was in Galatia.

The striking feature of Paul's personal identification in this case is the elaborate expansion regarding the *source* of his apostleship, which begins with a double negation before it is expressed in the more common positive way as an "apostle of Christ Jesus through the will of God." But it is this very negation that sets in motion both the concerns and the tone of the letter. He asserts at the outset that he is an apostle "neither from men, nor through a man," which means that his apostleship (and by implication his understanding of the gospel) had neither human origins nor human mediation. In the context of Galatians this means that his apostolic authority did not come from anyone, especially not from the leaders in Jerusalem, nor was he sent

---

[4] On the use of Torah instead of the standard term "law" see the Introduction, p. 5.

[5] This latter suggestion is based on the fact that this is the only instance in the Pauline letters where "co-authors" are mentioned and the person or (persons) is/are not named. Indeed, this element is missing in only two of the ten letters in the church corpus (Romans and Ephesians).

out to preach Christ on the basis of a human directive. Whatever else was true of the Apostle, and he is ready to take pride in this, he had not been properly "ordained" to his ministry through any human channels.

But why this emphasis?, one may rightly ask. To which question several answers have been offered. One may legitimately assume at the outset that the Galatians themselves would know precisely why Paul starts this way. What we cannot be sure of is whether Paul is putting himself forward in direct contrast to the agitators[6] themselves (that is, they have merely human credentials, while Paul's are divinely ordained) or whether it is in response to something the agitators have said about Paul's own "credentials." If it is the latter, as most think, then the question still remains as to what they have said about Paul. And here the answers are several, the most likely of which is that the agitators have denied the validity of his authority (and therefore of his "gospel"), since he does not come from Jerusalem as they themselves have and with the Jerusalem apostles' blessing.[7] This at least seems to offer the best possibilities for a good understanding of the various emphases of the narrative that follows, especially Paul's desire to distance himself from Jerusalem in 1:13–2:10. What the agitators saw as a positive for them and a negative for Paul ("in contrast to him we are authorized by Jerusalem"), he saw as exactly the opposite. They had merely human origins; Paul's apostleship was by divine appointment only.

One further feature in this clause, unique to this letter and therefore probably also a reflection of the situation, is Paul's adding to his mention of God the Father the fact that he "raised Christ from the dead." This is the piece of historical datum on which Paul's life and apostleship ultimately rest. Two matters are important to note here. First, it is easy for the casual reader to miss the significance of the unusual word order, that Paul's apostleship is from "Jesus Christ and God the Father." This, however, is consistent in Paul. According to

---

[6] For the use of this term to identify the itinerant missioners from Jerusalem that are upsetting the Galatian churches, see the Introduction, p. 6.

[7] Other options are: that he has merely human credentials, not divine as he claims; that in contrast to the agitators he lacks the kind of authentication they bring, as those blessed by Jerusalem; without the contrast, that he is simply a renegade who lacks proper authority at all, not having been blessed by Jerusalem. Those who read the letter through the lens of Greco-Roman rhetoric (Betz, Matera, Witherington) doubt whether this responds directly to anything said by the agitators; but that seems to downplay the obvious passion of the letter and its fierce opposition to these renegade itinerants.

1 Cor 9:1, his apostleship is predicated first of all on the fact that "I saw the Lord," which is his own way of speaking about the Damascus Road experience.[8] It was the risen Christ who accosted him and thereby turned him from an enemy into a devoted servant; and thus it was the risen Christ who appointed him as his apostle.

Second, and related to this first reality, it was this revelation of the risen Christ that so utterly radicalized Paul. As we will discover in 3:13 of this letter, Paul's passionate hatred of the early believers was the direct result of their worshiping as Lord someone whom God had cursed by having had him crucified. And whatever else, a "crucified Messiah" was an unthinkable oxymoron, the ultimate contradiction of terms. People who worshiped as Lord someone whom God had cursed by having him crucified were deranged and needed to be stopped. So what an utterly life-changing surprise awaited Paul on the Damascus Road. The crucified One now confronted him as the living One; and that meant that everything Paul knew and understood about God and Jewish messianic expectations had been overturned and had to be rethought. The crucifixion, it turns out, was something God himself had planned and been a part of. Hence in this letter, with Paul's apostleship having been called into question by the agitators, Paul's first mention of Christ as the source of that apostleship includes God the Father. It was by virtue of the Father's having raised and exalted him that the Son now functions as the One who has been given the Name above every name,[9] before whom every knee shall bow and every tongue confess to his Lordship (Phil 2:10). Thus Paul's apostleship had come directly from the risen Lord, the Lord whom God the Father had raised from the dead. And this crucial point is made right up front in the letter.

Verse 2b – The Recipients
We have already noted that the simple "to the churches of Galatia" is the only instance in the corpus where the recipients of a letter are addressed so succinctly. But the lack of elaboration does not make the

---

[8] It is common (e.g., Betz, Matera) to speak of this as a visionary experience. But that is not Paul's view. He had had such experiences as well (2 Cor 11:1-4) and calls them precisely that – "visions." About this experience he uses quite different language: "the Lord appeared to ...," "I saw ..."

[9] That is, the "Name above every name" is not "Jesus," but "Lord," which in the Greek Bible had come to be used consistently as a way of avoiding the actual use of the unutterable name of God, Yahweh. On this matter, see my *Pauline Christology: An Exegetical-Theological Study* (Peabody, MA: Hendrickson, 2006), 399-401.

task of interpretation easier. That it is addressed to multiple churches[10] in a given area is unique to this letter,[11] and perhaps helps to explain the lack of other personal notations that might have helped us know more certainly who the "Galatians" were.

Our problem lies with the phrase "of Galatia," which at the time of Paul was a geographical designation for a province created by the Romans in the central-southern interior of Asia Minor (contemporary Turkey). The Roman province was a purely political creation, without regard to the natural "people boundaries" that marked the area. It therefore included ethnic "Galatians" (a people who had migrated from Gaul [modern France] in the third century BCE), who lived in north central Asia Minor,[12] as well as other ethnic groups such as Lycaonians in the south. The phrase "of Galatia," therefore, is in this instance most likely a reference to churches somewhere in the Roman *province* of Galatia. But when Paul in 3:1 speaks of them as "foolish Galatians," this has all the earmarks of ethnicity, not of arbitrary political boundaries imposed by the Romans on other people groups. In the end there is very little else in the letter that might help one decide, except for the twofold mention of Barnabas in 2:1 and 13, as though he were someone known to the recipients. This would seem to favor churches in the south, since according to Acts 15:36-41 Barnabas did not accompany Paul when he went through the northern region. In any case, the one thing certain from the designation, "the churches of Galatia," is that the agitators have created trouble for Paul and the gospel in several of *his* churches in at least part of the province of Galatia.

Verses 3-5 – The Greeting
The greeting in this letter is the other place in the opening salutation where its unique and considerable elaboration seems to offer further clues as to what will follow later in the letter.

Verse 3. The greeting proper is the one that by now had become standard in Paul's letters to his churches. As elsewhere, here is a

---

[10] On Paul's use of the term "churches" see the comment on 1:13 below.

[11] The other exception is 2 Corinthians, where Paul adds, "along with all the saints in all Achaia," which would include believers at least in Cenchreae (see Rom 16:1-2) and perhaps Lechaion, the two port towns under Corinth's domain that were on either side of the 4 and 1/2 mile wide isthmus of Corinth, where goods were carried overland from one port to the other in order to avoid going around the treacherous southern coast of the Peleponnesus.

[12] Which today would include the Turkish capital, Ankara, known in early church history as Ancyra.

marvelous example of Paul's "turning into gospel" everything he sets his hand to. The traditional greeting in the Hellenistic world was *chairein* – the infinitive of the verb "rejoice" – but in salutations it simply meant "Greetings!" (see Acts 15:23; Jas 1:1). In Paul's hands *chairein* now becomes *charis* ("grace"), to which he adds the traditional Jewish greeting *shalom* ("peace," in the sense of "wholeness" or "well-being"). Thus instead of the familiar "greetings," Paul salutes his brothers and sisters in Christ with "grace to you – and peace."[13]

It is worth noting that this is the invariable order of Paul's words, not "grace and peace to you" as in most translations. Very likely there is significance to this order: the grace of God and Christ is what is given to God's people; peace is what results from such a gift. Hence, "grace to you – and peace." In a profound sense this greeting therefore nicely represents Paul's larger theological perspective. The sum total of God's activity toward his human creatures is found in the word "grace"; God has given himself to his people bountifully and mercifully in Christ.[14] Nothing is deserved, nothing can be achieved. The sum total of those benefits as they are experienced by the recipients of God's grace is "peace,"[15] God's eschatological *shalom*, both now and to come. The latter ("peace") flows out of the former ("grace"), and both together flow from "God our Father" and were made effective in our human history through our "Lord, Jesus Christ."

Some further observations are needed regarding Paul's use of this fulsome title-name. First, as has become commonplace for him by now, he begins with the appellation, "Lord," which is always titular, even when as here it is not accompanied by the definite article. In Galatians this title is used far less than elsewhere in Paul's letters,[16] since his focus is not on Christ's present reign as the exalted Lord in heaven,

---

[13] It should perhaps be noted that one cannot be sure that Paul himself is responsible for this "transformation into gospel" of traditional formulas. But his is the earliest evidence for it, and it is quite in keeping with what he does elsewhere.

[14] Thus the letter also signs off with "the grace of our Lord Jesus Christ be with you."

[15] In Paul "peace" can refer in turn to (1) peace with God (= cessation of hostilities), (2) peace within the believing community, (3) inner peace in place of turmoil, and (4) rest or order within a context of worship. Other commentaries express more confidence than I could muster that one can isolate any of these nuances in the Pauline salutations. In the context of greetings to a community it at least includes (1) and (2), and perhaps (3).

[16] Only 5 times altogether, 3 times in this threefold combination (here; 6:14 and 18); the other two are simple titular references to Christ as "the Lord" (1:19; 5:10).

but on his saving activity. This is the reason for the comma after "Lord," to separate the title from the combined "name," Jesus Christ.

"Jesus" is our Lord's earthly name. It is therefore of some interest, but not surprise, that it occurs less frequently elsewhere in Paul's letters as a stand alone name than the other names/titles.[17] This is almost certainly because its first referent is to Jesus' earthly life as such, and Paul's emphasis in this letter is primarily on Christ's saving work in our behalf.

The "name" Christ is also first of all a title, having to do with Jesus as the Messiah, a usage that still prevails in Paul, as Roman 9:5 makes clear. Nonetheless in Galatians, as throughout the corpus, it is Paul's most frequent referent to our Lord: 37 times in all, 22 of which stand alone. This is the clear indication that by the time of this letter the title had become for Paul much more of a name than a title; and its frequent usage in this letter can be accounted for because of Paul's emphasis throughout on Christ's saving work in our behalf.

Verse 4. The unique part of the salutation lies in the elaboration that follows, which happens in no other letter but this one. Note first that the divine names given in v. 1 are now reversed, and thus appear in their more normal order — and always so in Paul's salutations. But just as the order "Jesus Christ and God the Father" in v. 1 gave Paul opportunity to elaborate on the latter as the one who exalted the crucified Jesus to be the now risen Lord, so the conventional order of "God our Father and the[18] Lord Jesus Christ" offers him the opportunity to elaborate now on Christ. And again, the elaboration anticipates concerns in the letter itself. Three crucial things are said here about "the Lord, Jesus Christ."

First, Paul puts forward the *means* of salvation: The Lord, Jesus Christ "gave himself for our sins." This very personal language regarding Christ's death in our behalf is used only by Paul in the New Testament; it will occur again in this letter in a still more singularly personal way in 2:20 ("who loved me and gave himself up for me").[19]

---

[17] It occurs 16 times in this letter, 15 of these in combination. It stands alone only in 6:17, where Paul makes direct reference to our Savior's earthly sufferings.

[18] Paul's word order here (God the Father of us and the Lord Jesus Christ) suggests that his "our" very likely does double duty, especially in light of the "blessing" with which 2 Corinthians begins: "Blessed be God, even the Father of our Lord Jesus Christ." It is precisely because the eternal God is now known to us as the Father of the Son that we now use the Son's language "Abba" (see 4:6 below) and thus now know God as our Father as well.

[19] It occurs elsewhere only in Eph 5:2; 5:25; it occurs also in 1 Tim 2:6 and Tit 2:14, with the simple form of the verb, "give," rather than "give up" = to "hand

The present passage seems clearly to anticipate the next one. Here Christ is the one "who gave himself *for our sins*"; in 2:20 he speaks of the "Son of God, who loved me and gave himself *for me*." For the most part Paul tends to speak of Christ's sacrifice in less personal terms: as the means of redemption, for which he uses several metaphors depending on the view of sin involved (e.g., redemption from sin's slavery).

Although the Old Testament sacrificial system ultimately lies behind the imagery used here, in this case the language itself echoes three verses from Isaiah 53 in the Greek Old Testament (LXX): v. 4 "the one who bore *our sins*"; v. 6 "the Lord *gave him up for our sins*"; and v. 12 "he was *given up because of our sins*." It is of some interest that this kind of language is not as prominent in Paul's letters as one might have been led to think. Indeed that one might think otherwise is almost certainly the direct result of the influence of Romans on our overall understanding of Paul's theology. The fact is that the noun "sin" (ἀμαρτία) occurs 65 times in Paul's letters, 48 of these in Romans[20] and always in the singular except for the citation of Isa 27:9 in 11:27. Of the seventeen occurrences outside of Romans, nine of them are in the plural, and almost all of these in contexts where Paul is clearly reflecting his Jewish heritage. While the larger issue for Paul is our sinfulness in general (thus "sin" in Romans), this "sin" that is woven into the very fabric of our fallenness expresses itself in individual "sins"; and the incredible good news is that God's Son, our Lord, Jesus Christ, "gave himself [in his 'sacrifice' on the cross] for our [many] sins."

In the context of the present letter, of course, this clause anticipates the whole question as to whether Gentiles need also to become obedient to (certain aspects of) Torah in order to qualify them further as full members of God's newly constituted Israel. And this is the matter that drives our letter from beginning to end. Paul's answer is a decidedly forceful "No!" Since "Christ died for[21] our sins" and we have

over." In Rom 4:25 and 8:32 the same idea is expressed in the passive, with "God" as the implied subject. The only thing that comes close to this uniquely Pauline usage in the NT is Heb 9:14 ("how much more will the blood of Christ, who offered himself unblemished to God" TNIV), where the verb and concepts are quite different.

[20] And 42 of these in chs. 5-8 alone, thus 65% of all the occurrences in his letters in these four chapters, where "sin" (not "sins") is the issue.

[21] There is a considerable textual variation in the Greek manuscripts as to whether Paul wrote ὑπέρ (commonly = "in behalf of") or περί (commonly = "concerning"), both of which end up in most English translations with the more ambiguous "for our sins." In all other cases with this idiom Paul uses ὑπέρ; and only here is there a

"received the Spirit" (3:3), there is no place for Torah at all in the newly formed people of God, both Jew and Gentile together.

Second, Paul expresses the *goal* of our salvation in terms of "in order that he might deliver us from the present evil age." What first catches our attention here is the uniqueness of this clause – not only in Paul but in the entire New Testament. The closest thing to it in Paul is Col 1:13, where with a quite different verb he speaks of God as having "delivered[22] us from the power of darkness and transferred us into the kingdom of his Son." Nonetheless, the clause is quite in keeping with Paul's eschatological view of salvation that finds expression in ever so many ways – this being one of them. And the very ambiguity of the expressed purpose, whether it is present or future, or more likely both simultaneously, is fully in keeping with Paul's understanding of redemption not simply as "forgiveness of sins," but also as deliverance from the bondage of "the powers" of darkness. The "why" of this clause here in the salutation is best understood as anticipating the double mention of the Galatians believers' former bondage to "the powers" in 4:3 and 9, which in turn also suggests that the emphasis in this verse is therefore on *present* deliverance.

If this is the correct view of things, then one need only note further that for Paul the severest form of bondage in this present evil age is not to the "powers" as such, but to one's own sinfulness. "Sins," therefore, are not to be understood simply as expressions of disobedience to God's moral laws, but in a much more profound way are to be understood as a form of bondage to the present evil age from which Christ died to deliver us.

Third, Paul concludes this brief soteriological moment by reminding his readers of the ultimate *source* of their salvation. What Christ did was "in conformity to the will of our God and Father." With this remarkable concluding moment Paul puts the entire saluta-

---

significant number of manuscripts, many important ones, that have περί. While this has not been an easy choice for textual critics, I happen to side with the minority and think Paul in this one instance wrote περί under the influence of the Septuagint, and later scribes conformed it to Paul's otherwise consistent usage. Some want to fine tune Paul's doctrine of salvation at this point in ways that go far beyond the evidence. In all kinds of instances these two prepositions overlap with regard to "meaning," and they are clearly sometimes interchangeable for Paul. So one must in such circumstances avoid creating a theology of prepositions where there is none. The good news is that Christ died in our behalf and in so doing, removed our sins from us.

[22] The two verbs are synonyms; the one used here (ἐξαιρέω) occurs only here in the letters of Paul, while the ῥύομαι of Col 1:13 is both more common in Paul and is found in the LXX of Exod 6:6, which Paul is echoing in the Colossians passage.

tion in a kind of "inclusio," which typically for Paul encloses the work of Christ the Son within the overall comprehensive will of God the Father. The "grace and peace" Paul desires for his readers (v. 3) are first of all from "God our Father" as well as from "the Lord Jesus Christ." But mention of Christ in this case causes Paul to elaborate in a way that anticipates much that he will say in the letter itself. Having now done so he returns to where he began, with mention of God our Father, whose eternal will lies behind everything: Christ's redemptive work and thus our eternal salvation. It really cannot get any better than that, so Paul does the right thing – bursts into doxology.

Verse 5. The doxology itself is expansive, "to whom (i.e., our God and Father) be glory for ever and ever. Amen." This is the first of six such outbursts of praise to God the Father in the Pauline corpus,[23] all of which are basically like this one (except 1 Tim 1:17), with an occasional slight variation. And as with this one they come at moments where Paul is obviously full of his subject matter and simply bursts into praise, that all that God has done for us in Christ Jesus is ultimately to his own glory, a glory that God's people themselves should also be mindful of and live in keeping with.

Galatians 1:6-9 – A Curse on Paul's Opponents

> [6]*I am astonished that you are so quickly deserting the one who called you by the grace of Christ and are turning to a different gospel* – [7]*which is really no gospel at all. Evidently some people are throwing you into confusion and are trying to pervert the gospel of Christ.* [8]*But even if we or an angel from heaven should preach a gospel other*[24] *than the one we preached to you, let that person be under God's curse!* [9]*As we have already said, so now I say again: If anybody is preaching to you a gospel other than what you accepted, let that person be under God's curse!*

Under anyone's understanding of Paul, we are hardly prepared for the content of this paragraph. Especially we are not prepared to find it at the very point where in every other letter to a believing community Paul begins with either a thanksgiving or a *berakah* (a blessing of God; 2 Cor 1:3; Eph 1:3), and in many of these instances he reports how he

---

[23] The others occur in Rom 11:36; 16:27; Phil 4:20; 1 Tim 1:17; 2 Tim 4:18.

[24] A large part of the manuscript tradition has the dative "to you" (ὑμῖν) either before or after the verb, while some significant early MSS do not have it at all. The different order of words, equally supported by a large number of manuscripts, is most easily explained if the ὑμῖν was not original, but was inserted by early scribes on the basis of how the sentence ends.

prays for them. This is obviously neither prayer nor thanksgiving; it is Paul coming out with guns blazing as it were.

The paragraph comes to us in three sentences, the first of which (vv. 6-7), although a bit convoluted, spells out the problem. In setting out the issue itself (from his own perspective, of course), Paul begins with his own distress that they have so readily fallen for a false gospel, which of course is a contradiction of terms. There is only one gospel, so what the "troublemakers" are doing in fact is perverting the gospel of Christ. This is then followed by the double curse, the second (v. 9) basically repeating the first (v. 8), except that in the first instance the gospel is described as the one "*we preached* to you," while in the second it is the one "*you received*."

Verses 6-7. Hard on the heels of vv. 4 and 5, where Paul has concluded his salutation with an extraordinary affirmation of the saving work of Christ and a doxology to God the Father whose will has thereby been accomplished by Christ, Paul begins the letter proper with an expression of utter amazement that his Galatian friends could possibly do what they are now doing: "I am astonished that you are so quickly deserting the one who called you." And lest one read this too quickly as something personal, namely their deserting Paul himself for the agitators, he sets out as the very first thing that in moving away from the gospel, they are thereby in process of abandoning God himself, since it was God "who called you into the grace of Christ."

Thus while there is some initial ambiguity as to whether the "who" in this clause refers to God or to Paul, that it refers to God is made certain by the fact that elsewhere in Paul the language of "being called" with regard to becoming a believer always has "God" as the expressed or implied subject.[25] Although it was indeed through Paul's preaching that God called them (see v. 8), Paul's emphasis is on the fact that in responding to "our" preaching,[26] they were thereby responding to God's own calling them to himself.

Despite the fact that the issue itself is thus very clear, some of the details are less so, and we need to take them up in turn. First, Paul says that this is happening "so quickly" (οὕτως ταχέως), which is as ambiguous in Paul's Greek sentence as it is in English. Is it purely temporal, so that he means "so soon" after their conversion, or perhaps so soon after Paul and his companions had left them? Or is it

---

[25] See, e.g., 1:15; 5:8, 13 below; cf. Rom 8:30; 9:12, 24; 1 Cor 1:9; 7:15-24; Eph 4:1, 4; Col 1:15; 1 Thess 2:12; 4:7; 5:24; 2:Thess 2:14; 2 Tim 1:9.

[26] Note the use of the plural pronoun throughout the paragraph, probably picking up the inclusion of "all the brothers" from v. 2 as noted above.

attitudinal, meaning that when exposed to this new teaching, they "so quickly" abandoned what they had believed at first. Most likely it is the latter, although the very ambiguity may include the former as well. Thus Paul "marvels/is astonished" (θαυμάζω) not only that they are abandoning the God who called them into a relationship with him based on grace, but that they are doing it "so easily," just like that, as it were. From Paul's perspective this is a cause for wonder.

Second, and much more difficult to decide, are the complexities that surround the modifying prepositional phrase, "in/by [the] grace [of Christ]" (ἐν χάριτι [Χριστοῦ]). In the first place, although there is considerable difference of opinion as to whether Paul actually wrote "of Christ,"[27] its very difficulty, evidenced in the diversity among the English translations, makes an omission easy to account for. Since that same difficulty makes a frequent addition very unlikely, we may be quite sure that Paul himself is responsible for the "of Christ."

But more difficult is to determine the intended sense of the preposition itself, whether Paul intended agency ("by the grace of Christ") or locative ("in/into the grace of Christ"); and here the many English translations are fairly evenly divided. In moments like these Pauline usage elsewhere should be determinative, which in this case thus points toward the latter as Paul's intent: that God has called them to exist within the sphere of the grace that has come to them through Christ. Elsewhere when Paul speaks of grace as the means of our calling or existence he tends to use the straight dative without the preposition (χάριτι; see Rom 11:6; 1 Cor 15:10; Eph 2:8). Moreover, in the very next section of the letter, when referring to his own calling, Paul very clearly expresses agency ("through his grace") by means of a different preposition (διά). If this, then, is Paul's intent – to remind them that God had called them to an existence that was not only predicated on the grace of Christ but was also the sphere of their entire existence – then the translators of the KJV seem to have had the better of it over most modern versions: "called you into the grace of

---

[27] For reasons not at all clear this word (Χριστοῦ) was put in brackets by the editors of the UBS/Nestle-Aland Greek text. Here is a case where the reading supported by the best and majority of Greek MSS, and the basic textual criterion, "the more difficult reading is to be preferred as the original" (because scribes frequently made changes to the text for the sake of easier reading), should prevail. It has been put in brackets in the published Greek text, although preferred by the majority of the committee. Those who think otherwise base their support on its apparent absence from the earliest papyrus manuscript (𝔓[46]); but that is too high a price to pay textually for what is at best uncertain, while its very awkwardness can easily explain its omission.

Christ." This radically new sphere of existence, where all is of grace, is what Paul sees them abandoning for an existence hemmed in by Torah observance.

In abandoning life that is to be lived as it began, constantly within the framework of grace – grace that comes to them through Christ – the Galatians are turning to "another gospel." But having said that, Paul immediately catches himself. They are turning to something "other" all right, but it is certainly no "gospel" (εὐαγγέλιον), which in this instance probably carries both nuances of this word: the message itself as *good news*, and the *content* of the message having to do with the "grace of Christ." Thus the rest of Paul's sentence (v. 7) moves from his sense of amazement that the Galatians should abandon Christ for a false "gospel" to spell out in terse detail what he knows about their present situation: Some people are throwing them into confusion by their desire to change the gospel of Christ into something that is no longer "good news."

This is the first mention of these specific troublemakers in Paul's letters, although a good case can be made that they are related theologically, if not actually, to the itinerants in 2 Cor 2:14–3:6 (and 11:1-11).[28] In any case the present troublemakers are certainly of the same ilk as those in Phil 3:2-3. In the present letter they are specifically mentioned three more times: in 4:17-18 ("They make much of you, but for no good purpose; they want to exclude you [from us], so that you will make much of them"); 5:7-12 ("whoever it is who is confusing you will pay the penalty; I wish those who unsettle you would castrate themselves"); and especially 6:12-13 ("It is those who want to make a good showing in the flesh that try to compel you to be circumcised – only that they may not be persecuted for the cross of Christ. Even they themselves do not obey the law, but they want you to be circumcised so that they may boast concerning your flesh"). These latter two passages specifically indicate that the ultimate issue for the Galatian believers is the circumcision of the men in this nascent Gentile Christian community. The rest of the letter indicates that these troublemakers are on the verge of success in this matter, which suggests that they have presented their case in a way that on the surface

[28] On this matter see G.D. Fee, "'Another Gospel Which You Did not Embrace': 2 Cor 11.4 and the Theology of 1 and 2 Corinthians," *To What End Exegesis? Studies Textual, Exegetical and Theological* (Grand Rapids: Eerdmans, 2001) 240–61 [first publ. 1994]. On the matter of where Galatians fits into the chronology of Paul's letters, see the Introduction, pp. 4-5.

will have appeared to be very convincing. But Paul recognizes it for what it really is, "a perversion of the gospel of Christ."

Verse 8. Paul is about to pronounce an *anathema* on the men he has just mentioned in the preceding sentence. Part of his problem in writing this letter is that the agitators have apparently offered a persuasive case for their point of view. Otherwise it is hard to imagine how the Galatian men would find the option of yielding to circumcision – both its pain and, from the Greek point of view, its shame – as viable, unless they had found the arguments both convincing and not all that truly different from Paul's gospel. Thus to heighten the effect and dramatize the seriousness of the aberration these outsiders are foisting on the Galatians, he begins with the most remote of hypothetical possibilities:[29] "even if we ourselves or an angel from heaven." At this point Paul used the verb "proclaim the good news" (εὐαγγελίζηται), which he will use three times in vv. 8 and 9. The verb itself has been created from the noun "good news" (εὐαγγέλιον), which therefore has the object of the preaching built into the verb.

The point is that the gospel Paul preached among the Galatians is the only true one. As he will point out in vv. 12 and 15-16, just as with his apostleship, Paul's gospel came to him directly from God through Christ's own personal revelation. So any deviation from the divinely given revelation can only be from a human source, and cannot be tolerated even if the unthinkable were to happen – that he himself or an angel were to come to them with a deviation from the pure gospel divinely revealed to him. Those who do such are thereby turned over to God as subject to his curse; they are themselves *Anathema* ("cursed"), who bear such a curse for their distortion of the pure gospel of Christ.

This is the third (and v. 9 is the fourth) of five instances in Paul's letters where he uses the Greek equivalent of the Hebrew term for "something devoted to a deity," which in the Old Testament regularly refers to something set apart for God because it is cursed, and thus by implication the "curse" is from God himself. The two uses that precede the present two occur in 1 Cor 12:3 and 16:22, and are especially intriguing.[30] The latter instance is part of a most unusual conclusion to that letter. For after his own personal greeting (16:21), and without breaking stride, Paul pronounces an *anathema* on anyone

---

[29] The two conditional sentences are textbook grammatical examples of the difference between purely hypothetical and actual conditions.

[30] The final one occurs in Rom 9:3, where Paul could wish himself *anathema* from God if that were to bring about the conversion of the Jewish community.

"who does not love *the Lord*." This in turn is most likely a pickup of
12:3, where the basic Christian confession "the Lord is Jesus (κύριος
Ἰησοῦς)," spoken especially as an utterance of the Spirit, is preceded
by the strange contrast, "no one speaking by the Spirit can say *cursed is
Jesus* (ἀνάθεμα Ἰησοῦς)." Thus the concluding word in 16:21 may
suggest that some believers in the Corinthian community, for reasons
not fully known to us, were saying this very thing, and that Paul at the
end of the letter reverses the curse – that it rests on those who do not
love the Lord.

In any case, Paul now picks up this same theme with regard to the
gospel. So confident is he that the gospel that had been revealed to
him through Christ is the *only* gospel there is, he boldly asserts that
God's own curse should rightly rest on Paul himself, not to mention
an angel, if ever[31] he were to come to them with a different "gospel"
from the one he had preached earlier – the gospel which, by the
empowering of the Spirit (3:3), had brought about their becoming a
part of the new-formed people of God.

Verse 9. What is said so confidently in v. 8 is now repeated in
slightly different form in v. 9, this time with the agitators specifically in
view. That Paul is aware of the somewhat repetitive nature of what he
will again assert is made evident by the "and now again I say," where
the "now again" (ἄρτι πάλιν) is intended to reinforce what was said
in v. 8. While it is absolutely unthinkable that he or an angel would be
party to preaching a different "gospel," the less unthinkable has unfortunately actually happened. Thus Paul's more hypothetical conditional sentence yields to an actual condition, where the "if anyone"
points directly to those who are in fact "preaching to you a 'gospel'
different from the one you have already received." God's own curse
rests upon those who would dare to do so.

Since Paul has often been subjected to criticism for this kind of
curse, two further things need to be said. First, the curse is not spoken
because the agitators disagree with Paul himself. That is, this is hardly
personal on Paul's part. Rather, he recognizes far more clearly than his
later detractors that everything is at stake here – both the gospel of
grace itself and the no-strings-attached inclusion of the Gentiles as full
and equal members of God's household (see esp. Eph 2:11-22).
Second, Paul's detractors would themselves never have the benefit of
the gospel of Christ had Paul lost this battle. Subjecting Gentiles to

[31] This first "if-clause" is purely hypothetical in the Greek (ἐάν with the subjunctive), what is known as a present general condition. The next clause suggests (εἰ with
the indicative) an actual condition.

circumcision in order to belong to God's people would have soon brought the Gentile mission as a whole to an end, and thus would have changed the entire course of European history. Here is a clear case where one needs to be careful of biting the hand that has fed it.

Reflection and Response – Part One

Reflection

I have purposely kept these two opening sections of the letter together, not only because they belong together, but also because they should elicit different forms of response from the reader, and therefore offer us an opportunity to be a bit more reflective. Because of the way the salutation begins, one might get the sense that Paul is simply being defensive, a point of view that could easily be encouraged by vv. 6-9. And this is certainly a way these paragraphs have been read. In fact, for Paul's many detractors – and there are many, even in the Christian world – who think of themselves as more "liberal-minded" than Paul, and thus more godly than he (although they would never actually say this), this is the damning passage.

Unfortunately, one of the reasons they condemn Paul for talking this way about "brothers" in Christ with whom he disagrees, is that there has been an unfortunate history of the use of this passage by ever so many who think of themselves as "orthodox" and thus condemn those with whom they disagree. But one should ask reflectively on what grounds one would use Paul's anathema in this way. His authority comes directly from a personal revelation and calling by the risen Christ, who also revealed to him the content of the essential gospel. Perhaps if one has not had Paul's own kind of revelation – and it is doubtful whether any of us has had such – then we need to ask some different kinds of questions about what this text might mean for us, rather than the purely attitudinal one.

We might begin our reflections by asking whether or not we stand on the other side of Paul's gospel – with those who here stand condemned – because we, too, have added our own set of rules and regulations to the pure gospel of Christ. Is it not possible that in our eagerness to "help God out" as it were, we have added conditions to grace that lie on the "law-keeping" side of things that have almost nothing to do with the gospel itself? It is amazing how historically Pentecostals, who often know about the Spirit the most, trust him the least, and have found it easy to add external regulations regarding food, dress, and entertainment, as a means of "hemming people in," as it were. Having begun in the Spirit (3:3), do I myself find it easier to keep myself and others faithful to Christ by establishing rules of conduct that give me a sense of confidence in my obedience to the "rules" rather than living out of profound and pure gratitude to the God who in grace would include me among his children? Is my identity to be found in some modern form of "circumcision" rather than in trusting God's grace, so that his Spirit produces his character in me (5:22-23)? Why is it, I wonder, that we find law-keeping so attractive? Is it because we have a hard time believing that God accepts and forgives us, just as we are, warts and all? Or am I driven by a need to prove myself before God, since I do not show evidence of the Spirit's fruit as much as I would like?

And if my suggesting this causes the reader to squirm, is this because we really do think that the agitators had it right after all, that God really does require us in our day to abstain from wine, despite the fact that the Bible itself speaks so favorably of wine as a gift from God? And if it does cause us to squirm, perhaps we should admit honestly that we line up far more easily with the agitators than with Paul, and maybe need a rebirth of freedom that comes from a genuine experience of grace.

In any case, this kind of reflection more likely puts us as readers on the less presumptuous side of things in this passage, rather than assuming that we have Paul's own authority to call down God's curse on those who do not agree with our understanding of the gospel. But to reflect in this way will also mean that I have listened more closely to the encouraging words of the salutation itself, that everything is of grace, including the peace that ensues. And that grace has found its ultimate expression in our Lord, Jesus Christ, who gave himself for our sins. Here is the place to learn the humility that will keep me from standing on the wrong side of vv. 6-9; here is the constant reminder that I am a sinner, saved by the grace of him who gave himself for our sins, which means not only forgiveness in the present, but the final rescue of us from this present evil age. And to think that this rescue is precisely in keeping with the will of the eternal God who through Christ and the Spirit has become my own heavenly "Abba"! Here is the place to learn anew that being good is far more important in God's eyes than being right. Arguments may move heads, but love will move hearts.

So how do I respond to this passage overall? First, it reminds me that the gospel is all about Christ, not about me. The constant amazement is that God in his mercy has included me among those who have come to know the grace of Christ; and the constant cause for concern is that I am also called to live in the context of that grace. While it is obviously possible to please God, the plain truth is that God does not like me better if I serve him well. Christ gave himself for me when I was his enemy, not his friend; and serving him well must flow out of a heart of gratitude, not out of a desire to get him to like me better.

Second, it reminds me that some have perverted the gospel of grace by adding law-keeping to it. The question is, how much have I been party to the very thing on which Paul calls down an anathema? And how much have I been party to trying to get others to conform to my "law" rather than to join me in sheer wonder at the grace of God, which alone, by the empowering of the Spirit, is able to cause us to reflect God's true character?

Response

In response, one might ask: In what ways have I assessed my relationship with God as an act of pure grace? Am I among those who like the idea of grace for myself, but readily impose law-keeping on others? In what ways might I have taken the side of Paul's opponents on matters of "law-keeping" as conditions for the continuing experience of God's grace? And if I am guilty of the latter, do I really believe that God's anathema rests on the likes of me? If you are a pastor, do you have a small group of people who will hold you accountable, and with whom you can be honest about such matters?

1. Identify ways in which you are tempted to supplement your trust in God for salvation with trust in a modern-day version of "circumcision." Perhaps making a written response to the above questions would assist you in this matter.
2. Test your response by examining your list against Scripture to evaluate biblically the nature of the items listed.
3. In consultation with one or more trusted brothers or sisters in the community seek to discern the nature of your response to such items.
4. Enter into times of prayer for the purpose of confession of any misplaced trust and again affirming your faith in Christ alone as the basis of salvation.

Galatians 1:10–2:21

The Text

Paul Defends Himself and His Gospel

The way Paul moves from the preceding introductory matters to this
first main section of the letter suggests that part of the strategy of the
Jewish-Christian agitators, in calling Paul's gospel into question, was
first of all to call into question his apostleship. One can easily see how
these two matters are essentially related. If Paul lacks proper authentication, in this case from the present leaders of the church in
Jerusalem, then one can make a considerable case that his version of
the gospel is also not authentic. The itinerants would thus have argued
that converts in Paul's churches need the correctives they bring –
ostensibly under the authorization of Jerusalem (whether they actually
were or not is moot, but they apparently presented themselves in this
way). In light of what Paul says in v. 10, which is the very first thing
up in the letter, it seems likely that with a bit of reverse psychology
they had accused Paul of trying to be a "people pleaser" – because he
did not insist on his converts' also adhering to certain aspects of the
Torah. From their point of view, Paul is trying to make following
Christ "easier" than it actually should be.

Both the subtlety of this argument and its viciousness toward Paul
led him to begin the letter with a long defense of his apostleship itself.
What was ultimately at stake was the authenticity of the gospel itself,
and thus the genuineness of the Galatians' present faith in Christ and
experience of the Spirit. But to get there Paul must first address the
issue of his own authenticity as an apostle. Thus in turn he addresses,
first, the issue of his being a "people pleaser" (v. 10), and then the
authenticity, and thus the source, of his gospel (vv. 11-12). What
follows is a narration of Paul's story as to his (basically non-)
relationship with Jerusalem. He begins by capitalizing on what was
apparently the primary accusation against him by the agitators – that he
lacks proper authority because he has not been sent out by Jerusalem.
Instead of defending himself at this point, he takes up their accusation
and turns it on its head. Rather than having come to Galatia on the
basis of human authority (from Jerusalem) as his detractors have done –
even though he never directly makes this latter point – Paul lacks

human authority altogether. Thus he begins with a brief recital about his prior life *in Jerusalem*,[1] both as an avid persecutor of the church and as having advanced in Judaism beyond his peers (vv. 13-14). The rest of this first part of Paul's narrative (vv. 15-24) then recounts his (basically) lack of relationship *with the believers in Jerusalem*: just fifteen days over a span of some seventeen years, and that was limited to his staying with Peter and becoming acquainted with James, the Lord's brother.

Having thus distanced himself from Jerusalem in terms of acquaintance, and thus of their non-authorization of his apostleship, he moves on to narrate his first significant trip to Jerusalem (2:1-10). In this case he went up deliberately, in keeping with a prophetic word, to talk about the gospel he and Barnabas had been preaching among the Gentiles (2:1-10). The result of this meeting was an agreement by both parties as to spheres of ministry, plus an affirmation on the part of Jerusalem of Paul's message ("they added nothing to my gospel," v. 6). Moreover, the implied assumption is that they agreed to a Torah-free gospel for Gentile converts, since "Titus was not compelled to be circumcised" (v. 3).

But the next incident, which took place in Antioch (2:11-14a), makes it clear that the issue was not only over the circumcision of Gentiles, but included the food laws as well. For some time the Jewish Christians in Antioch, including Peter and Barnabas, had been eating together with Gentile believers without strict adherence to the stipulations of the food laws. At the instigation of some Jewish believers from Jerusalem (specifically "from James"), they chose to join the latter at separate meals. Outwardly this had the appearance of being innocent enough – a legitimate compromise one could well argue. But Paul saw it as putting pressure on Gentile believers either to conform to a strict interpretation of Torah at this point, or else making them second-class citizens in God's newly constituted kingdom under the rule of Christ[2] and empowered by the Spirit. So Paul uses the content of his "speech" to Peter on that occasion as the way of launching directly into the issue now facing the believers in Galatia (2:14b-21).

For those who dislike the apostle Paul, as arrogant and intolerant, this entire passage is used by them as grist for their mills; for those of us Gentile believers who appreciate that we exist only because Paul

[1] Although this is not said, it is assumed by the content; and offers a substantial reason for starting this way at all. It is further supported by the narrative in Acts (chs. 7-9).

[2] For this reality, see e.g. 1 Cor 15:24.

won this battle, this passage helps to explain not only the battle that Paul waged for our sakes, but also to recognize that God had called and inspired this spirited apostle so that we might come to faith through "the truth of the gospel" (2:5, 14).

Galatians 1:10-12 – The True Source of Paul's Gospel

> [10]*Am I now trying to win human approval, or God's approval? Or am I trying to please people? If I were still trying to please people, I would not be a servant of Christ.* [11]*I want you to know, brothers and sisters, that the gospel I preached is not of human origin.* [12]*I did not receive it from any human source, nor was I taught it; rather, I received it by revelation from Jesus Christ.*

This paragraph serves as a transition from the salutation and curse formula to the body of the letter. This is clearly the case for vv. 11-12, both of which begin with an explanatory "for" (γάρ)[3] and by direct echo pick up the concerns expressed in v. 1. But whereas v. 1 dealt with the source of Paul's *apostleship*, vv. 11 and 12 deal with the source of Paul's *gospel*. Most of our difficulties as readers lie with v. 10, which also begins with a "for" and seems to be equally transitional, while at the same time it implies an added dimension to what was said in vv. 6-9.

Verse 10. This verse has long been a source of difficulty for scholars, especially regarding its role in the present argument. Part of the reason for this lies with the transitional "for" with which it begins, and which is so difficult to account for that it is usually bypassed in English translations.[4] Nonetheless its presence is sometimes recognized by the paragraphing, where it is included as a sort of conclusion to the double curse of vv. 6-9.[5] In any case, the sentence must be taken seriously as

---

[3] Thus Danker puts the one in v. 11 under the category, "marker of clarification," which he explains as "appear[ing] to be used adverbially like our 'now' (in which the temporal sense gives way to signal an important point of transition), 'well, then.' 'you see'" (BDAG 2 [under γάρ]).

[4] This is true even of the NET Bible, which has a copious footnote system that would allow them to explain the omission in this case. The exceptions are the standard ones, KJV and NASB, and (more surprisingly) the ESV. This passage is unfortunately not referenced in BDAG, perhaps in itself another piece of evidence for the difficulty it presents here.

[5] So, e.g., the NJB and NET Bible, which include it as the conclusion of the paragraph that begins with v. 6; it is especially so of translations that use paragraph titles (NIV, TNIV, ESV, NET, GNB, NLT, NASB), while the NAB does the same thing by putting a space after v. 10. Most of these translations, which follow the UBS[4] paragraphing in this case, also set it off as a separate paragraph within the section (the

intentional by Paul, and thus as offering an "explanation" for what is most likely an otherwise hidden piece of information, known to both Paul and his readers regarding the charges brought by the agitators against Paul and his gospel: that he avoided requiring circumcision as a way of trying to "please 'men'."[6] If that be the case, and it seems the most likely explanation for the "for" (γάρ), then in a certain sense it does indeed belong to the paragraph that precedes. But since it also moves considerably beyond the concerns of the curse – which have to do with those who preach "another gospel" – and deals with Paul's own relationship to the gospel, it may more legitimately be seen as introducing the "defense" of Paul's ministry and gospel that follows.

If its role in the context of the epistle can be thus explained with a relative degree of certainty, its actual content is another matter altogether. The sentence begins with an (apparently) emphatic repetition of the "now" (ἄρτι) from v. 9. In direct response to his own calling down God's curse on the agitators, Paul asks rhetorically, "*Now* am I seeking 'men's' approval?" Since nothing before this sentence specifically prepares us for its content, it seems most likely to be a direct response to yet another accusation brought against Paul by his detractors: by avoiding preaching circumcision, Paul has deliberately offered a gospel that has as its goal an attempt to curry human favor in order to make converts. Thus the verb that ordinarily means "to persuade" in this case seems to carry a slightly pejorative sense of trying to gain someone's approval. This understanding of the verb seems demanded by the follow-on phrase, "or God." That is, by means of the double curse (in vv. 8-9) am I trying *now* to win the approval of human beings – or even of God himself?[7] That this is the best way to understand this first clause lies with the semi-repetition that immediately follows, "or am I seeking to please 'men'?" which in turn is followed by his own denial of such a possibility with a

---

NJB and NET are notable exceptions, the former using paragraphs but no titles). The paragraphing that I have adopted for the commentary is that of NA[27], which I am convinced makes much more sense of what Paul actually does here.

[6] Paul's ἀνθρώπους ("men") is nicely ambiguous here; it would primarily seem to be generic (= human beings), but in this case it could also be gender specific, since it is especially the men who would have to come under the knife.

[7] The addition "or God" to this question is difficult enough to have engendered several alternative explanations as to what it means here. I take it as a negative in both cases (i.e., Am I trying to please either "men" or God?). It is possible to take it as positive (i.e., Am I trying to please "men," or [as I should be, only] God?), while others see it as disjunctive (i.e., Who am I trying to please? men or God?).

contrary-to-fact conditional sentence: "If I were yet seeking to please 'men,' Christ's slave I would no longer be."

Nonetheless, if this is the best explanation of the "what" of this verse, it still leaves us on the outside looking in as to the "why." Nothing that is said in the preceding curse quite prepares us for this particular form of denial. That is, it is one thing to offer a double curse on the troublemakers, and then move on to a rebuttal of their charges; but it is quite another thing to begin that rebuttal with a denial that he has been seeking human (and perhaps divine) approval. That he begins with an emphatic, "*now* am I doing this?" which is quite unrelated to anything actually said in vv. 8 and 9, can best be explained if this accusation had actually been brought against him by the agitators.

If so, then it seems highly likely that his detractors are offering this as the real reason why Paul does not advocate circumcision for his Gentile converts. The agitators probably well knew that Paul by his own admission, "became all things to all people that by *all means* he might win some" (1 Cor 9:22). Thus when he was among Jews (only) he lived like a Jew, but not in his case for the sake of "harmony," but for the sake of evangelism. He could do this precisely because he had learned that none of these things, including circumcision and food laws, count for anything with God (see 5:6 and 6:16; cf. 1 Cor 7:19). Paul has come to realize that God simply does not care whether men are circumcised or not, or whether people eat or do not eat certain foods. Thus when he is in a strictly Jewish context Paul eats "kosher" so as to evangelize Jews, because in Christ, who has made food laws irrelevant, he is free to do so; and when he is with Gentiles he eats "non-kosher" for the same reason. But for people who believe otherwise – that God really does care about these things – then Paul's doing one thing when with Jews and not doing it when with Gentiles is to be explained as an attempt "to please people."

Paul knows well from previous history that his fully redeemed attitude toward circumcision, food, and special days (including sabbath) does not sit well with those who take such "divine matters" with special seriousness as irrevocable. So his immediate response to the twofold "curse" of vv. 8 and 9 is to speak directly to what he otherwise knows about his detractors, who have argued that he lives like this because he is a man without conviction and is interested only in currying the favor of the people he preaches to. Thus Paul responds, "in light of what I have just said [in vv. 8-9], am I *now* trying to curry favor either with people or God?" If this were in fact the case, he concludes, I am no longer Christ's slave. Rather, by implication, he is enslaved to his own personal point of view.

It is of some further interest that many contemporary believers, who tout Paul as the apostle of grace and freedom, are not at all prepared to go this far with Paul regarding their own pet aspects of Torah. Some, for example, rather than seeing Sabbath as a gift to be appreciated, see it as a law that must be "observed" in a certain way. But not so Paul: God regards all days alike (Rom 14:5-6). And thus on these matters Paul is not seeking to please people but to be faithful to the freedom of the gospel.

Verses 11-12. With another set of "for's" (γάρ) Paul now proceeds from the denials of v. 10 – that his gospel was not a matter of trying to please people – to a twofold explanation as to the nature (v. 11) and source (v. 12) of his gospel. These two sentences thus pick up the negating prepositional phrases from v. 1 regarding Paul's apostleship, that it is "neither from human beings nor through human instrumentality, but through Jesus Christ."

Using the first of eight vocatives ("brothers and sisters") in the letter, Paul speaks directly to the Galatians, now "making known" to them the true source of "the gospel that was 'gospeled' by me."[8] In doing so, Paul picks up a redundancy that had occurred in almost identical fashion in 1 Cor 15:3, except in this case it is even more emphatic. Thus it is not now simply "the gospel I 'gospeled' *to you*," as in 1 Corinthians, but "the gospel that has been 'gospeled' *by me*," not just in Galatia, but everywhere, being implied.

Paul's concern now lies altogether with the divine character of his gospel, not its human agency, a point made clear by the present tense verb that follows: "that it *is* not in keeping with human design (κατὰ ἄνθρωπον)." The emphasis with the phrase is thus not on its origins as such, but on its nature; its content lies totally outside what would be in keeping with the merely human thing to do. This is why Paul cannot possibly have been trying to "please human beings." His gospel lies quite outside that frame of reference.

So with yet another explanatory "for" (γάρ), Paul moves from a negation as to the nature of the gospel he proclaimed, that it was not in accordance with what is merely human, to an equally strong negation as to its source. The "for" reinforces his point: what is not in

---

[8] This awkward "translation" is an attempt to help the reader see that both the noun and the verb appear in this sentence, and that the verb does not mean "preach" as such; rather it has to do with telling/proclaiming the gospel, with all the emphasis on the gospel that is being told.

keeping with what is merely human, by that same token cannot possibly have a human source. Thus, "I neither had it handed on[9] to me from a human being [= from any human source at all], nor was I taught it," which does not mean that he is opposed to "teaching" as such, but that he himself had not been taught the content of the gospel by any human being. At the same time this negation moves him toward the narrative that follows in which he so strongly and deliberately distances himself from Jerusalem – that, whatever else, his understanding of the gospel does not come from there.

Rather (ἀλλά), he insists, his gospel came to him "through revelation of/from Jesus Christ" (δι᾽ ἀποκαλύψεως Ἰησοῦ Χριστοῦ). At face value Paul's preposition could be ambiguous, whether he intended Christ as the object (content) of the revelation[10] or the (grammatical) subject, the one who did the revealing of the gospel to him. And even though in the end these probably come out very close to the same place (i.e., the revealer is also the revealed), in this case the genitive is most likely subjective (as TNIV, "I received it by revelation from Jesus Christ").[11] After all, at issue in this particular sentence is the source, not the content, of the revelation. It was neither "handed down" to him from a human being,[12] nor did it come to him by way of (human) instructors. Rather he received his gospel by direct revelation – from Christ himself. And with that he launches into a brief accounting of his non-relationship with Jerusalem.

Galatians 1:13-24 – Paul's lack of Relationship with Jerusalem

> [13]*For you have heard of my previous way of life in Judaism, how intensely I persecuted the church of God and tried to destroy it.* [14]*I was advancing in Judaism beyond many of my own age among my people and was extremely zealous for the traditions of my fathers.*

---

[9] In Paul this verb (παρέλαβον), which can mean simply "I received," is used consistently for the handing down of traditional teaching; see e.g., 1 Cor 11:2, 23; 15:1 and 3. Given that ordinary sense in Paul and the present context, that is almost certainly its intended sense here.

[10] As in the commentaries by Burton, Bruce, Betz, Fung, Morris, Dunn, Matera, and Martyn.

[11] So also Lightfoot, Longenecker, Hansen.

[12] Gk. οὐδὲ γὰρ ἐγὼ παρὰ ἀνθρώπου παρέλαβον αὐτό (*for I neither received it from a human source*), where the παρέλαβον is a semi-technical term for the passing on of tradition from generation to generation. In Paul's case, the "tradition" he received came directly from Christ himself, not from a merely human source.

[15] *But when God, who set me apart from birth[a] and called me by his grace, was pleased* [16] *to reveal his Son in me so that I might preach him among the Gentiles, my immediate response was not to consult any human being.* [17] *I did not go up to Jerusalem to see those who were apostles before I was, but I went into Arabia. Later I returned to Damascus.*

[18] *Then after three years, I went up to Jerusalem to get acquainted with Cephas[b] and stayed with him fifteen days.* [19] *I saw none of the other apostles – only James, the Lord's brother.* [20] *I assure you before God that what I am writing you is no lie.*

[21] *Then I went to Syria and Cilicia.* [22] *I was personally unknown to the churches of Judea that are in Christ.* [23] *They only heard the report: "The man who formerly persecuted us is now preaching the faith he once tried to destroy."* [24] *And they praised God because of me.*

[a] Or *from my mother's womb*   [b] That is, Peter

With this series of four brief paragraphs Paul sets out to explain the two assertions in v. 12: that the origin of his gospel had no relationship of any kind with "men," but rather that it came directly from Christ. The narrative itself is in four distinguishable parts, recognized by the paragraphing in the TNIV. He begins by establishing his impeccable Jewish credentials when he had lived in Jerusalem before his "conversion" (vv. 13-14). The final three parts set forth his non-relationship with the Jerusalem church and its leaders in the years following his conversion (vv. 16b-24). That this is the primary concern of the passage is made evident by the (very long) sentence that makes up our vv. 15-17. What begins as a narrative of Paul's conversion (vv. 15-16a) concludes not with its having resulted in his becoming a proclaimer of Christ, but with emphasis on the fact that there was a three year hiatus before he went up to Jerusalem for the first time as a believer (vv. 16b-17). The final two paragraphs narrate in turn his one (quite brief) visit to Jerusalem as a believer, whose aim was to become acquainted with Peter (vv. 18-20), and his subsequent return to home turf in Syria and Cilicia (vv. 21-24), again with emphasis on his non-residence in Jerusalem.

Once one sees the narrative in these terms, that is, in light of what Paul actually says, then one must of necessity ask the "why" question:[13] why would Paul tell his "story" only in terms of his non-residence in

[13] Or at least one would think that would be the case; it is therefore a small cause for wonder that this question is so seldom raised in the literature, and when it is raised the emphasis is basically on his not having received his gospel from "men," without noting the more dominant motif of his distancing himself from Jerusalem.

Jerusalem as a follower of Christ, and thus of his basically non-acquaintance with the apostles except for a brief visit with Peter in which he also met James? Whatever else, this is not a conversion narrative as such, but a narrative intended to distance himself from the Jerusalem apostles during the first decade and a half of his life as a Christian believer and apostle. While a variety of answers to this "why" question have been brought forward, the most common is that his opponents had accused him of having only human credentials, if at all, and certainly not the right ones, meaning "authorized" by Jerusalem, as they claimed themselves to be. Therefore, Paul cannot be a truly "authentic" apostle; so the Galatians should now pay attention to those who have such authority.

But that seems to make little sense of the way the narrative itself develops. Rather, Paul gladly acquiesces to the fact that he lacks proper human credentials, especially that he was not "credentialed" by Jerusalem. Indeed, he argues by way of narration, he had almost no personal relationship at all with the Jerusalem apostles. Thus, what his detractors glory in – having the blessing of Jerusalem (whether true or not) – Paul dismisses altogether. In so doing, he will validate the point made in vv. 11 and 12, that he did not receive his gospel from a human source of any kind, especially not from Jerusalem; rather he received it by direct revelation from Christ himself. Thus the major part of this opening narrative is a deliberate distancing of himself from Jerusalem, that they had nothing at all to do with his apostleship. What his detractors thus saw as a debility, Paul is quite ready to glory in: his apostleship and his gospel are altogether independent of Jerusalem.

Verses 13-14. This long sentence is the first of two instances in his letters[14] where Paul feels compelled to speak about his former life as a religious zealot, well-trained in the Judaism of his day. In both cases he puts his own credentials forward as evidence that he was far more advanced in the ways of Judaism than his present opponents. His former zeal evidenced itself in two ways: first, with regard to training in, and adherence to, the Torah; second, with regard to his unspeakable antipathy toward those who had become followers of Jesus as the Messiah. It is of interest that in this telling of his story he puts these two items in reverse order, mentioning his religious zeal against believers in Christ before he speaks of his advancement in Judaism.

---

[14] See Phil 3:4-6; cf. 1 Tim 1:12-15, where it occurs in a slightly different way as evidence of the greatness and universality of God's abundant grace.

This is now the fourth sentence in a row that begins with an explanatory "for" (γάρ), and as with the one that began v. 10, it is also somewhat elusive as to what is being explained. Most likely in this case, the "for" is not just about the content of this long sentence, but rather is intended to introduce the entire narrative that follows (at least through v. 24). What he sets out to explain first is his role in "Judaism," a word that occurs only in these two instances (vv. 13 and 14) in the New Testament and seldom elsewhere, and which at the same time anticipates the cognate verb in 2:14, where Paul accuses Peter of "Judaizing" with regard to food laws. The word had apparently been coined by the author of 2 Maccabees to describe "the Judeans" who had remained absolutely loyal to Jewish faith and practice, which in that author's case included both loyalty to Jewish practices and antipathy toward those who failed to do so.[15] Thus Paul begins the present narrative by highlighting these same two aspects of his former absolute loyalty to "Judaism."

The purpose of this present sentence, however, is not simply to offer a kind of "before" to set the stage for the "after" that follows – although it does that as well. Rather, while deliberately setting himself in contrast to the agitators who have disrupted life in Galatia, he makes two crucial points with regard to his own former life in "Judaism." First, and especially in light of the present accusations against him, he acknowledges that as one deeply loyal to his Jewish heritage he had had plenty of "relationship" with the church before his encounter with the risen Christ.[16] But it was entirely antagonistic; he "persecuted the church of God and tried to destroy it," so much so that this reality in itself gave him good reason to stay aloof from Jerusalem after his divine encounter. Whatever else, Paul did not return to Jerusalem as a kind of "trophy," to be put on the circuit, as it were, as evidence of Christ's saving power. Indeed, his former antipathy was such that many had good reason to hold him at arm's length,[17] since for them this might be just another ploy for him to worm his way into their confidence so as to know who should be executed. After all, he not

[15] See 2 Macc 2:21; 8:1; 14:38(2x); and 4 Macc 4:26. Apart from a synagogue inscription, these are its only known occurrences prior to these two instances in Paul.

[16] Indeed, we will learn in the next sentence that this life-changing encounter was of such moment that his first response was to abandon both Damascus and Jerusalem for a long stay in Arabia – the place where God had first revealed himself to Israel in the Exodus (see v. 17).

[17] Just as Luke describes in his own report of Paul's first visit to Jerusalem as a believer (Acts 9:26).

only "had persecuted the church of God," but had done so in a deliberate attempt "to destroy it."

Second, the reason for his former antipathy is found (in a somewhat circuitous way, to be sure) in the rest of the sentence (our v. 14): his own significant role in Judaism. He was not simply another young man from the Diaspora who had come to study Torah in Jerusalem; he had in fact excelled in his studies, so much so that he could claim to have been advancing toward "the head of his class" as it were, "beyond many of my own age among my people." And whatever else was true of the young Saul of Tarsus, he was absolutely devoted to – "extremely zealous for" is his own language – "the traditions of my fathers." Indeed, even a casual reading of Paul's letters, especially the present one, reveals a man with a brilliant mind, a passionate disposition, and learned in the Jewish Scriptures. It is safe to surmise that the (Jewish) world would surely have heard of Saul of Tarsus had it never heard of Paul the apostle.

Although not said directly in this case, it seems very likely that much of this second clause is therefore also intended to function in a way similar to the companion passage in Phil 3:4-6, namely that whatever "credentials" his opponents may bring to the table when attempting to upset his churches, he quite outstripped them at two crucial points: in his knowledge of and zeal for "the traditions of my fathers." And one should not miss the "my" in this clause. As will become clear in the arguments that follow (3:6–4:7; 4:21-31), Paul does not consider himself a renegade with regard to his place among his own people. Although Christ has brought the *traditions* to an end, Paul still thinks of himself and his churches as belonging most truly to the ancient people of God; they are "*my* fathers," whatever else. This alone explains his own passionate zeal for the Gentile mission evidenced throughout his letters, but especially in Galatians and Romans. As we will learn in 3:6-9, for Paul it is primarily related to the fulfillment of God's promise to Abraham, picked up regularly in the prophets, that God's Story that began with Abraham always had the eventual inclusion of the Gentiles as a crucial part of the Story.[18]

---

[18] See the promise to Abraham (Gen 12:2-3), which concludes: "… and all peoples on earth will be blessed through you." This dimension of Israel's reason for being is especially pronounced in Isaiah, beginning at 2:3 ("Many peoples will come and say, 'Come, let us go up to the mountain of the Lord, to the house of the God of Jacob. He will teach us his ways, so that we may walk in his ways'"); cf. e.g., 11:10; 52:15; 55:5; 56:3; 66:18.

We need also to note Paul's language in v. 13 for the newly formed people of God, namely "the assembly (ἐκκλησία) of God." The popular myth that this term means "the called out ones" needs to be laid to rest. While that is indeed the derivation of the word, usage had become so fixed by the time of Paul that that derivation was no longer in its present range of meaning. The happy choice of this word for Paul – and other New Testament writers – is that it does double duty: it was a term of familiarity in the Greek world that also had deep roots in the Old Testament. Thus, long before the Old Testament had been translated into Greek (the Septuagint), the term had been used for the "assembled citizens" in the Greek city states, a usage found in Luke's narrative in Acts 19 of the "riot" in Ephesus (vv. 32, 39, 40). Precisely because it already had such usage in the Greek world, it was the word chosen by the Greek translators of the Old Testament for the Hebrew term translated "congregation" (*qahal*) in such phrases as "the whole congregation of Israel," which in the Septuagint became "the whole assembly of Israel." In this way it became the natural term of use in the Gentile churches, since it was a familiar term that also had Old Testament roots. Thus the various Greco-Roman towns and cities where Paul had established Christian communities now had another "assembly" in their midst, one which belonged to the living God, and their true "citizenship" was in heaven.[19]

Of particular interest in the present sentence is that it is not being used in its normal sense, referring to specific churches, but to the "church universal," as it were. Although he does not do so often,[20] Paul is here stretching its meaning beyond that of the local gathering of God's people. And thus, apart from the unfortunate transference of the term to the building in which the people gather (an idea totally foreign to the NT), Paul himself is the forerunner of our other present uses of the term "church." He had already used it in the plural in v. 1 to designate the individual congregations in Galatia and will do so again in v. 23 of those in Judea. But the present usage makes it clear that for him the term can be used as a collective to refer to the entire "body of Christ." Thus the language "assembly/church of God" had by the time of this writing already become a standard designation for the people of God newly constituted through Christ and the Spirit. As with the term "Christians" (Acts 11:26), it almost certainly arose among believers in Gentile settings as a way of distinguishing them in

[19] See Phil 1:27 (esp. in the TNIV) and 3:20.
[20] Cf. the similar usage in Phil 3:6; such usage has previously occurred in 1 Cor 10:32 and will occur on a regular basis in both Colossians and Ephesians.

two ways: first, they did not continue to use the Jewish designation
"synagogue," as apparently was the case among some Jewish
believers;[21] second, they formed an entirely new kind of *ekklesia* in the
Greco-Roman cities, where both Gentile and Jew together formed the
newly-constituted people of God.

Verses 15-17. Although our English translations must do otherwise,
vv. 15-17 are a single long, convoluted Greek sentence in which Paul
begins with some immediately important points about his calling and
mission, and then concludes with what is clearly his main concern: his
lack of contact with Jerusalem in his early years as a believer. At the
same time there is a striking contrast between Paul's own achievements in vv. 13 and 14 and God's activity in vv. 15 and 16*ab*. Thus,
when Paul again picks up his own role in the narrative in v. 16*c*
(through v. 22), the emphasis is not at all on his (apostolic)
achievements, but on his singular lack of relationship with the apostles
in Jerusalem.

Grammatically, the sentence is a temporal clause, whose protasis (the
"when" clause, vv. 15-16ab) speaks of matters that preceded, and thus
led to, the apodosis (the "then" clause, vv. 16*c*-17). The sentence in its
barest form thus reads: "When [God] was pleased to reveal his Son in
me, I at once did not consult with 'flesh and blood' [= human
beings]." The complexity of the sentence lies with the further
modifiers and additions, including a very important purpose clause, all
of which from Paul's perspective are necessary to get at the main point
he is trying to make: that his calling to Christian discipleship and
apostleship came directly from God, totally without human mediation.
At the same time the added purpose clause anticipates the primary
concern of the rest of the letter: Gentile inclusion apart from doing
works of Torah. To ease the task of interpretation, I offer the
following structural display of the whole sentence (mention of God is
in **bold**, Paul underlined, and other people in *italics*; the lines are
"lettered" for the sake of the comments that follow):

---

[21] See James 2:2; the usage in Rev 2:9 and 3:9 ("synagogue of Satan") is more
ambiguous, as to whether it refers to actual Jewish synagogues that are acting contrary
to God's will, or Christian communities that are doing the same. In any case, Luke,
himself a Gentile, begins to speak of the early believers as the "church" (ἐκκλησία)
right up front (as early as Acts 5:11); but this is very likely the later term being used of
an earlier time.

a. When	**he was pleased**		[start of protasis]
b.	**(who had set**	<u>me</u> **apart** from <u>my mother's womb</u>	
c.	and **called**	<u>me</u> **through his grace)**	[description of God's activity]
d.		**to reveal his Son** <u>in me</u>	[basic protasis]
e.	so that	<u>I might preach</u> him *among the Gentiles,*	[God's purpose]
f.	at once	<u>I did not consult</u> *with flesh and blood*	[neg. apodosis]
g.		<u>nor did I go up</u> *to Jerusalem to the* <u>before me</u> *apostles,*	[elaboration]
h.	but	<u>I went away to Arabia</u>	[pos. apodosis]
i.		<u>and returned again to Damascus.</u>	[elaboration]

You will note that God's threefold activity with regard to Paul (lines b-d) dominates the protasis, concluding with the ultimate goal of that activity (line e): Gentile inclusion in the people of God. The apodosis, by way of contrast, is dominated by a single, repeated concern: where Paul did not go immediately following God's call.

These several features also indicate that even though in a sense the sentence begins as a "conversion narrative," that is neither its main point nor its main thrust. Indeed, it lacks the essential element of Luke's thrice-repeated narrative of Paul's "conversion" in Acts[22] – his being confronted by the risen Christ. Paul's own version of that event is expressed as a rhetorical question in 1 Cor 9:1: "Have I not seen Jesus the Lord?" In his view this encounter on the Damascus Road was in fact an out-of-the-ordinary "resurrection appearance," but of a kind with those that had preceded his (1 Cor 15:8).[23] Precisely this element is what is lacking here, where the emphasis in not on Paul's "conversion," but on his divine calling to be an apostle to the Gentiles. According to Luke's account, even though this calling was first revealed to Paul at his conversion (Acts 26:17-18),[24] it took effect when Christ appeared to him later in the temple in Jerusalem (22:17-21). In the present version Paul goes right to the heart of things – and with a threefold emphasis. First, picking up what he had said in v. 12, he stresses that his apostleship is altogether the result of divine initiative and thus of divine grace; second, he makes the point that God's

---

[22] See Acts 9:1-19, whose essence is repeated in his address to the mob in Jerusalem (22:1-21) and before Agrippa, Bernice, and Festus in Caesarea (26:4-23). It should also be noted (a) that Paul's role in the Gentile mission is a key feature in each of these narratives (9:15; 22:21; 26:17-18, 23), and (b) that each of them speaks of his one visit to Jerusalem as endangering his life (9:29; 22:17; 26:17).

[23] That is, Paul's language forbids one to think of this experience as a vision of some kind. He is quite explicit; as one "born out of due season" he saw the risen Lord, the last in a sequence of such appearances.

[24] As well as to Ananias (Acts 9:15).

revelation of his Son *in Paul* was for the purpose of the Gentile mission; and third, Paul deliberately (and understandably) chose not to consult any human being about this calling, including the apostles in Jerusalem. These features together thus distance the content of this sentence from a conversion narrative as such; instead they put the emphasis on Paul's calling to take the gospel to the Gentiles, and that without human approval or mediation.

Lines a and b. Although not mentioned by name, God[25] is the implied subject of the verbs and the antecedent of the repeated "his" in the protasis. Thus the "*God* [who] was pleased to reveal *his* Son in me" is identified first as the "*One who* set me apart ..." and then as the "*One who* called me by *his* grace." Thus Paul's own emphasis is altogether on God, who is described first as "being pleased" to act in this way. Paul's calling and appointment were first of all an expression of God's eternal purposes, purposes which God himself delighted to bring to pass in human history. While this kind of language has engendered a great deal of theological conversation, Paul is not here trying to make a theological statement as such. Rather he was a child of a worldview that put proper emphasis on what God is doing in the world. After all, Paul's story is not that of a seeker, nor of a "converted sinner." Rather he had thought of himself as actually doing God's business when he was intercepted by and stood face to face with the risen Christ – the one whom he believed God had cursed by having him hanged on a cross. It would have been unthinkable for him that such an extraordinary life-changing encounter, which was entirely by divine initiative, was not already present in God from the time that Paul came from his mother's womb.

Furthermore, with something of a coup, and certainly as an intentional contrast with the agitators, Paul deliberately refers to his calling in language reminiscent of Israel's prophetic tradition, especially Jeremiah: "Before I formed you in the womb, I knew you, before you were born I set you apart; I appointed you as a prophet to the nations [= Gentiles]" (Jer 1:5; cf. Isa 49:1). Thus from Paul's time-bound

---

[25] The word "God" (ὁ θεός) is missing in the earliest and best manuscript evidence (𝔓[46] B G Old Latin) and early Fathers (Origen, Eusebius, Ambrosiaster, Victorinus of Rome, Epiphanius, Chrysostom, Jerome, and Theodoret). Cf. B.M. Metzger, *A Textual Commentary on the Greek New Testament* (2nd ed.; New York: American Bible Society, 1994), pp. 521-22 ("The reading with ὁ θεός has every appearance of being a scribal gloss making explicit the implied subject of εὐδόκησεν ['he was pleased'], nor is there any good reason why the words should have been deleted if they had been original").

existence, and looking back on his experience of grace, he recognized that his "calling" was already a part of God's purposes from the time he was born, and in so doing, as with Jeremiah, God called him precisely to carry the good news to the Gentiles.[26]

Line c. While the first clause in this narrative places Paul's calling within God's eternal purposes, this second one, "and called me by his grace," brings it forward to the event itself. Thus in a moment of internal "echo" within our letter Paul picks up his own language about the Gentiles from v. 6 ("the one who called *you* into the grace of Christ") and uses it to remind them that his own coming to faith was similar to theirs. Since in some ways this clause is unnecessary to the point of the present narrative, it almost certainly exists because of the present situation in Galatia, where the agitators are urging Gentiles to add a plus factor to grace in the form of law-keeping. Here is a man who, according to vv. 13-14, had impeccable credentials as a law-abiding Jew; by his own later testimony he had been circumcised and had kept Torah blamelessly (Phil 3:4-6). Yet his becoming a follower of the risen Christ had nothing at all to do with that. Rather, God called him and redeemed him on the basis of grace, and grace alone. There can be little question, given what we know from Paul's other letters, that this experience of grace established for him the absolute paradigm of God's gracious acceptance of all people, including Gentiles – quite apart from the observance of Torah, which he had done blamelessly.

Line d. With this phrase, "to reveal his Son in me," Paul moves on to the crucial matter with regard to God's purpose in having called him by his grace. In what must be considered one of the more surprising moments in Paul's letters, he here speaks of the result of his "conversion" in terms of "God's revealing his Son *in me*." The surprise (in terms of our expectations) is twofold: (*a*) that Paul thinks of his "conversion" in this case not in terms of what happened *to* me, or as in 2:20 in terms of what Christ lovingly did *for* me (and by implication for all others), but in terms of the revelation taking place *in* me; and (*b*) that who is revealed in Paul is not "Christ" or "the Lord Jesus," but God's own Son. Both of these realities need brief discussion.

First, despite the way many scholars and translators have read this sentence, one must take seriously that Paul's preposition "in" (ἐν)

---

[26] The term "from my mother's womb" (ἐκ κοιλίας μητρός μου) is not used elsewhere by Paul; but it does occur twice in Acts (3:2; 14:8), where it clearly means "from birth." From the perspective of the present narrative it is ultimately irrelevant as to whether it also means "while in the womb."

carries its ordinary locative force, having to do with the location, not the means, of the revelation. The point is that Paul is not here trying to establish that God revealed his Son *to* him, as though this were a different way of speaking of his encounter with the risen Lord noted first in 1 Cor 9:1-2. That point is made earlier in v. 12. He could have repeated that clearly and easily enough[27]; Paul's point rather has ultimately to do with his apostleship and the true source of his gospel. Thus his emphasis here is that he himself is the *locus* of that revelation, meaning in context that the revelation of/from Christ that he has spoken of in v. 12 has taken place *in Paul* in such a way that both the gospel itself and Paul's apostleship should be visible to others. In effect, Paul himself is Exhibit A of God's saving grace. That the implacable enemy is now a promoter of what he once sought to destroy is for Paul supreme evidence of "the grace of God." Thus Paul's "in me" has little to do with his own inward sense of God's grace; rather it must be kept closely related to the purpose clause that immediately follows.[28]

Second, the fact that in a letter where "Christ" (Χριστός) is by far the most common way of referring to his Lord (six times to this point),[29] it should probably catch our attention that Paul here refers to God as revealing *his Son* in Paul. This usage would seem to set the stage for the next two occurrences (2:20; 4:4-6), which together suggest that near the center of Paul's gospel is a "Son of God" Christology, which has Jewish messianism deeply embedded in it.[30]

---

[27] The evidence is quite certain – and consistent – with regard to how Paul uses the verb "reveal" (ἀποκαλύπτω). When he speaks of the revelation as coming *to* someone, he uses the dative (1 Cor 2:10; 14:30; Eph 3:5; Phil 3:15); when he indicates the locus of the revelation he uses ἐν (Rom 1:17, and here); the usage in 1 Cor 3:13 is probably a dative of means. The greater problem with the prevailing view is that there is no known instance where Paul uses ἐν to indicate the recipient of something.

[28] This was clearly recognized by Lightfoot (83); but through most of the last century (Dunn [64] is a notable exception) the phrase was understood to have implications for Paul's own deep inward experience of grace. Whatever may be true of Paul's own inward experience, that seems not to be his point here; rather God did this with the Gentile mission in view. At least that is what is implied by the grammar.

[29] See the discussion of v. 3 above for Pauline usage when referring to Christ. The statistics for the letter are striking, and quite out of character with most of the rest of the corpus: "Christ" occurs in 37 of the 44 referents, either alone (22x) or in combination (15x), while "Jesus" occurs 16x, all but one in combination, and "Lord" occurs but 5x, three in combination.

[30] That is, the designation "son" which God used of both Israel (Exod 4:22-23; Hos 11:1) and of the davidic king (Ps 2:7; Hos 11:1) was eventually transferred to the expected messianic king.

Although the present usage could be simply "off-handed" as it were, it is worth noting that this emphasis on Christ as "messianic Son" occurs in a letter where Gentile believers are being cajoled into accepting a degree of "Jewishness" in order to be completed as believers. The Jewish Messiah, Paul counters, whom he will later identify as Abraham's true "seed" (3:16), has been revealed *in me*; how that revelation has taken place emerges in the next occurrence of "Son of God" language in 2:20. And both of these anticipate 4:4-6, where the Son is clearly pre-existent and eternal,[31] and the believer's *Abba*-cry to the Father is the direct result of the indwelling Spirit of the Son, whose own language this is. Thus this revelation of Christ as Son of God has already occurred in Paul himself, who will be God's agent to make him known to the Gentiles.

Line e. Paul now concludes this very full protasis with a purpose clause, which at first blush seems quite beside the present point, since nothing is made of it either here or in the rest of this opening narrative (through 1:24). Nonetheless it is a crucial moment in the narrative, since it spells out the nature of Paul's calling: "to preach him [God's Son] among the Gentiles."[32] Thus it anticipates the two narratives that follow (2:1-10, 11-21), where it is the central matter. The revelation of God's Son that has taken place in Paul was to serve as "a light to the Gentiles." Picking up the same verb that appeared four times in vv. 8-11, meaning "to announce the good news," Paul now makes the Son of God the object of the preaching for which God had set him apart and called him. What is of importance for him is the phrase "among the Gentiles." That he understands this to be his calling is writ large in his preserved letters; and since the Galatians owe their own lives to his obedience to this calling, he can well expect them to hear their own names, as it were, in this clause.

Lines f-g. With the words of the preceding purpose clause the protasis had come to an end, and the natural expectation for the apodosis would be some indication as to how he had fulfilled his calling. But what he does rather is to take up the main concern of the narrative, a concern for which we were somewhat prepared by v. 12: "I did not receive [the gospel I preach] from any human source, nor was I taught it." In that instance the concern had to do altogether with

[31] See the discussion in ch. 14 in Fee, *Christology*.

[32] This is also, incidentally, another reason why he stayed away from Jerusalem. After all, according to Luke, first Peter and then Jerusalem itself had to be persuaded by an act of divine intervention that the Gentiles were to be included in the newly formed people of God. See further on lines f-g below.

the *source* of his gospel; so nothing in what he has said to this point quite prepares us for this actual turn in the narrative. That is, given the content of the protasis, with its concluding purpose clause about Paul's calling to the Gentile mission, we might well have expected him to spell out in some measure how he had fulfilled that calling. But what we get rather is a series of sentences whose whole purpose is to distance himself from the apostles in Jerusalem. Thus what his detractors see as a debility, Paul himself sees as providential; he is not dependent on human approval but on God alone.

Therefore, even though from one point of view this long sentence does not seem to hold together, from the perspective of the concerns of this letter it makes perfectly good sense. What Paul has done in the protasis is to verify the reality of his calling and gospel, that they are altogether the work of God and thus "not from any human source." What he sets out to do now is to put that reality into the context of another reality, that with regard to both his mission and gospel he is absolutely independent of the apostles in Jerusalem.

The clause itself takes the form of a typical (for Paul) not/but contrast, expressed with a pair of doublets. What he did *not* do immediately[33] was to "consult with flesh and blood" (line *f*). The verb "consult," which occurs again in 2:6, has to do with laying something out before other people either for counsel or consideration. The phrase "flesh and blood," which occurs twice elsewhere in Paul (1 Cor 15:50; Eph 6:12), is a Jewish idiom that puts special emphasis on the humanity of the persons involved. So what Paul did not do after his encounter with the risen Christ was to consult with others about it. And especially, he adds immediately (line *g*), "I did not go up to Jerusalem to visit those who were apostles before me."

As a matter of simple historical record, it should be noted that Paul had no good reason to go to Jerusalem at all. He was not native to Jerusalem; and although his first reason for being there was to study Torah under Gamaliel (Acts 22:2), he had in the meantime become a vigorous champion of historic Judaism against the upstart followers of the crucified Nazarene. So his encounter with the risen Christ basically made him a man without a country as far as Jerusalem was concerned. He certainly would be wary of returning to see his former compatriots, who were trying to stamp out the nascent faith he had now come to embrace; and he would have no reason to seek out the

---

[33] By fronting this adverb in his clause, Paul puts special emphasis on the nature of his "immediate response" (as the TNIV rightly has it), that he did not consult with anyone about it.

leaders of the church in Jerusalem, who reasonably would be at least wary of him, if not highly suspicious, and in any case who had shown no interest in a Gentile mission. Thus his language in this passage suggests nothing about his "going *back*" to Jerusalem, but simply of "going *up* to Jerusalem to those who were apostles before me."

Nonetheless, with the phrase "go up to Jerusalem" we come to the heart of things regarding this narrative, as is made clear by its repetition in v. 18 and 2:1 and by the fact that the word "Jerusalem" occurs more times in this short epistle (five in all) than anywhere else in Paul's letters. This is further confirmed by the negative press it receives in the analogy in 4:25-26, although in this latter instance the city no longer refers to the Christian apostles, but unbelieving Judaism. In its present context it refers especially to "those who were apostles before me." This is made clear not only by how v. 19 responds to v. 18 ("I did not see any other of the apostles"), but also especially in 2:1-2, where Paul's "them" in the phrase "laid before them" has "Jerusalem" as its antecedent. All of this together confirms that his long period of non-relationship with the Jerusalem apostles is the real issue for Paul in this extended narrative.

What is of further interest is his designation, "who were apostles before me," the significance of which is twofold. First, he not only recognizes them as fellow-apostles, but he also recognizes, as he notes in 1 Cor 15:5-8, that they were on the scene well before him. At the same time, secondly, and now surely for the sake of his present readers, he places himself among those who have been given the special designation "apostle." While it has been common at a later time to speak of "the twelve apostles,"[34] Paul himself knows of no such limitation in number. When he refers to Jesus' earthly disciples, for example, he does what the Gospel writers regularly do – simply calls them "the Twelve." Paul's concern is not with the number of apostles, or who they are specifically; rather "apostle" is for him a designation for a special kind of ministry given to those who have been witnesses

---

[34] This phenomenon has its roots in the Gospels of Matthew and Luke (it is a corrupt addition to Mark's text; see the note on 3:14 in the TNIV), where the Gospel writers use this language to refer to those whom they otherwise call by their known title, "The Twelve." So fixed is this latter title in the early church that Paul uses it of the group even when it consists of only eleven (1 Cor 15:5). That he has no concept of "the Twelve Apostles" as such is made clear by the mention of "and then to all the apostles" in v. 7. Later (Rom 16:3) he designates Andronicus and Junia as "outstanding among the apostles." Later in the present passage (v. 19) he also includes James the Lord's brother among the apostles. For bibliography see next note.

of the risen Christ.[35] Although no further point is made of it here, this phrase, especially as it is worded in Paul's sentence as "the before me apostles," is surely for the sake of his Galatian readers, since those who have come from Jerusalem and are upsetting them are not themselves apostles; they merely represent themselves as coming from (some of?) the Jerusalem apostles. So with these words Paul is deliberately distancing himself from Jerusalem. His opponents have come from Jerusalem, but theirs is only secondary authority. The apostle who founded the Galatian churches is not secondary in any way; he has full standing as one of *the* Apostles.

Lines h and i. With these final two clauses in his sentence Paul indicates what he did do instead of going up to Jerusalem. He first "went away to Arabia," for how long he gives us no hint, and then later "returned to Damascus." Both of these clauses are filled with presuppositional data that Paul assumes his Galatian readers will understand, but which are not totally clear to us – although the second is a bit easier than the first. Our difficulties with the first clause have to do with both *where* Paul went and *why*, and one's guesses about the former are integrally related to one's guesses about the latter. At the time of Paul "Arabia" covered most of what is today the Arabian peninsula, going north beyond Damascus and as far south as to include Mount Sinai, as Paul himself bears witness to in 4:25 of our letter ("Mount Sinai in Arabia").

At issue in part is *why* Paul went first to Arabia (whatever that means), the answer to which lies with whether one thinks of this clause in relationship to line *e* ("that I might preach the Son among the Gentiles") or line *f* ("I did not consult with flesh and blood"). If it is the former (for purposes of evangelizing among the Gentiles), then "Arabia" would probably refer to the regions of the province not far from Damascus itself. If it is the latter (to be away from human contact with regard to what had happened to him) then Mount Sinai would be a logical place for him to have gone. Whereas one's sympathies might lie with his immediately carrying out an evangelistic mission, the actual structure of the whole sentence as analyzed above suggests otherwise. As noted, the purpose clause, "so that I might preach him among the Gentiles," is not the main point of the present sentence, but is rather anticipatory of what is to come. Paul's sentence itself

---

[35] On this matter see G.D. Fee, *Commentary on the First Epistle to the Corinthians* (NICNT; Grand Rapids: Eerdmans, 1987) 728–34. One might note that from Paul's perspective it is therefore a term limited to the first generation of believers who actually *saw the risen Lord and were commissioned by him.*

indicates that his going away to Arabia was the flip side of his not consulting "with flesh and blood" (I didn't do the one but the other). In which case his reason for going to Arabia would be for the sake of "consulting" with the Lord about what had happened to him; and where better to go, given his deep and passionate love of his people and their history, than the mount of revelation itself.[36] In any case, conjectural as this latter point might be, grammatically the purpose of his going "to Arabia" is less up for grabs; whether at Sinai or elsewhere in Arabia, Paul deliberately avoids talking with other believers about his experience, but seeks out a place of solitude to be alone with the Father and the Son. Most of his former categories had been blown away, and since Christ himself had blown them away, it would have to be Christ alone, not "flesh and blood," who would help him through the reconstruction process.

At some point thereafter he shows up again in Damascus; in his own language "I returned again to Damascus." The fact that he says this without explanation suggests that this part of his story must have been known by the Galatians; otherwise why the verb "returned" and the mention of Damascus as though that should be known by them? It is most likely after this "return" to Damascus that he became so effective as a witness to Christ that the governor under the Nabatean King Aretas was bent on arresting Paul, from whose grasp he escaped by being lowered in a basket through a window in the city wall (2 Cor 11:12-13). In any case, Paul's point is for him verifiable history: for three years he had no immediate contact with Jerusalem after Christ claimed him as his own. That first contact is what the next sentence is about.

Verses 18-19. The adverb "then" (ἔπειτα), with which this sentence begins, stands at the beginning of v. 21 and 2:1 as well. In each case it indicates the next item in a chronological sequence. The present two verses narrate Paul's first visit to Jerusalem as an apostle of Christ, which took place "after three years," meaning after the events narrated in v. 15-17, thus dating back to the beginning of his life as a follower of Christ. Although according to Luke's account (Acts 9:26-30) Paul had had considerable ministry in Jerusalem as well, and Barnabas was a key figure in his acceptance in Jerusalem, Paul's interests lie singularly with *his relationship with the apostles.* Thus he relates his stay with Cephas (Peter) and his meeting James, and this not only because they

---

[36] It should be noted that this is a decidedly minority view; but most of those who take the opposite position deal with the historical options available to Paul, but never deal with the clause within its own sentence structure.

were apostles, but because they would be two of the key players in the next two events he will narrate. This also explains why Barnabas is not mentioned at this point, since Paul never puts him among the apostles.

It is of some interest that Paul here continues the habit found in 1 Corinthians of referring to Peter by his Aramaic name, Cephas ("rock"), which had been given him by Jesus.[37] Paul in fact mentions Peter only in these two letters; in 1 Corinthians he uses the name Cephas exclusively, and predominantly so in this letter,[38] switching to "Peter" only in 2:7 and 8, where he notes the division of labor between Peter and him to the Jewish and Gentile communities respectively. From the perspective of this narrative, Paul's purpose for the visit was singular: "to become acquainted with Cephas" (ἱστορῆσαι Κῆφαν), a verb that implies no previous acquaintance. He stayed only a fortnight, and in the process met only one other apostle, "James, the Lord's brother" (cf. 1 Cor 15:7). This latter description gives clear evidence that Paul had some knowledge of the historical Jesus; at the same time it is clear by Paul's non-deferential way of speaking about James that he did not consider James' relationship to the earthly Jesus to have given him one whit of advantage over other apostles, who had also seen, and been sent by, the risen Lord. Furthermore, this designation of James as an "apostle" verifies the point made above in v. 17 which was based on what Paul says in 1 Cor 15:6-8 and 9:1, that for him at least, if not in the early church as a whole, the term "apostle" was reserved for those who had seen and had been commissioned by the risen Lord.

Paul's point in this paragraph is singular – not to explain anything about the visit as such, but to point out how brief and limited his initial acquaintance with the Jerusalem apostles actually was. And it is regarding this point that he adds the mild oath in v. 20: "I assure you before God that what I am writing is no lie." This is the second of four such moments in his letters, each of which is in the interest of verifying some aspect of his apostolic calling or ministry.[39] In this case it is added to establish in the eyes of the Galatians that Paul's early

[37] The only other use of this name is found in John 1:42, where the author actually interprets the Aramaic for the sake of his Greek-speaking audience ("whom he called Cephas, which means Peter [in English, 'Rock']).

[38] For 1 Corinthians, see 1:12; 3:22; 9:5; 15:6; in Galatians see 1:18; 2:9, 11, 14. It is of some interest that later scribes changed "Cephas" to "Peter" in each of the instances in Galatians except 2:9, where it occurs in the combination, "James and Cephas and John," but never so in 1 Corinthians.

[39] See 2 Cor 11:31; Rom 9:1; and 1 Tim 2:7. In the first three instances he calls on God as witness to his truthfulness.

relationship with Jerusalem was not only three years after his calling as apostle to the Gentiles, but also was of minimal time and acquaintance. This point is quite in keeping with the narrative to this point – that as a Christian believer and apostle he had almost no association of any kind with Jerusalem; and what he did have was minimal at best.

Verses 21-24. This second "then" in the narrative pushes Paul's story forward to include the next fourteen years (2:1). And here especially one can see that his only interest throughout is to distance himself from any significant contact with Jerusalem. He mentions only his stay in the Roman provinces of Syria and Cilicia (v. 21). His home town, Tarsus, is the major city in Cilicia; according to Luke he returned there for some years before Barnabas sought him out to help with the work in Antioch, which is the major city in Syria.[40] That Paul has no present interest in his actual ministry in these parts is made clear by the follow-up sentences about these fourteen years. Three brief points are made.

First (v. 22), he was unknown personally (lit. "by face") to the churches of Judea, which are further identified as being "in Christ." This latter phrase, which recurs in this letter only in 2:17, is one of Paul's common ways of identifying God's new covenant people formed by the work of Christ and the Spirit. There is nothing mystical intended by this phrase; rather it is simply Paul's way of indicating the sphere of existence for these newly formed people of God; they now exist "in Christ." One should also note that, as with "the churches of Galatia" in 1:2, Paul thinks of the church in Judea in its collective sense as "the churches (that is, the individual congregations) of Judea," where "Judea" is an adjectival, or descriptive, genitive.

Second (v. 23), though unknown to them "by face," Paul had nonetheless become well known by reputation. Of interest is Paul's way of putting that reputation. Picking up on how he begins in v. 13, and thus serving as a kind of "inclusio" for this first section of the narrative, he reiterates that what they knew was that he was "the man who formerly used to persecute[41] us," and that this man "is now preaching the faith he once tried to destroy." It is of some interest that Paul would here describe the Christian message as "the faith." In some circles that usage in the Pastoral Epistles is seen as evidence against Pauline authorship; but here in the letter where "by faith" is a kind of shorthand catchword for how one is identified as a Christian, Paul himself uses the same word to describe the entirety of the Christian message. He

---

[40] See Acts 9:30 and 11:25-26.

[41] This is the best way to handle the imperfect ἐπόρθει, which in this case implies an ongoing occurrence of some time past.

obviously does not fit comfortably into some of the straitjackets with which many scholars would wish to restrict him.

Third (v.24), the final outcome of this brief narrative of the fourteen intervening years is that news about Paul's now preaching the faith he once tried to destroy regularly resulted in these Judeans giving glory to God.[42] For Paul this is always the goal of everything believers are and do; they are themselves "to the praise of God" (Eph 1:14; Phil 1:11), and thus they also regularly offer praise to God (as in Phil 4:20), and all to his eternal glory. And so Paul concludes by noting that even though he had no significant post-resurrection contact with Jerusalem, the believers in Judea themselves had reason both to know about him and to glorify God "in me." Thus what God had done *in* Paul for the sake of the Gentiles (v. 16) is also cause for the Judean believers to give glory to God.

Galatians 2:1-10 – Jerusalem Affirms Paul's Gospel

[1]*Then after fourteen years I went up again to Jerusalem, this time with Barnabas. I took Titus along also.* [2]*I went in response to a revelation and, meeting privately with those esteemed as leaders, I set before them the gospel that I preach among the Gentiles. I wanted to be sure I was not running and had not been running my race in vain.* [3]*Yet not even Titus, who was with me, was compelled to be circumcised, even though he was a Greek.* [4]*This matter arose because some false believers had infiltrated our ranks to spy on the freedom we have in Christ Jesus and to make us slaves.* [5]*We did not give in to them for a moment, so that the truth of the gospel might remain with you.**

[6]*As for those who were held in high esteem – whatever they were makes no difference to me; God does not show favoritism – they added nothing to my message.* [7]*On the contrary, they saw that I had been entrusted with the task of preaching the gospel to the Gentiles,[a] just as Peter had been to the Jews.[b]* [8]*For God, who was at work in Peter as an apostle to the Jews, was also at work in me as an apostle to the Gentiles.* [9]*James, Cephas[c] and John, those esteemed as pillars, gave me and Barnabas the right hand of fellowship when they recognized the grace given to me. They agreed that we should go to the Gentiles, and they to the Jews.* [10]*All they asked was that we should continue to remember the poor, the very thing I had been eager to do all along.*

[a] Greek *uncircumcised*   [b] Greek *circumcised*, also in vv. 8 and 9
[c] That is, Peter; also in vv. 11 and 14

---

[42] "Regularly" is my way of handling the imperfect ἐδόξαζον, which in this case implies a regularly recurring phenomenon.

The "then" (ἔπειτα) with which this section begins is the third in a row and thus marks the passage as the fourth item in the chronological narrative that began in 1:13, regarding Paul's (non-)relationship with Jerusalem. At the same time the present section has some notable contrasts to 1:13-24. The former is basically a simple narrative, easy to follow in its various parts, which apart from vv. 15-16a has very little complexity regarding sentences and very little emotion (except for the oath in v. 20). What Paul has done to this point is to outline in its barest form (*a*) his preconversion activities in Judaism, (*b*) his conversion (as a call to proclaim Christ to the Gentiles), and (*c*) his limited association with Jerusalem for a seventeen year period, whose main point (at least from v. 17 on) seems to be to distance himself from Jerusalem as far as his gospel is concerned. The present, slightly longer narrative, on the other hand, deals with a *single* event of a *brief* duration and is full of emotion and impossible sentences,[43] which are not fully clear at some key points.

Here Paul now sets forth the second major stage in the narrative regarding his relationship with Jerusalem. His point in the preceding passage was to capitalize on what his detractors saw as a defect, namely, that they came from Jerusalem but Paul had not. But what they saw as a defect Paul saw as to his great advantage. His gospel came directly from Christ and therefore had nothing to do with "men," either in terms of source or approval; and this stands in stark contrast to his detractors, who had only a merely human source and approval. But if Paul's gospel is *independent* of the leaders in Jerusalem, it is not in fact *different from* theirs, which is the point of the present section.

Thus the whole of vv. 1-10 narrate a visit whose sole purpose was to lay before the leaders in Jerusalem the gospel Paul preached *among the Gentiles,* and for the sake of his Galatian friends to point out Jerusalem's agreement with Paul at two points: (*a*) Titus was not compelled to be circumcised; hence by implication they agreed that Gentiles do not need to be circumcised; (*b*) they added nothing at all to Paul's gospel; hence by implication the agitators are quite wrong about his gospel and its relationship with Jerusalem. These matters are taken up in order in the narrative. *Verses 1-2* describe the occasion, purpose, and participants of the meeting. *Verses 3-5* describe the first result, with Titus serving as a kind of test case; at the same time they offer clues as to the cause of the issue. *Verses 6-10* then describe the

---

[43] Indeed, two of them are *anacoloutha*, sentences that "do not follow" in the sense that they totally break down grammatically.

second result: an agreement in terms of "division of labor" between the Jewish and Gentile missions, spearheaded by Peter and Paul respectively.

In terms of the actual narrative, one could easily go from vv. 1-2 to 6-10 without breaking stride – and could also thereby eliminate some of the difficulties. In such a reading, the only strange thing in vv. 1-2 would be the mention of Titus. But in fact, all the passion resides in vv. 3-5, which thereby tell much of the tale. From Paul's perspective the issue is singular: whether or not a male Gentile believer needs to be circumcised in order to be a full member of the newly formed people of God. The reason for the conference, we learn indirectly in vv. 4-5, is the insistence on the necessity of the circumcision of Gentiles on the part of some Jewish believers – men very much like those currently distressing the Galatians. This not only accounts for the passion with which Paul expresses himself in vv. 4 and 5, but also for the same passion he had expressed in the earlier curse on those who have broken faith with that agreement and are currently unsettling things in Galatia (1:6-9). This issue had already been settled by a conference in Jerusalem, and these interlopers are not only breaking faith with that agreement, but allegedly are doing so with the blessing of Jerusalem. There can be little wonder that Paul is upset.

Verses 1-2. The two sentences that make up these two verses begin by picking up the thread of the narrative: Paul's presence/non-presence in Jerusalem, with its singular concern over his (lack of) contact with the Jerusalem apostles. At the same time they set the stage for the present narrative, and thus we learn several important things. First, he had had a fourteen year hiatus of contact with the Jerusalem apostles; second, in this instance he was accompanied by Barnabas and Titus, neither of whom has been mentioned heretofore; third, he went up as the direct result "of a revelation"; and fourth, from Paul's point of view the *specific purpose* of the visit was to lay before the significant men of Jerusalem the gospel he had been preaching, so as not to have been "running in vain." The very way these several items are narrated makes it especially difficult to escape the conclusion that these latter three items are intimately related.[44] We take up each of the items in turn.

---

[44] Each of these items also presents special difficulties for those who wish to make this visit correspond to the "famine visit" recorded in Acts 11:27-30 (see the Introduction, pp. 4-5). Here is a clear case where one must let what is technically known as "primary evidence" (Paul's letter in this case) have priority over "secondary evidence" (Luke's narrative in Acts).

First, picking up the sequential thread from 1:18, Paul indicates that his next visit to Jerusalem occurred fourteen years later, thus some seventeen years after his conversion. Although some have attempted to read Paul's phrase as inclusive of the first three years, thus making the "fourteen years" apply to the entire time since his conversion,[45] that runs contrary to both the data and the concern of Paul's narrative.[46] Paul's point to here has been to distance himself altogether from Jerusalem, so as to verify the *independence* of his gospel from them – that his gospel came by direct revelation from Christ. Paul's point now is that after all these many years (seventeen in all), when he finally did go up to Jerusalem with the express purpose of "laying out before them the gospel I preach among the Gentiles" (v. 2), the church in Jerusalem not only did not add anything to his gospel (v. 6), but signally offered him the right hand of fellowship with the commission to continue working among the Gentiles (v. 7).

Second, he was accompanied in this instance by at least two men, presumably known to the Galatians: Barnabas and Titus.[47] This is the piece of evidence that suggests that the "Galatians" of this letter belong to the province, not necessarily to the territory (see above on 1:1). Although one needs to be properly cautious here, the way the two of them are introduced, and especially the further mention of Barnabas in v. 13 below, suggests that the Galatians knew him as well – and perhaps Titus. It further seems certain, given the way Paul speaks of his present companions in 1:2, that neither of these brothers was present with Paul at the time of this writing. Since in Luke's account (Acts 13-14) Barnabas accompanied Paul only when he was evangelizing the southern portion of the province of Galatia, it is very

[45] This attempt is the result of trying to harmonize Paul with Luke's accounting of Paul's *visits* to Jerusalem. But Paul's narrative is dealing not with "visits" as such, but those specific times that had to do with his "visiting" so as to discuss his ministry and its relationship to the church in Jerusalem.

[46] In a narrative designed to minimize his relationship with Jerusalem it would be exceedingly strange for such a specific time reference as this one to go back to vv. 15-17 rather than to pick up from vv. 18-19; furthermore Paul's use of the preposition διά (lit. "through") is a standard Greek idiom to express "after an interval of time" (cf. Mark 2:1; Acts 24:17; see further BDAG A.2.c.); so also, his use of "again" is a clear pointer back to vv. 18-19.

[47] Because of the complexity of the sentence that follows in v. 2 (all of v. 2 in the Greek text), translators have had various ways of breaking up Paul's Greek sentences to make them work better in English. Thus despite the TNIV, the taking along of Titus is not an afterthought but is the crucial conclusion to this first sentence: "... I went up to Jerusalem with Barnabas, accompanied also by Titus."

likely that "the Galatians" of this letter live in this region. In any case, the present significance of mentioning these two brothers as "with" Paul is that each of them would be known to the Galatians and each of them will play a further role in the narrative (Titus immediately; Barnabas in 2:13). Barnabas, it should be noted in passing, was also a Diaspora Jew (a Levite from Cyprus according to Acts 4:36) who had for some time taken up residence in Jerusalem, which accounts both for his befriending Paul and the fact that their first journey together began in Cyprus.

Third, the more important feature of this narrative from Paul's perspective lies with the way he begins the next sentence: "I went up in keeping with a revelation and I laid before them the gospel I preach among the Gentiles." It is important for us in this case to keep Paul's two clauses closely together, precisely because it was "the revelation" that prompted them to go up to Jerusalem with the express purpose of "laying before *them*"[48] Paul's gospel. In light of the evidence from 1 Cor 14:6 and 26 (and 30), one can be sure that "revelation" in this case refers to a prophetic word in the community in Antioch. Thus from Paul's point of view, this meeting in Jerusalem did not happen because of a human request or decision, but as the direct result of the Spirit's direction: "I went up *in keeping with* (κατά) a revelation." This also means that this clause is not parenthetical, as some translations and commentators suggest, but is for Paul the primary impetus for the meeting that followed. It was the Spirit who brought about the meeting in Jerusalem for the express purpose of dealing with the issue of Paul's law-free (= circumcision-free) gospel among the Gentiles.[49]

Fourth, the specific purpose of this meeting had to do with what is clearly the main concern of this entire letter: whether Gentile believers in Christ must also practice certain aspects of the Jewish law in order to be full citizens of the newly-formed people of God – although that issue is not actually spoken to until the next sentence (v. 3). Paul's way of presenting the issue here, and almost certainly with his Galatian readers in view, is, "I laid before them the gospel I preach among the Gentiles." The verb "laid before them" implies "with a view toward consultation"; and by putting "the gospel I preach" in the present tense, he implies that there has been no change on his part all this time. What he preaches now is what he preached in Galatia; and it is

[48] As noted above on 1:17 (line *g*), "Jerusalem" in this sentence refers to the primary leaders of the church there, as this personal pronoun, whose grammatical antecedent is "Jerusalem," but whose elaboration is the "esteemed leaders."

[49] See further Fee, *GEP*, 372-73.

what he had preached from the very beginning: that Gentiles who believe in Christ and live by the Spirit do not need to observe Torah as well. But his sentence also becomes convoluted at this point because, instead of moving right on to the outcome (expressed in v. 3), he concludes on an unexpected double note, having to do (*a*) with the participants of the meeting and (*b*) Paul's own stated purpose for having the meeting with this select few.

The clearly interrupting phrase, which the TNIV has translated "meeting privately with those esteemed as leaders," has been the source of some difficulty for Pauline scholars over the years, as to both the reason for it and whether or not, in light of how he qualifies it in v. 6, he intended it to be slightly pejorative. Taking up the second issue first, one may conclude with a measure of confidence that Paul does not intend to be putting them down, as it were. Our difficulties lie with the phrase itself, which is a plural noun formed by the participle of a verb whose basic meaning is "to consider as probable," thus "to suppose" or "to believe" something to be so. The noun in this case could indeed have a pejorative cast to it, "appear to be, but may not really be." But that is most unlikely here, given the nature of Paul's argument. Rather, in this case the verbal aspect of the noun carries the further sense of "be recognized as."[50] The fact that he repeats the phrase again in v. 6d without a qualifier, as here, suggests that it has become a kind of honorary title for the triumvirate in Jerusalem (James, Cephas [Peter], and John); they are "the recognized leaders." Indeed, in v. 9 Paul repeats the title with the qualifier ("pillars"), which is not only not pejorative but properly honorific. He can do that in this latter instance because the honorific is also a verbal noun; and this is what he will play on in v. 6. It is very likely that Paul uses this title throughout this passage because his opponents in Galatia referred to them in this way. If so, in their case it would have been deliberately over against Paul, who was definitely *not* one of "the recognized leaders" in Jerusalem.

In any case, it would be self-defeating for Paul to put Jerusalem down in any way. Rather his concern is to point out how *the recognized leaders* in Jerusalem gave him and Barnabas their blessing for

---

[50] See BDAG, whose two main entries are (1) "think, believe, suppose, consider" and (2) "seem, be recognized as." Since the participle is a verbal noun in this case, and is used by Paul precisely because it was used in Jerusalem as an honorific for their three primary leaders, there is every reason to believe that Paul is first of all using it in a deferential way; the fact that it is also a *verbal* noun is what allows him his own qualifier in v. 6.

the mission to which God had called them.[51] Thus in this case the phrase is neutral and important. The men he met with privately are the "influential leaders," those who have been "recognized as leaders" by others. Thus it here has little or nothing to do with reputation and everything to do with the reality that had actually emerged in Jerusalem over the years. Furthermore, the meeting itself was "private," in the sense that whatever may have happened in a larger gathering, such as that described by Luke in Acts 15:1–35, the basic essentials had already been hammered out privately among the primary players. And Paul clearly has interest only with these major players, almost certainly because of how the agitators have presented themselves to the Galatians with regard to their own relationship with the leaders in Jerusalem.

But the phrase about meeting privately with the primary leaders in Jerusalem is quite interruptive; and this is the reason English translations have had a variety of ways of dealing with it. Paul's reason for going up to Jerusalem, however, which is the point of the sentence, is expressed not in terms of "the truth of the gospel" as such, but in terms of whether or not he was currently, or had in the past been "running my race in vain." The latter metaphor is one of several that Paul borrows from the games in the stadium. It will reappear in Phil 2:16 with the companion idea "labor in vain," the latter a probable echo of Isa 65:23, that God's eschatological people will "not labor in vain." In any case, as with the Philippians passage, Paul is concerned about his Galatian converts, that if they succumb to the wiles of the agitators, he will have lost this particular "race."

Verse 3. This sentence ("yet not even Titus, who was with me, was compelled to be circumcised, even though he was a Greek") is the certain evidence that one of the issues on the table at this conference was that of the circumcision of Gentile believers in Christ. And here is where the final phrase in v. 1 becomes significant. It is very likely that Paul knew full well that this was going to be the crucial matter dealt with in Jerusalem, thus the primary reason for his "taking Titus along" with them. What this move disallowed on the part of Jerusalem was any handling of the issue at a merely theoretical level. That is, even though the "theoretical" issue was the "circumcision of Gentiles" who had become believers, Paul had forced on them a non-theoretical test

---

[51] For the role of the qualifier in v. 6, see the discussion of that verse below (p. 64).

case – whether or not Paul's and Barnabas's Gentile companion Titus, "being Greek,"[52] would be "compelled" to be circumcised.

As is usually the case, theoretical issues are much more complex when they are dealt with at a personal level, but they are also much more certain to be done in the right way. Indeed, the fact that Paul uses the strong verb "compelled" is sufficient evidence that, as with Luke's account in Acts 15:1-2, we here come to the real cause of the issue in the first place, since it is this phrase that Paul sets out to explain – or elaborate – in vv. 4 and 5. Moreover, Paul's use of this same language in 6:12 with regard to what the agitators are urging on the Galatians is the sure indication that this is the primary issue in Galatia as well, which also accounts for Paul's bringing it forward precisely at this point in the narrative. Whether or not some of the leaders themselves actually exerted pressure to have Titus circumcised cannot be known; but Paul's language, and especially the immediate interruption of the narrative in vv. 4 and 5, suggest that he was at the center of the controversy.[53]

Verses 4-5. With this (broken) sentence, which explains the "compelled to be circumcised" at the end of v. 3, we come to the real issue for Paul, an issue that is still so hot for him that he starts his sentence in one way and finishes it in another – but which is thereby also the more striking. What is lacking is a grammatical subject and verb, which are implied in the preceding clause, "[Titus] was not compelled to be circumcised." Since that needs explanation, Paul sets out immediately to do so. Thus our v. 4 is a clause given wholly to a description of these interlopers, including their ultimate aim, while v. 5 is a clause

---

[52] By calling him "Greek" Paul puts emphasis on both his cultural milieu and his being Gentile. This usage also helps to resolve some of the tension many have had with the fact that according to Acts 16:1-3 Paul yielded on this matter with regard to Timothy. But the latter was born of a Jewish mother and therefore was *not* considered "Greek" but Jewish. His circumcision was therefore a legitimate expression of Paul's being "all things to all people, so that he might win some" (1 Cor 9:22). An uncircumcised Jewish companion would not go over well in the Diaspora synagogues where Paul always began his ministry, since circumcision was one of the matters (along with food laws and Sabbath) that gave Diaspora Jews their identity. But this would pertain to a "Greek" only if one chose to become a proselyte.

[53] In an idiosyncratic moment of interpretation, F.C. Burkitt, *Christian Beginnings* (London: University of London, 1924) 118 (followed by Duncan [*Commentary*, 43-44] and D.W.B. Robinson, "'The Circumcision of Titus, and Paul's Liberty,'" *Australian Biblical Review* 12 [1964] 24–42) argues that Titus was in fact circumcised, but it was not a matter of compulsion but of choice. That not only misses the point, but it also neglects the sense of the "not even" that precedes and the "who was with me" that follows the mention of his name.

that then explains how it is that they failed. At least they failed in that
earlier attempt. Paul's problem is that similar "spies" have infiltrated
the believing communities in Galatia; thus this brief parenthetical
explanation, which at the same time gives the modern reader insight
into the issue at hand, turns out in fact to speak to the Galatian
situation in a very direct way.

Indeed, one can scarcely imagine that the Galatians are not to read
this scathing indictment of these earlier "spies" of Christian freedom in
light of those who have invaded their own churches and are doing the
same thing. Thus what has recently happened in Galatia is not the first
time up; and Paul's present concern is that the Galatians handle their
interlopers as this earlier gathering in Jerusalem did to their
counterparts. All of this is made clear by the sudden change of
pronouns. In vv. 1-3 Paul talks to the Galatians about "I" and "them,"
the latter referring especially to the "influential" three: James, Peter,
and John. Here the pronouns are "we" and "you," where the "we" is
not just about Paul, Barnabas, and Titus, but is clearly directed toward
his Gentile readers as well, as the final clause suggests. Thus: "the
freedom *we* (all) have in Christ … so that the truth of the gospel might
remain with *you*."

Several further matters about these two clauses need our attention.
First, the indictment of the "false brothers" in v. 4 is fivefold – and
severe. In turn, (*a*) they are "false brothers." This is not an indictment
regarding their eternal salvation; rather, they are "brothers" who have
given themselves to a false understanding of the nature of the gospel.
Their "falsehood" lies in their trying to persuade others to adopt their
understanding of what it means to follow Christ. Thus (*b*) they are
castigated as having been "smuggled in" (παρεισάκτους), a word that
is always pejorative and usually refers to people who have been secretly
brought into a group by others in order to gain information or create
unrest within the group. In the present case it is unlikely that Paul
thinks of them as brought in by others; rather they have become
"sneaks" by the way they have gone about pressing their cause. This is
made clear by the next word (*c*), "sneaked in" (παρεισῆλθον), a word
that is likewise only pejorative, implying that their action was sur-
reptitious. They presented themselves in one way but in reality desired
only that the whole group go their way. Their purpose is then
described as (*d*) "to spy out our freedom," a word that implies lying in
wait for someone to catch them in their snare. The final result (*e*) is
that they want "to enslave us," a word that in a purposefully ironic
way echoes language from the Septuagint about Israel's "bondage" in

Egypt.[54] The key words in all of this are to be found in the contrasts at the end of the clause: "our *freedom* which we have in Christ, so that they might *enslave* us." As will be made clear in the rest of the letter, "freedom" here means freedom from the bondage of Torah observance, and it is ours "in Christ" because of what he has done in our behalf, which Paul will go on in the next clause to refer to as "the truth of the gospel."

Losing the grammatical thread altogether, Paul in v. 5 proceeds immediately to describe his and Barnabas's response to these "spies," and in so doing he speaks directly to the Galatians themselves. He begins with another clause that gets a bit overloaded because of his concern for them. "Not for a second[55] did we yield to them[56] by way of submission." This latter, otherwise unnecessary, phrase ("by way of submission") is in fact what ties this clause, that is aimed at the Galatians, to the prior clause which described the earlier intruders in terms of bondage and enslavement. And the reason, Paul goes on, for our resisting yielding to them was ultimately – even if not known specifically so at the time – for the sake of the Galatians: "that the truth of the gospel might remain for[57] you."

We should perhaps note finally that even though the sentence is not grammatical as such, Paul has certainly not lost his way. Thus the whole is enclosed by the contrast between "false" (in "false brothers") and "true" (in "the truth of the gospel"), while the central section (the end of v. 4 and beginning of v. 5) is dominated by the contrast between freedom and enslavement. These are precisely the concerns that will be picked up when Paul gets to the argument itself; but this parenthesis serves for now as an anticipation of what is to come.

Verses 6-10. It turns out that one ungrammatical sentence calls for another, which in this case is so broken as to require fixing by translators. It is easy enough to see what happened. Paul begins by

---

[54] See e.g. Exod 1:14 and esp. 6:5.

[55] Paul's Greek idiom is "not for an hour" (πρὸς ὥραν), but there is sufficient evidence both in the NT and elsewhere that it functions in a figurative way, precisely as our "not for a moment" or "a second."

[56] This pronoun refers specifically to the "spies" who obviously put pressure on the whole assembly to yield on this matter. What cannot be known – and conjecture is worth nothing here – is whether any of "the recognized leaders" were also persuaded by them at some point. The outcome certainly suggests not.

[57] The TNIV takes this preposition (πρός) as associative, but since its basic sense with the accusative is "movement or orientation toward someone" (BDAG), it seems much more likely that in this case it is purposive" (= "for your sakes" or "with you in mind"; cf. "for your benefit" [NAB]; "for you" [NEB]; "to safeguard for you" [JB]).

picking up the thread from the interruptive phrase in v. 2 about "those recognized as leaders" and intends to make the point that nothing was added to his gospel by them. So he starts by saying, "*From* those esteemed as leaders ..."; but he immediately adds a parenthetical note on the very idea that some are "so esteemed by others." When he finishes that aside, he starts his sentence all over again, so that the first phrase no longer fits into this new beginning of a sentence that now carries all the way to v. 10 at the end of the paragraph. Thus a brief outline of the structure may help the reader to see what Paul is doing, so that one can also appreciate how it works as a whole.

In *verse 6a* Paul begins to describe the results of this meeting in Jerusalem, and thus starts with a prepositional phrase "from [them]," which would then of necessity continue with him (Paul) as the grammatical subject of the sentence. But fortuitously he pauses at the end of the phrase to qualify it; and I say "fortuitous" because what follows is not about what *Paul* did, but about what *Jerusalem* did.[58] So Paul starts his sentence all over again in *verse 6b*, with what turns out to be the basic "thesis" statement: "to me these influential leaders added nothing." This is then followed with an "on the contrary," whose main clause is picked up in *verse 9b* as, "they gave me and Barnabas the right hand of fellowship," and concludes with its twofold result: a division of labor between Jerusalem and Paul and Barnabas (*v. 9d*); and the further qualification that "we remember the poor" (*v. 10*). But to get there he fronts his main verb (*v. 9c*) with twin participial phrases that offer the reasons for their action: They "*saw/realized* that he had been entrusted with the Gentile mission in a way similar to Peter's having been entrusted with the mission to the Jewish community" (*v. 7*), and "they *knew* the grace that God had given him in this regard" (*v. 9a*). All of this appears more complicated than it really is because our *verse 8* is yet another parenthesis, explaining that the same God who worked through Peter for one mission was also working through Paul for the other. Thus in brief outline, the various parts look like this:

6a   An opening prepositional phrase that is qualified in 6b and then left to hang

6c   The first main clause of the paragraph ("They added nothing to me")

7   The first reason given ("they saw that I had been entrusted with the Gentile mission, just as Peter had been with the Jewish mission")

---

[58] The point is that Paul's prepositional phrase, "from those esteemed leaders," requires a sentence that has "I" as the grammatical subject, such as "I received no additional instruction." So in starting his sentence over again, he gets the proper emphasis: "*They* added nothing to me."

8   A parenthetical explanation about God's working in both of them
9a   The second reason given ("they knew the grace that had been given
       to me," with the "they" being given specific names [9b])
9c   The second main clause ("they gave [us] the right hand of fellow-
       ship")
9d   The concluding purpose/result clause ("we to the Gentiles; they to
       the circumcision")
10   The final qualifying clause ("remember the poor").

For obvious reasons all of this must be reworked a bit in order to be
put into readable English, as in the TNIV. But for the purposes of
understanding our further comments, it is important to see how Paul's
own (very long) sentence actually works in Greek.

Verse 6a-b. With his opening phrase ("as for those who were held in
high esteem") Paul returns to the honorific title for the leaders in
Jerusalem from v. 2 and thus picks up the thread in the narrative that
was dropped at the end of that verse. Only in this instance, precisely
because the "title" is in fact a verbal noun, he plays on the verb's
primary meaning ("believe," "suppose," "appear") and thus adds the
infinitive "to be" plus a predicate noun, "something." When one adds
to that the parenthetical qualifier that "whatever they were[59] makes no
difference to me; God does not show favoritism,"[60] it is easy to see
how some would regard this as a kind of putdown. But as noted above
such an understanding would be self-defeating. Rather, what he does
is to play on the meaning of the verb itself, which he can do precisely
because the "title" has been created from this particular verb. One
must therefore assume that this parenthetical qualifier has only the
Galatians in view, and that because of how the interlopers have
presented themselves in Galatia as to *their* relationship to these primary
leaders vis-à-vis their view of the secondary character of *Paul's*
apostleship. So this phrase has little to do with Paul's own attitude

---

[59] The reason for the past tense of this verb is not at all certain. In light of what
follows it can hardly mean they were formerly recognized as such but are no longer.
Most think it is an oblique reference to their special privilege as having known Jesus
and thus going back to the beginning (thus, "whatever special privileges they may
have once had" is of little present importance"). But it could also have an indefinite
sense, thus "whatever sort of people they have been known to be" (so Matera), or
more likely be in the past tense simply because he is narrating an event that took place
in the past (so Martyn).

[60] Paul's Greek clause says (literally), "the face, God, of man, does not receive"
(πρόσωπον θεὸς ἀνθρώπου οὐ λαμβάνει). "Receiving a person's face" is a Greek idiom
for "showing partiality"; the strange word order puts the two key words ("face" and
"God") up front.

toward Jerusalem; that comes out in the rest of the passage and is altogether positive. Rather this is for the sake of the Galatians, that those who are indeed (properly) recognized as leaders in Jerusalem are not thereby to be seen as possessing an apostleship superior to his. Thus what is being said to the Galatians by this qualifier simply reinforces what he has demonstrated in the narrative thus far. That God chose him as an apostle, to take the gospel to the Gentiles, and thus his apostleship is quite independent of Jerusalem and is in no way inferior to theirs, even though they are indeed "the recognized ones" in the mother church in Jerusalem. Whatever else, Paul did not consider himself to have gone to Jerusalem to get their "approval"; rather he went as their equal, and submitted his mission to them so that they would understand the nature of his mission to the Gentiles – that it was "law free," in the sense that Gentiles did not need to submit to purely Jewish boundary markers in order to belong as full members of God's new household.

Verses 6c-8. With that matter off his chest, as it were, which has little to do with his own attitude toward "the pillars" and altogether with an unbalanced view on the part of the agitators in Galatia, Paul proceeds to narrate the outcome of their (Paul, Barnabas, Titus) visit. But to do so properly he must now start over, which he does by fronting "to me" followed by an explanatory "for" (γάρ), the first one since the string of four in 1:10-13. With this "to me," Paul begins, as he did in vv. 1-2, a series of first person singular pronouns (five in all) that carry through to v. 9c, where he then adds "and Barnabas," and thus returns to the "we" of vv. 4 and 5.

What is about to be explained, since he had already addressed the issue of the (non-)circumcision of Titus (v. 3), is that "*to me* the recognized leaders (TNIV, 'those who were held in high esteem') added nothing." Paul's verb in this case is the same as that used in 1:16, and translated there as "consult." But here it refers not to consultation but to their communicating something further regarding Paul's message. Thus, "they *added* nothing." This, of course, is the absolutely crucial matter with regard to the situation in Galatia. *What* has not been added, of course, is the circumcision of Gentile converts, the matter already spoken to in v. 3. Thus Paul's real concern in the rest of the present narrative is to emphasize what this event meant with regard to his own ministry. These "recognized leaders" not only did not add anything to Paul's ministry, but in fact they in turn "recognized" (TNIV, "saw")[61] that God had entrusted Paul with the gospel for the "uncircumcised."

Paul's way of putting all this needs special notice. First of all, he continues in the first person singular (*I was entrusted*) because his concern at this point is not with the ministry that Paul and Barnabas shared for a time, but with his own calling and ministry, as already noted in 1:16. Furthermore, by putting it in the first person with a passive verb, he does two things at once: stay with the present subject matter – his own ministry – but put his emphasis on God's activity without actually mentioning God by name. In this case he has used the verb "believe" in its extended sense "to entrust" something to someone; and it appears in the Greek perfect tense, implying that this is something that began at a point in time and holds good to the present moment. The "someone" in this case is the grammatical subject of the sentence, "I"; the "something" is "the gospel to the uncircumcised."[62] Then Paul adds, "just as Peter [was entrusted] with the gospel to the circumcised." The issue of whether or how much the believing Jews continued to observe aspects of Torah matters nothing to Paul. What alone matters, as the final episode in the present narrative makes plain (vv. 11–14), is whether such matters of observance are "enforced" when Jew and Gentile share life together at a common table.

Second, by identifying the primary "apostle" to the Jewish community as Peter, rather than James, Paul is not so much trying to identify the principal leader among the three, but to identify him as the primary leader in the actual "mission" of taking the gospel to the Jewish world, including especially that in Palestine. But as 1 Cor 9:5 makes clear, Peter's mission extended also to the larger Gentile world as well – although his ministry may very well have been primarily among the Jews of the Diaspora rather than Gentiles as such. Most likely this itinerant ministry on his part is what caused leadership in the believing community in Jerusalem eventually to fall into the hands of James, the Lord's brother. It is, after all, precisely these two men

---

[61] The Greek participle ἰδόντες is used exclusively in the NT as the aorist (past tense) of the verb "to see" (ὁράω). Its first meaning in BDAG is "perceive by sight of the eye." This is almost certainly its meaning here; they "saw" in the sense that they "perceived" that Paul had been entrusted with the gospel for the "uncircumcised."

[62] For the sake of a contemporary English-speaking audience, the TNIV translators have chosen to go with its ultimate intended meaning, "Gentiles," and put the literal Greek in a note. But that seems to miss too much in terms of the present concern in the letter, which is the circumcision of the "uncircumcised" Gentiles.

whom Paul deliberately notes as his having visited in his first trip to Jerusalem some fourteen years earlier (1:18-19).

Third, in this first instance when Paul expresses the "division of labor" between himself and Jerusalem (the latter in the person of Peter), he deliberately delineates the two groups not as Gentile and Jew, but as "uncircumcised" and "circumcised." The reason for such deliberation is clear enough. Paul's concern is not simply with the different spheres of ministry as such, but that his ministry is specifically *"the gospel of the uncircumcised,"* where the genitive "of the uncircumcised" is a genitive of destination, and means *"for* the uncircumcised."[63] And this is precisely what is at stake: whether uncircumcised Gentiles, whose "uncircumcision" distinguishes them from the Jewish community, must also become circumcised in order to be full members of the new community created by Christ and the Spirit. Paul is the one person who recognizes clearly what is ultimately at stake. If these Gentile converts must also submit to circumcision, what will finally identify them is not their trust in Christ and the presence of the Spirit (4:6), but their circumcision, which the whole world will recognize is but another way of becoming Jewish. So Paul deliberately sets out the key issue in this verse, by identifying both types of believers in Christ, not as Gentile and Jew, but as "uncircumcised" and "circumcised." Indeed he sees clearly not just the theological ramifications of such an action on their part, but the ethnic ones as well. Gentile believers in Christ must be identified only by the markers that are specifically Christian: Christ and the Spirit. Otherwise the gospel is for naught, and the whole Christian enterprise will simply become a sect of Judaism.

That this is the reason for this identification is made certain by the parenthetical explanatory clause that is our *verse 8*. "For," Paul interrupts to explain to the Galatians, and now taking the clauses in v. 7 in reverse (thus chiastic) order, "the One who (= God) was at work in Peter for his apostleship to 'the circumcision' was at work also in me for the Gentiles." Thus with this explanatory clause, whose first purpose is to identify both ministries as enabled by God (and thus not by merely human resources), Paul at the same time keeps the identification of the Jews as "the circumcised," but now switches the second identification as "the Gentiles." Paul has already scored his point about their uncircumcision in the preceding clause (v. 7); here

---

[63] On this question see D.B. Wallace, *Greek Grammar Beyond the Basics: An Exegetical Syntax of the New Testament* (Grand Rapids, MI: Zondervan, 1996), 100-101.

he puts the emphasis back on the biblical language that God also intends to include "the Gentiles" in his eschatological salvation that is already at work through Christ and the Spirit. This same twofold identification is then repeated in the purpose clause at the end of v. 9.

Verse 9. Although most English translations, including the TNIV, make this a new sentence on its own right, in fact it is a second clause that deliberately corresponds to v. 7. Now using a different verb ("knowing"), but one with an overlap in meaning with "seeing" in v. 7, Paul adds that they "recognized the grace given to me." Although "grace" is a favorite word, and will be used in 2:21 in its usual sense of "totally undeserved divine favor toward someone," in this case it probably had the extended meaning of the effects of that grace in his being especially given the privilege of taking the gospel to the Gentiles.[64] And again as with "entrusted" in v. 7, the implied subject of the giving is God.

But we are not quite prepared for what Paul does at the beginning: name the "recognized leaders" by name, "James, Cephas, and John."[65] We have already met James and Cephas in 1:18 and 19, but not in this order. Since the next mention of the two of them by name is in vv. 12 and 13 below, where James is still in Jerusalem and Peter in Antioch, it seems most likely that the present order is that which eventually emerged in Jerusalem, where James apparently had assumed the primary role of leadership, as Luke also acknowledges in his account in Acts 15. This is the only mention of John in the entire Pauline corpus; but the fact that he is included in the acknowledged three adds considerable historical weight to the accounts in Acts, where John plays a prominent role in the early years. The more significant designation is the one that occurs next, "these esteemed as pillars." This is a clear – and complimentary – indication of their prominent role in the church in Jerusalem. The imagery is almost certainly that of a "temple," which in earlier and later letters Paul uses as a metaphor for the church.[66] If Christ alone is the foundation for his church, Paul recognizes the essential

---

[64] On this see BDAG under χάρις, item 4.

[65] There has been considerable tinkering with Paul's usage and word order here on the part of later scribes, especially in the Western church, who under several influences changed it to "Peter, James, and John." This both eliminates the familiar Aramaic "Cephas" by which he was known in the Aramaic-speaking community and puts him in first position.

[66] See esp. 1 Cor 3:16-17, where the church in Corinth, not individual believers, is in view; cf. also Eph 2:21-22.

nature of leadership in the church by designating them as "pillars," those who serve as part of the supporting structure.

What these "pillars" did was to offer him, and now also to Barnabas, "the right hand of fellowship." While this is the kind of language that seems to slight left-handed people, the fact is that this particular idiom has a history in the Greek world that goes back as far as Homer in the eighth century before Christ. And this is the same world where the word for left in Latin is *sinister*, which can only have evolved as a borrowed word in English with such negative connotations because these have been carried over from antiquity. Paul of course means nothing at all about there being actual significance in the right hand. By his time this is simply the common idiom for a handshake that acknowledges full acceptance of one another as an equal.

This present clause finally ends on a repeated note from vv. 7 and 8, only in this case the two parties are now plural: "They agreed that we should go to the Gentiles, and they to the circumcision [TNIV, 'the Jews']." So what in v. 7 was expressed in language that singled out Paul and Peter for their respective apostolic missions, is now expressed in the plural so as to include Barnabas, on the one hand, and James and John, on the other. And as with the elaboration in v. 8, the ministries are noted respectively as "to the Gentiles" and "to the *circumcision*."

Verse 10. With this "exceptive" clause Paul brings his now very long sentence to a conclusion. The "exception," of course, is no exception for Paul at all. In their mission to the Gentile world, he and Barnabas were "to remember the poor," which here almost certainly refers not "the poor" in general – although by extension it would surely include them – but "the poor" in Jerusalem and Judea in particular. According to Acts 2–6 this was a regular part of the church's mission in Jerusalem, especially to its widows – probably of diaspora couples who came to Jerusalem in their later years, where the husband had died and the wife no longer has her lifelong home and friends elsewhere in the Greco-Roman world. Likewise, according to several passages in Paul,[67] an offering on the part of the Gentile churches for the sake of the Jerusalem poor had long been an item on Paul's missional agenda. This was his way of allowing the Gentile believers to express their gratitude to Jerusalem for their part is sending out the Gospel to their cities and lands. Thus Paul concludes with "the very thing I had been eager to do all along," as is evidenced by the space given to it in 1 & 2 Corinthians and Romans.

---

[67] See 1 Cor 16:1-4; 2 Cor 8 and 9; and Rom 15:23-32.

Galatians 2:11-13 – Jerusalem Reneges on Paul's Gospel

> [11] *When Cephas came to Antioch, I opposed him to his face, because he stood condemned.* [12] *For before certain people came from James, he used to eat with the Gentiles. But when they arrived, he began to draw back and separate himself from the Gentiles because he was afraid of those who belonged to the circumcision group.* [13] *The other Jews joined him in his hypocrisy, so that by their hypocrisy even Barnabas was led astray.*

This paragraph is the third and final episode in the long narrative about Paul's relationship with Jerusalem, all of which is for the sake of the Galatians because of misinformation they had received from the agitators. In the preceding narrative, Paul had gone to Jerusalem; now "Jerusalem" has come to Paul. He has thus moved from a narrative demonstrating his independence from Jerusalem (1:13-24), to a narrative demonstrating Jerusalem's approbation of his gospel and mission (2:1-10), to this narrative demonstrating that when someone actually broke faith with the agreement, it was Jerusalem, not Paul. By their actions in Antioch some "people from James" not only reneged on the prior agreement, but did so in such a way as to persuade both Peter and Barnabas of the rightness of their point of view. And we must take that seriously in order to understand the vehemence of Paul's response. For him again, as with the "compulsion to have Titus circumcised" (v. 3), the "truth of the gospel" (v. 14), meaning a Torah-free gospel for the Gentiles, is at stake. So in this case he narrates (at least the beginning of) his response to Peter, which very early on evolves into an introduction to the argument of the rest of the letter.

There are also some striking features to this narrative that need to be noted before looking at the details. First, Paul neither argues directly with (or against) the agitators from Jerusalem (whom the Galatians are expected to see as forerunners of the agitators who are upsetting them), nor does he appeal to the results of the conference which he has just narrated. That is, he could easily have argued, "This issue was settled in Jerusalem by the leaders in conference with Barnabas and myself, and therefore these 'people from James' should back off." But he does not do that in this present recounting of the event for the sake of the Galatians. Nonetheless, Paul clearly intends his Galatian friends to read what happened here in light of the preceding narrative.[68]

---

[68] One of the more idiosyncratic moments in NT scholarship is the suggestion by some that this event *preceded* vv. 1-10 in time. That surely misses the "logic" of Paul's

Second, the argument of the "people from James" must have had a
high degree of persuasive force (again, "believers in Galatia take note")
since both Peter and Barnabas saw its merits and chose to go along
with them, although Paul also attributes to Peter the further motive of
"fearing those who belonged to the circumcision group." Since Paul
does not mention the issue of food per se, we can only guess what the
primary issue was: the Jewish food laws as such, or the fact that Jews
were having table fellowship with Gentiles. Very likely it was a
combination of both (the Gentiles were "unclean" because they ate
"unclean" food), but at least it involved eating food that was
proscribed in the Torah. After all, in his speech to Peter (v. 14) Paul
further describes this event in terms of Peter's having once "lived like
a Gentile," but now of reverting to "living like a Jew" and thus
"forcing Gentile believers" to do the same.

The relationship of Christ, both in his earthly life and through his
death and resurrection, to the issue of the Old Testament food laws is
in fact writ large in the New Testament. According to Mark 7:19 Jesus
radically restructured the meaning of "clean and unclean." Not what
goes into the mouth defiles, but what comes out, Jesus said, which
Mark then interprets explicitly to refer to the food laws ("In saying
this, Jesus declared all foods clean"). Peter himself was one of the slow
learners, since it took a divine intervention for him even to visit a
Gentile home (Acts 10:9-22), of which event he explains to Cornelius:
"It is against our law to have close association with Gentiles or to visit
them" (Acts 10:28); and it was for this "breaking of the law" that he
was "called on the carpet" in Jerusalem (11:1-18). But it obviously
took the Jewish Christian community a long time to catch on, since
Paul feels impelled to speak to this issue on several occasions (here;
1 Cor 10:23–11:1; Rom 14:1-12); and it is the basis for his Christian
understanding of "becoming all things to all people, so that by all
means I might win some" (1 Cor 9:19-23). As our present text
indicates, this is still a matter of high value for some Jewish believers;
and for whatever reasons, both Peter and Barnabas are persuaded by
their arguments.

Third, the vehemence with which Paul speaks, and the fact that he
reports the speech to have been made "in front of them all" (v. 14),
suggests that the event took place in a semi-public setting in which the
larger community of faith in Antioch was involved. The most likely

presentation, where Peter and Barnabas stand condemned precisely because they
should have known better, given what has preceded.

scenario for such an event would have been the believers' common meal of which the Lord's Supper was also a part. We cannot be sure of this, of course, and in the end it does not affect our overall understanding of the passage; but it does make more sense of the narrative if such were the case. This also helps us to understand how Paul, according to 1 Cor 9:19-23, can do exactly the opposite when he is in non-mixed company, that is, when with Jews he ate "like a Jew" and when with Gentiles he ate "like a Gentile." In private matters, God simply does not care at all; one may or may not, depending on one's own comfort zone; but in public matters for Jews to insist on Gentiles eating as Jews do is to insist that they must "live" like Jews in order to be full members of God's family. And that is what causes "the truth of the gospel" to be at stake.

Finally, in our seeking to understand both the what and why of this brief episode, we must keep in mind that this is the last event in the long narrative having to do with Paul's relationship with Jerusalem. For whatever else may be true about it, Paul intends the Galatians to hear that his response to this episode also ultimately had Gentile believers like them in view. The possibility that the issue in Galatia included the food laws would help to explain Paul's present vehemence and his calling Peter's "innocent" action an attempt to "force Gentiles to live like Jews." In any case, the issue as it appears in this narrative is not whether people are saved by grace or by doing law, but that salvation by grace alone is the only way Jew and Gentile can become one people in the newly formed eschatological people of God; for if Gentiles are forced to "live like Jews" on any matter that is based merely on Torah, then the theological result is that their salvation rests ultimately on "doing Torah" not on grace.

Verses 11-12. In a very condensed way the opening sentence (v. 11) sets out the basic features of the narrative to follow. The issue had primarily to do with an action by Cephas (Peter), who is the grammatical (and actual) subject of all the verbs in this and the next two sentences (v. 12) and the antecedent to the two pronouns ("him," "himself," vv. 11 and 12). Following the agreement of vv. 2 and 6-10, Peter subsequently "came to Antioch" and pursued a course of action regarding the Jewish food laws that to Paul seemed contrary to that agreement. So Paul "opposed him to his face, because he stood condemned," meaning his own actions condemned him just as the act of stealing itself condemns a thief. Only in the fourth sentence (v. 13) does Paul pick up on the fact that "the rest of the Jewish believers" in

Antioch, not to mention Paul's own companion Barnabas, one of the founding fathers of this church, also joined Peter in "the hypocrisy."

With an explanatory "for" (γάρ) Paul then proceeds in *verse 12* to spell out the basic details of Peter's action that called for Paul's "dressing him down" publicly, whose emphases come out in his Greek sentence in ways that cannot be duplicated in good English. The sentence is "enclosed" by the two verbs "came" and "used to eat," causing the "people from James" and "with the Gentiles" to be juxtaposed in the middle. Thus, "before came certain people from James, with the Gentiles he used to eat." The important point is the last one, that Peter and other Jewish Christians in Antioch "used to eat with Gentiles," which, as noted above, is most likely to be understood in terms of Jewish food laws, one of the key ways that diaspora Jews maintained their Jewish identity in Gentile settings. But all of this changed when "certain people came from James." We cannot know from Paul's designation whether these "certain people" were actual envoys from James, or whether they were simply itinerants, very much like the agitators in Galatia, who had put themselves forward in such a way.[69] In any case, Paul defines them in terms of "those of the circumcision," which is the same language Paul had used in vv. 7-9 regarding Peter's role in the church.

When these itinerants arrived, Paul goes on, Peter "began to[70] draw back and separate himself from the Gentiles." It is unlikely that this means all association with Gentile believers, but only (especially) at meals, which would probably have included a celebration of the Lord's Supper. The one truly surprising element in Paul's account is that Peter did this "because he was afraid of those who belonged to the circumcision group." From this distance we simply cannot know how to account for this "was afraid of" (reputation? relationship with/influence in Jerusalem? relationship with James? division in the Jewish-Christian community?). One could well understand how a series of arguments could have been presented that for the sake of all parties concerned, Jewish believers and Gentile believers should eat separately. After all,

---

[69] The evidence from James's letter in Acts 15 suggests this latter to be the case: "we have heard that some went out from us without our authorization and disturbed you" (v. 24).

[70] The language "began to" is an attempt on the part of the TNIV translators to give proper ("inceptive") force to the Greek imperfect tense, the same tense as in the verb that concluded the preceding sentence in terms of "he used to" ("iterative"). See Wallace, *Greek Grammar*, pp. 544 and 546. Some (e.g. Burton) take it as iterative here, but that seems contrary to the force of the argument itself. How many times, one wonders, would this have happened before Paul blew the whistle?

the agreement in Jerusalem implied at least that Jewish Christians would still keep the law. As with the matter of Peter's "fear" we cannot be sure of the exact nature of "separately" (separate tables? separate times? or separate houses altogether?). Most likely it is the first of these, since Paul can address Peter in the context of his and the others' action.

Verse 13. The apparent innocence of what happened in Antioch, at least on the part of many within the believing community, comes to the fore in this sentence, since "even/also[71] the rest of the Jews" joined Peter in this action. Given the way the narrative is played out, these "other Jews" would most likely have been the Jewish Christians in Antioch, some of whom would have been part of the founding of that church. But the shocker comes with the final word, that "even Barnabas was led astray." Given that Barnabas was one of the leaders in the Gentile mission in Antioch, one might think that Paul would have assailed him instead of Peter. But Paul recognized that, given the preceding narrative, the key player in this event was Peter, the enormity of whose action is signalled by the fact that Paul begins and ends his sentence by calling it "a hypocrisy," thus identifying its true character. The Greek word "hypocrisy" (ὑπόκρισις) has to do not with a false motive as such, but with trying to make something to appear differently from what it actually is. In Peter's case that might have been spelled out as "caring for the visiting brothers"; but in fact, Paul says, he "feared" them, even though the "why" of that fear is not known to us. In any case, from Paul's perspective it is Peter's action that is crucial because he apparently took the lead; and he is obviously the key figure in the preceding agreement, or at least Paul considers him so and turns his full attention on Peter in the speech that follows.

At the same time this event also brings Paul's narrative about his relationship with Jerusalem to conclusion – without actually specifying that he is doing so. So before going on to the speech itself and looking at how it functions in the letter, we need here to sum up the points Paul has made with the Galatian churches. In a narrative of three parts, he has first of all (1:13-24) emphasized his non-relationship with Jerusalem as far as both his apostleship and the content of his gospel is concerned. Whether accused of having had only human origins, as many scholars

---

[71] Although this καί ("even, also") is missing in a goodly number of the better manuscripts (𝔓⁴⁶ B 1739 1881 a f vg cop), it is found in other early manuscripts (ℵ A C D F G) and became the majority text. Both its difficulty and its redundancy suggest that it is the original reading in this case; it is easy to see why it would have been omitted, but much more difficult to see why anyone would have added it.

think, or of not having proper credentials (read: "having not come from Jerusalem as his detractors brag they have"), he puts all of his emphasis on the fact that for a period of seventeen years he was in Jerusalem for only fifteen days with the express purpose of visiting the apostles. The second part of the narrative (2:1-10) emphasizes one thing as well: that when he finally did go up to Jerusalem – at the Spirit's behest – the issue was over the circumcision of Gentile converts, on which matter Jerusalem was in full agreement with Paul, evidenced by their not "compelling Titus" to submit to it. Furthermore, Paul is pleased to report that neither did Jerusalem "add anything" to the gospel he has preached; indeed the only "requirement" was about something he was already doing: to continue to remember the poor. With the present narrative (2:11-14+) he makes the further point that when someone actually broke faith with the earlier agreement, it was Jerusalem who did so, in the person of Peter under the influence of some men "from James." They did this probably by agreeing to separate tables for Jewish believers so that they would not have to eat with their Gentile brothers and sisters. But Paul saw the full ramifications of such an action and "opposed Peter to his face." The basic content of that opposition is what he offers next; and this is given in such a way that it also introduces the basic argument of the letter.

Galatians 2:14-21 – Paul's Speech Introduces his Gospel

[14] *When I saw that they were not acting in line with the truth of the gospel, I said to Cephas in front of them all, "You are a Jew, yet you live like a Gentile and not like a Jew. How is it, then, that you force Gentiles to follow Jewish customs?*

[15] *"We who are Jews by birth and not sinful Gentiles* [16] *know that a person is not justified by observing the law, but by faith in Jesus Christ. So we, too, have put our faith in Christ Jesus that we may be justified by faith in*[a] *Christ and not by observing the law, because by observing the law no one will be justified.*

[17] *"But if, in seeking to be justified in Christ, we Jews find ourselves also among the sinners, doesn't that mean that Christ promotes sin? Absolutely not!* [18] *If I rebuild what I destroyed, then I really would be a lawbreaker.*

[19] *"For through the law I died to the law so that I might live for God.* [20] *I have been crucified with Christ and I no longer live, but Christ lives in me. The life I now live in the body, I live by faith in the Son of God, who loved me and gave himself for me.* [21] *I do not set aside the grace*

*of God, for if righteousness could be gained through the law, Christ died
for nothing!"* [b]

^a Or *but through the faithfulness of … justified on the basis of the faithfulness of*
^b Some interpreters end the quotation after v. 14

With this speech Paul slowly moves his attention away from his
relationship with Jerusalem to the situation that has emerged in
Galatia. In so doing he uses his speech to Peter as the point of
transition; but this also can make the present passage a difficult one for
contemporary readers. So we begin with an overview of the whole,
pointing out its various parts and suggesting how they relate to each
other in a sequential way, and then offer an overview of the
theological "logic" that lies behind everything.

We begin by noting that the TNIV translators have chosen to put
quotes around the entire passage, from v. 14b through v. 21, but with
a marginal note at the end that reads: "Some interpreters end the
quotation after v. 14." Among these are the majority of modern
English translations, including the NRSV, whose note (on v. 14)
points to the real difficulty: "Some interpreters hold that the quotation
extends *into the following paragraph*" (italics mine). This seems to be the
plain matter of fact, as a simple analysis of the argument itself, and
especially Paul's use of pronouns, suggests. That Paul intended to be
quoting himself at least through v. 16, seems to be made certain by his
change from "you" singular in v. 14 to the first person plural "we/us"
in v. 15 that carries through v. 17. The surprise comes with the
sudden appearance of "I" in v. 18 that carries through to the end. And
one must remember in all of this that Paul is ultimately speaking to the
Galatians themselves.[72]

Thus Paul begins (v. 14b) by giving the basic content of his
"speech" to Peter regarding his personal failure in the Antioch matter.
But then in typical fashion, when the resolution includes something
which Paul himself has experienced, he resorts to "we."[73] Thus in vv.
15 to 17, having to do with what Jewish believers have experienced in

---

[72] Cf. Lightfoot (113): "St. Paul's narrative in fact loses itself in the reflexions suggested by it. Text and comment are so blended together that they cannot be separated
without violence."

[73] This happens often enough in Paul that most readers simply don't notice. For an
example of this phenomenon in a single sentence, see Col 1:9-14, which is a single
long sentence in Greek. The shift comes in vv. 12 and 13, where he thanks God for
what he has done for "you" Colossians, but when further elaborating on the
redemptive work of Christ, he shifts to "us."

common, it is all "we." But in v. 18 Paul chooses to identify with Peter, whose action is rebuilding in Antioch what had once been destroyed. In the rest of the passage Paul thus becomes the "representative Jew" in terms of what God has done for him (them). But his attention is now turning altogether toward the Galatians, as the sudden challenge in 3:1 makes clear. Thus his own experience sets the stage for his argument with them.

It seems likely, however, that Paul's turning his attention toward Galatia begins as early as v. 15. In any case, they are surely in view in v. 17, where Paul is wrestling with Jews like himself and Peter, who have trusted Christ and thereby have also abandoned any definition of "sin" in terms of law-keeping. To revert now to law-keeping, as Peter is in effect doing, has the ultimate effect of making Christ the one who promotes sin, since his death and resurrection is responsible for their no longer keeping Torah. But Paul is not willing to be party to such a betrayal of Christ – to rebuild what had been destroyed – so the rest of the paragraph plays on the themes of "death" and "life" with respect to Torah and the work of Christ, all of which is finally expressed in an intensely personal way.

Before going through the passage in detail, one needs to be aware of three *fundamental premises* that lie behind everything. First, from the Jewish point of view, sin = *not* keeping Torah. Thus, to be uncircumcised means to be a sinner, because it means not to keep Torah on this matter. Gentiles, being uncircumcised, are therefore sinners *by nature* (by birth). At the same time, second, the fundamental premise of the gospel – for *both* Paul and *all other Jewish Christians* – is that salvation has now come through Christ, for *both* Jew *and* Gentile. Because of his mission to the Gentiles, Paul will insist that everyone follow the logic of the second premise as it relates to the first. Third, inherent is a third premise, broached here, but not fully articulated: that breaking Torah in terms of "identity markers" – those aspects of Torah that identify diaspora Jews in their Gentile settings – *does not in fact constitute sin.* Behind all this is Paul's transformed understanding of sin (see on 5:13–6:10), that it is a matter of yielding to the "flesh," and therefore is not a matter of Torah at all.

Thus Paul's urgency – and his "logic." By compelling Gentiles to "live like Jews" (by keeping kosher in Antioch; and by being circumcised in Galatia) Peter in Antioch, and the agitators in Galatia, are in effect insisting that the old distinctions between Jew and Gentile, thus between being righteous and sinner, still hold. Paul, on the other hand, is committed to a position that Christ's death and resurrection have in fact *abolished* the old distinctions (which will be argued with force in chap. 3). Jew and Gentile *alike* are *sinners* (because they have both "broken law" and have lived "in keeping with 'the flesh' [κατὰ σάρκα]); therefore Jew and Gentile *alike* are *given rightstanding with God* on the basis of grace alone, which means further that *neither* Jew nor Gentile need any longer be circumcised or keep kosher. It is okay for Jews, if they wish, but absolutely irrelevant to God himself. Thus Paul sees clearly the "logic" of compelling Gentiles to be circumcised. It means that even though they have trusted in Christ, without circumcision they are in effect still sinners, in the sense that the old "rules" which make them sinners are still in effect. For Paul, therefore, this is no mere quibble; for him the "truth of the gospel" is at stake.

Verse 14. The first part of this verse ("when I saw that they were not acting in line with the truth of the gospel") is in fact the continuation of the narrative that began in v. 11. As in v. 5 above, Paul sees Peter's action as a betrayal of "the truth of the gospel." His way of putting it is a picture word, "to walk straight" ("acting in line with" TNIV), implying that with this action Peter is veering off on a tangential, and therefore false, path with regard to what the gospel is all about. The "truth of the gospel," therefore, in this case is not a phrase that is all-embracing, and thus a kind of theological compendium that Peter and others must adhere to. For Paul "the truth of the gospel" is about what Christ has done on behalf of all people, so that trusting him is all that is necessary for both Jew and Gentile to belong together as the one people of God. To revert to Jewish food laws by eating at separate tables is to rebuild what Christ demolished and thus to make oneself a transgressor against Christ himself (v. 18).

So in the presence of "them all" Paul addresses Peter directly: "If you, being a Jew yourself, live like a Gentile and not like a Jew, how is it that you now force the Gentiles to live like Jews?" With this question we come to the heart of the matter for Paul, because nothing in Peter's and the others' action would necessarily intend that *Gentiles* must "live like Jews." Rather, they would have argued, "we are trying to be loving toward our *Jewish* brothers who have come from Jerusalem and sit at table with them, since they are offended to sit at table with Gentiles and their non-'kosher' food" – especially so since it very well may have included food sold in the marketplace that had once been offered to an idol. We know from many sources that Jews simply could not bring themselves to eat anything that had ever been "corrupted" by its appearance in a pagan temple. But what one does in private is one thing; in the corporate community, where Christ himself has declared *all foods* "clean" (Mark 7:19), there simply can be no food laws that would make Gentiles second-class citizens in the newly formed people of God. After all, the Jewish believers could simply skip eating any food that would be offensive to them. Thus for believers in Christ to give credence to food laws in a way that excludes others from Christ is for Paul a betrayal of Christ himself. By such action they are in effect "compelling" Gentiles to "live like Jews," whereas the gathering in Jerusalem chose deliberately *not* to "compel" the Gentile Titus to be circumcised (v. 3). The inherent irony for Paul, of course, which he capitalizes on, is that Peter himself had already chosen to "live like a Gentile" with regard to the food laws.

Verses 15-16. This next step in Paul's argument with Peter, which consists of a long, quite complex sentence in Greek, is in many ways the most important sentence in the letter. Here Paul does three things simultaneously. First, he sets out the basic contrast noted above between Jew and Gentile as understood by the Jewish community, that Gentiles, because they do not have the law, are thereby understood automatically to be "sinners," while observant Jews would never understand themselves in this way. Rather, failure on their part would make them "transgressors" of the law (v. 18). Second, he sets out the basic contrast between Jew as Jew, and Jew and Gentile as Christian, in terms of the one as "based on works of law" (= *doing* law as a means of/expression of righteousness) and the other as "based on faith in Christ Jesus." Third, in so doing he is thereby also setting forth the basic premises on which the rest of the arguments of the letter are based, namely that to be "justified"[74] before God, Jew and Gentile alike have put their faith in Christ Jesus and not in doing works of law. It seems likely that Paul is here echoing language from the Septuagint of Psalm 143:2, "no living being will be justified (δικαιωθήσεται) before you," but where the Hebrew text uses the adjective, "For no living being is *righteous* before you." But whether so or not, the use of this verb makes Paul's sentence especially complex, which will require some close work with his text in order to get at the heart of things.

We begin by noting the overall structure of the sentence itself, since it should help to resolve some of the initial difficulties. Paul starts with two basic premises: (1) that Jews by nature (= circumstances conditioned by birth) are not sinners in the same way as the Gentiles

---

[74] Since this is a key word in this letter, I have chosen to put it in quotes until it can be discussed is some detail as item (a) below.

(v. 15); nonetheless (2) "we" Jews also have come to know that a person is "justified" before God not by "doing law" but by trusting in Jesus Christ (v. 16a). The rest of the sentence spells out what "we" (Jews by birth, including Peter and Paul) did about the two basic premises, and does so by a twofold repetition of "our" response to the second premise. Thus two more times he repeats, "not by doing law" but "by faith in Christ Jesus." This threefold repetition of "doing law" and "faith in Christ Jesus" is obviously intended to catch the reader's attention, especially that of Paul's friends in Galatia for whom all of this is being recounted. But for those of us who are not only distanced in time from the Apostle but also have had a long history of interpretation precede us, it is easy for us to assume we already know what all of this means. So we need to look at three items in detail, which appear together for the first time in v. 16a. What does Paul mean by "justified," by "works of law," and by "faith in Christ Jesus." For most of us these are easy; they have to do with our rightstanding with God based not on our doing works to gain God's favor but on our putting our complete trust in what Christ Jesus has done for us. But for several reasons, true as that is, it is a bit misleading with regard to the present passage in Galatians, since the "ease" for many of us entails a great deal of prior understanding that we bring to the text because of our place in the church. At issue, after all, is not how people gain their salvation, but whether "saved people" must also adhere to the law.

(a) The meaning of "justified." Our difficulty with understanding this verb is predicated on three factors: (i.) that Paul is here using what is basically a *metaphor* for salvation that is based on an understanding of sin as "breaking the law"; (ii.) that historically Protestantism has isolated this one as the primary Pauline metaphor for salvation; and (iii.) that its corresponding adjective in this case is not "just" but "righteous" and the corresponding noun is most often translated as "righteousness," but never (in the TNIV) as "justification."

Since most of our complications come from the third item, we need first to say a few brief words about the first two, mostly because "justification" is neither the predominant metaphor in Paul nor the most common one. It is well known that Paul uses several verbs (and their corresponding nouns) to speak about what God has done for us (that we could not do for ourselves) through the death of Christ and the gift of the Spirit. Most often these verbs emerge in contexts that have been determined by the view of sin that is under consideration. Thus when our sinful condition is thought of in terms of our being enslaved to it, the metaphor is "redemption." When the issue is enmity with God, the metaphor is "reconciliation"; and when the issue has to do with our being under God's wrath, the metaphor is "propitiation."[75] And these metaphors are seldom, if ever, mixed in Paul. A slave to sin is not "reconciled to God"; nor is the one standing under God's wrath "redeemed." So much is this so, that in several instances where Paul wants to emphasize the full measure of Christ's saving work, and where one specific form of our sinfulness is not in view, he piles up several of these at one time. Thus in 1 Cor 1:20, Christ has become for us our source of "righteousness (pardon?), sanctification, and redemption," while in 6:11 it is "you were washed, you were sanctified, you were justified." In Titus 3:5-7 it comes out as "washing of rebirth, renewal by the Holy Spirit, ... justified by his grace." The reason for this is simple: the redemptive work of Christ is so large, covering every aspect of our fallenness as it does, that no one metaphor can ever cover the whole ground, and therefore one metaphor simply does not predominate in Paul. Indeed, it almost always comes as a surprise to people raised in Protestant churches that the verb "justify" occurs in this theological sense only in Galatians and Romans, besides the one occurrence noted above in 1 Cor 6:11. All of this to point out that it is the predominant metaphor in Galatians precisely because the primary issue is over whether or not Gentiles must also "do law" in order to complete their relationship with God.

So what then does this metaphor mean here and elsewhere in Paul? Our problems here stem basically from our need to translate Paul's Greek into meaningful English, a language that grew out of a combination of two language groups: Teutonic (Germanic) and Romance (going back to Greek and Latin, but coming to England by way of Normandy [France]). Thus for ever so many ideas we ended up with two words that are often synonymous, but not always; and in most cases the simpler, shorter word is Anglo-Saxon while the longer word is ultimately derived from Latin. Thus "work" is a good Anglo-Saxon word (cf. German "Werk"), while "labor" comes straight from Latin. Our present problems begin with the adjective (δίκαιος), since it can mean either "just" or "righteous," which do not mean the same thing in English. Furthermore, the cognate noun for the condition of "being righteous" (i.e. "righteousness" [δικαιοσύνη]) seldom means "justifica-

---

[75] For a fuller exposition of this matter see G.D. Fee, "Paul and the Metaphors for Salvation: Some Reflections on Pauline Soteriology," *The Redemption: An Interdisciplinary Symposium on Christ as Redeemer* (ed. S.T. Davis, D. Kendall, G. O'Collins; Oxford: Oxford University Press, 2003) 43–67

tion." We can be sure of this in Paul's case because he is using an Old Testament word that has come to him by way of the Septuagint that is consistently used to translate the Hebrew *tsadek*, a word used most often to speak of God's own character of "righteousness."

Our real problems emerge with the use of the Greek verb translated "justify" (δικαιόω), because in English we have no verbal equivalent on the Anglo-Saxon side of our language, and are left with only the word "justify" which comes from our Latin heritage. But in both everyday English and legal contexts, "justify" means something quite different from Paul's usage. On the one hand, "justify" means "to show [something] to be just or right, or to show a satisfactory reason or excuse for something done," as in "they are justified in doing that" or "the end justifies the means."[76] Since neither of these comes even close to what Paul is about, an entirely different meaning is offered for theology, "to declare innocent or guiltless; absolve; acquit." But these do not work well either, since the one who has been "justified" through Christ is not innocent, but guilty, and is not "acquitted," since that means found not to have been guilty in the first place. Interestingly, the word "absolve," in the sense of "to grant pardon for" would seem to come the closest to it, but it is a word Protestants are loathe to use because of what they perceive to be abuses in Roman Catholic use of the word.

But all of this has to do with getting it right in English; at issue is what Paul himself intended by his use of this Greek verb, because even if we were to invent the word "righteousize before God," we would still have to ask what that meant, whether "given rightstanding with God" or "pardoned by God" or "made righteous by God." One may argue from all of Paul's uses that it minimally includes the first two of these in conjunction with each other. One is "pardoned," not acquitted, since the former recognizes the full measure of guilt for one's sins while the latter never means that. The result of such pardon also includes "rightstanding with God," which further means that through Christ and the Spirit we have ready access into God's presence even when we have been guilty of further sin. So in the end we must admit that Paul's concern is not precision with regard to this word, but that with regard to breaking or keeping the law, both Jews and Gentiles together have received their pardon and rightstanding with God through the work of Christ.

---

[76] Both of these definitions are taken from *The Random House Dictionary of the English Language* (2nd ed., unabridged; New York: Random House, 1987), 1040.

(b) The meaning of "works of law." In many ways this should be the easy one, but in this case that is not so either, since it is so often taken to mean "doing good works in order to gain salvation." One can say definitively that such is not its meaning here. Indeed, at the end of this letter as his final word in the argument itself, Paul, with a deliberately inclusive "we," urges the Galatian believers, first, "let us not become weary in doing good" (6:9) and finally, "let us do what is good [lit., 'work at the good'] for all people" (6:10). It is a simple matter of fact that Paul regularly urges his churches to "do good works." But here Paul is dealing not with "good works" but specifically with doing "works of law," meaning keeping certain requirements of the law as a means of gaining, or being in, rightstanding with God.

Furthermore, "doing/observing the law" does not in this argument have to do with keeping the *whole* law, as both 3:10 and 5:3 make plain. It is quite clear from the argument in 5:2 and 3 that the agitators in Galatia are not interested in these Gentile believers' "keeping the whole law," nor do they themselves keep the whole law, Paul says in 6:13. Rather, they are specifically interested in those aspects of the law that in the Diaspora identify the Jews as God's chosen people in their pagan surroundings. The three aspects of the law mentioned either explicitly or indirectly are circumcision (2:3; 5:2-6; 6:12-15), the observance of special "holy" days (4:10, something on which the Galatians have apparently already capitulated), and the food laws (2:11-13 above). These, then, are the "works of law" that are being urged on the Galatians, which Paul recognizes have the ultimate theological implication of basing one's relationship with God on "doing law," not in trusting Christ.

(c) The meaning of "faith in Christ Jesus." This would seem to be the simple one of the three, especially since Paul goes on in the next clause to spell it out in terms of "believing (putting one's faith in = trusting) Christ Jesus." But such is not the case, on two counts. First, as with the verb rendered "justified," so the verb "believe in" is another instance where the English language, for all its richness, is slightly impoverished, inasmuch as we have no verb that corresponds with the noun "faith." That is, we cannot say "one faithed God"; and the problem with the verb "believe" in English is that it has singularly to do with mental activity of having "confidence in the truth of something or someone." Whereas even though the Greek word (πιστεύω) can move in this direction, it more commonly has to do with "putting one's trust in someone or something," as our noun "faith" does. Fortunately in this letter the verb occurs only three times

(here; 3:6 [citing the LXX]; 3:22), so the problem is not as intense as with "righteousness." But one needs always to be reminded that in Galatians the verb singularly means "to have faith in (= put one's trust in)" God or Christ.

But the second issue with this phrase is far more complex, since there is something of a groundswell in New Testament scholarship which interprets this phrase as a subjective genitive, and thus as referring to Christ's own faithfulness that led to his death for us.[77] But there are several reasons for *not* going this way, attractive as it might be in terms of theological emphasis.

First, the data. This use of "faith" (πίστις) with Christ in the genitive occurs four times in Galatians (here [2x]; 2:20; 3:22), twice in Romans (3:22, 26), and once in Philippians (3:9). In each case it occurs in direct contrast to doing "works of law." Although there are places where the phrase might possibly refer to "the faithfulness of Christ" (e.g., Rom 3:22, on the pattern of "God's faithfulness" in 3:3, and Abraham's in 4:12, 16),[78] it is unlikely to do so here in Galatians, and thus in its other (very few) occurrences. Here are the difficulties:

(i) Most damaging to the subjective genitive view is its occurrence in this passage, the first in Paul's letters, where it is immediately explained (with the cognate verb) in terms of "even we *believed* [put our faith] in Christ Jesus." The common appeal to tautology (unnecessary repetition) as a reason for rejecting such a view does not hold up here, since the power of Paul's rhetoric lies precisely in the threefold repetition of "works of law" and "belief in Christ." And in this case, the very phrasing and emphases of this second clause speak against the "new look" view. That is, when Paul immediately qualifies the phrase with "*even we* have believed in Christ Jesus," the "even we" is a clear pick up from what precedes. Thus, since "we know" that a person is not justified by works of law "but through faith in Jesus Christ, *even we ourselves* (= Paul, Peter, Barnabas, and the rest), law-keeping Jews though we were, *even we* put our trust in Christ." The "even we" makes very little sense following "Christ's own faithfulness."

---

[77] See the TNIV marginal note; for this point of view, and thus the "groundswell," see the commentaries by Longenecker (87), Matera (100-101), Witherington (179-82), and Martyn (263-75); for the traditional view see the commentaries by Betz (117-18), Bruce (139), Dunn (134-39), and Hansen (69).

[78] It is also to be noted, however, that πίστις carries a considerably different nuance in these latter two passages.

(ii) It has been argued regarding the combination of the Greek word "faith" (πίστις) with the genitive "that when πίστις takes a personal genitive it is almost never an objective genitive."[79] But almost all the alleged analogies are not true analogies at all, since the vast majority of them are the personal *possessive pronoun* and thus they all have the Greek definite article with the noun πίστις to specify precisely that the author is talking about "*the* faith that [you] have."[80] This means that the one analogy to this (possible) usage in Paul is Rom 3:3, which in fact is not a true analogy, since *both* nouns have the definite article, so as to make certain that Paul is referring to "*the* faithfulness of *the* [one and only] God." That God in this case is the subject of "faith" is evident by the use of the definite article with both words. What is significantly overlooked in these discussions is the true analogy to this (double *non*-articular) usage of "faith" with the genitive, namely Mark 11:22, where Jesus tells his disciples, "Have faith in God" (ἔχετε πίστιν θεοῦ), and where no one would imagine translating, "have God's faith(fulness)."

(iii) Moreover, the apparent analogies of Rom 3:3 and 4:16, where πίστις does mean "faithful," are not precise. In all seven instances of πίστεως Χριστοῦ both words occur *without the definite article*,[81] thus implying "through faith in Christ," exactly as Paul has it grammatically in 2 Thess 2:13 ("by trusting the truth" [πίστει ἀληθείας]). In fact, this passage offers the real analogy to this phrase where Christ is in the genitive, but is overlooked in most of the discussions (cf. Mark 11:22 above). As with the usage in our present letter, this unusual expression owes its existence to Paul's rhetoric – as a way of expressing a sharp contrast between the Thessalonian believers and those destined for perdition because they do not "love the truth" (2:10). Moreover, although the usage in Rom 4:16 regarding Abraham may seem to be

---

[79] The NET Bible, p. 2176, n. **tn**. The passages offered in support are Matt 9:2, 22, 29; Mark 2:5; 5:34; 10:52; Luke 5:20; 7:50; 8:25, 48; 17:19; 18:42; 22:32; Rom 1:8, 12; 3:3; 4:5, 12, 16; 1 Cor 2:5; 15:14, 17; 2 Cor 10:15; Phil 2:17; Col 1:4; 2:5; 1 Thess 1:8; 3:2, 5, 10; 2 Thess 1:3; Titus 1:1; Phlm 6; 1 Pet 1:9, 21; 2 Pet 1:5). This looks like an imposing list (36 items in all), until one looks carefully at them.

[80] This occurs in no less than 32 of the genitives. Two of the other four have Abraham as the subject (Rom 4:12 and 16), and one "God's elect" (Tit 1:1). So the only true analogy in this list is the one always appealed to, Rom 3:3.

[81] Some object that Paul uses the definite article in Gal 2:20, but this is not analogous since the usage is appositional in this case, not truly articular. In typical fashion Paul has phrased his contrasts in poetic, chiastic fashion: ὁ δὲ νῦν ζῶ ἐν σαρκί, ἐν πίστει ζῶ τῇ τοῦ υἱοῦ τοῦ θεοῦ, where the word order ζῶ ἐν σαρκί, ἐν πίστει ζῶ calls for the defining τῇ because of the intervening ζῶ.

"an exact parallel," as some would have it, in fact it is quite dependent on 4:12, where the defining article makes Paul's sense certain ("*the* faith/fulness of Abraham"; cf. Rom 3:3).

(iv) Significantly, the "new look" rests altogether on an interpretation of this one phrase, which occurs but seven times in the entire corpus; and it does so by way of an understanding of the noun πίστις that can indeed be found (once at least) in Paul, but is only a secondary meaning at best. That is, nowhere else does Paul in plain speech (rather than in a prepositional phrase with an unusual [for Paul] meaning) say anything about our salvation resting on Christ's faithfulness.

(v) Not only so, but Paul does use a shortened version of the phrase (ἐκ πίστεως without a genitive qualifier) no less that seven times in Galatians alone,[82] and in each instance it refers to their "faith" in Christ, by which they were justified, not to the faithfulness of Christ that made such rightstanding possible. Since this shorter phrase by itself seems to be a pickup of the longer phrase, it would be especially strange for Paul to give it a *different* meaning from that intended in the two instances where the same phrase occurs with "Christ" as the genitive qualifier (2:16 and 3:22). That is, since ἐκ πίστεως means that we live "by faith" = trust in Christ Jesus, how is it that the longer version of the phrase makes Christ the *subject* of the "faith" rather than the object?

(vi) Even more damaging for this point of view is the way Paul immediately picks up these two phrases in the argument that immediately follows in 3:1-6. Only the contrast now is between "works of law" and "the hearing of faith," which can only mean "the hearing that produces faith," or as the TNIV has it, "by believing what you heard." Had this first contrast been between people's "observing the law" and "Christ's faithfulness," then the follow-up contrasts would seem of necessity also to reflect this understanding. But in fact Paul puts all his emphasis on the Galatians' faith, not on Christ's faithfulness.

(vii) Finally, the phrase itself was most likely coined in this, its first occurrence in the corpus, in antithesis to "by works of law" (ἐξ ἔργων νόμου), where "works" can only refer to what we do. By analogy, and in total antithesis, ἐκ πίστεως Χριστοῦ is also what we "do"; we put our trust in Christ. Thus, the only reason this phrase exists at all in the

---

[82] See 3:7, 8, 9, 11, 12, 24; 5:5.

Pauline corpus is rhetorical, as a way of expressing faith in Christ as the opposite, both grammatically and theologically, of "works of law."

All of this, then, to indicate that the traditional meaning is almost certainly the correct one, provided that by "traditional" one understands the word to involve the element of "trusting wholly in," not simply assenting to something that one believes to be true. It is further significant to point out that this phrase occurs with two different prepositions. In the first instance, it is "through (διά) faith," thus expressing the means whereby we enter into the state of being "justified." In the second two instances it is "based on (ἐκ) faith," where the contrast is with an existence "based on doing law." In v. 20 below Paul moves to yet a third way of speaking about our "faith," namely living "in (ἐν) [the sphere of] faith."

What this means, finally, is that Paul in these two verses is deliberately setting out Peter's activity in Antioch as reverting to "doing the law" and thus abandoning "faith in Christ Jesus" – although Peter himself would surely not have thought of it this way. But from Paul's perspective, by choosing to eat at separate tables from the Gentile believers, Peter was in effect *theologically* siding with Jewish sensibilities: that God's new people must still keep faith with the basic regulations of the law that gave them identity in the Gentile world. Paul not only says a loud "No" to that here, but in 3:2-5 he will go on to argue that only the Spirit gives God's people their identity under the new covenant.

Verse 17. With a quite complicated sentence in the form of a question Paul moves on to point out to the Galatians (by way of still speaking to Peter) the consequences of their adding certain requirements of the Jewish law to their faith in Christ Jesus: "But if, in seeking to be justified in Christ, we Jews find ourselves also among the sinners, doesn't that mean that Christ promotes sin?" The sentence is predicated on the assumptions of the preceding sentence. Its logic seems plain enough. The first premise (from v. 15): Jews, who have the law, are not "sinners" like the Gentiles. The second premise (from v. 16): nonetheless, even we Jews have to put our faith in Christ Jesus, since the gift of righteousness comes by trusting him, *not* by observing the law. The third premise is an implication based on Peter's action: by eating at separate tables you have implied that the food laws are still in effect, and if so, then eating forbidden food with Gentiles means that we have "sinned" in so doing; that is, we have become like the Gentile "sinners." Thus the logical conclusion: Since we ate this food because of our new relationship with God through Christ, that means that Christ himself is responsible for our becoming sinners; by thus making us "law-breakers" Christ is thereby "promoting sin."[83] No wonder Paul ends with a kind of, "Perish the thought!"[84] a denial that implies the absurdity of the argument and its logical implications.

The point of all this is that Christ has made the ground level between Jew and Gentile; neither is now advantaged or disadvantaged with God on the basis of having and doing, or not having and not doing, the law. But if Jews come along and argue that the food laws are in fact still in effect, that means that one's relationship with God is ultimately based on keeping these laws. And if Gentiles must also keep these laws (implied by the separated tables), then Christ died in vain. Or, to put it baldly as Paul does here, it also means that Christ has become responsible for our becoming "sinners" like the Gentiles if we, like them, do not keep the food laws.

Verse 18. The "for" with which this sentence begins[85] indicates that Paul is now offering his own explanation of what he has just said. But the explanation in this case is not about the role of Christ, but about the role of Peter and others who by their actions are "rebuilding" the structures of the former covenant. Thus he asserts, "if I rebuild what I destroyed, then I really would be a lawbreaker." What is of high interest is that Paul now shifts from the "we" of vv. 15-17 to an unexpected "I," which will continue through to the end of the chapter. By doing this Paul does not thereby exonerate Peter – what he has said to this point makes that clear – but he now clearly begins to shift the focus from the event in Antioch to the present issue in Galatians. And by taking the role of the bad guy here, he can thereby move easily to his own experience of grace in the sentences that follow, as a paradigm for them.

Thus, keeping the argument intact, and with a "present particular conditional clause,"[86] he repeats now in the more traditional language of law-keeping, that Peter's action, and especially now by implication,

---

[83] An alternative view is that this is actually a charge made by the "men from James"; but this seems less likely in view of the rhetorical nature of the sentence. The power of the rhetoric lies precisely in the absurdity of the conclusion that must be drawn if one may assume (as Peter's conduct does) that these early "Judaizers" are correct.

[84] This is the second occurrence of this denial in the corpus (cf. 1 Cor 6:15); in this letter see 3:21 and 6:14.

[85] Because the "for" is implied in the TNIV it was not rendered specifically.

[86] In the present particular condition, both the "if-clause" (the protasis) and the "then-clause" (the apodosis) are in the indicative mood and thus present a simple matter of fact. If one condition exists, so then does the other.

the action of the agitators in Galatia, means to "build up again" what
Peter himself (and others) had already "torn down" regarding the food
laws. What the "men from James" persuaded Peter to do is precisely
what the agitators are urging the Galatians to do, which apparently
they are on the very brink of doing. Paul recognizes clearly that if they
yield to this they are in effect abandoning Christ, because adding a
"plus factor" to grace is to eliminate grace altogether. The stinger thus
comes at the end, and again putting himself in the role of both Peter
and the Galatians, he says in the apodosis, "I demonstrate myself to be
a transgressor [of the law]." This is a strong indictment indeed. Adding
law-keeping to "faith in Christ" is thus double jeopardy. Under this
definition of sin, if I don't keep the law, Christ himself becomes a
servant of sin; and I am now a lawbreaker and thus a transgressor who
is liable for punishment for being/doing so.

Verse 19. With yet another explanatory "for" Paul goes on to offer
his own theological understanding of the real trouble with the law as
legal requirement for righteousness. In many ways he says here in
shorthand what he will say later about the law in "longhand" in Rom
7:14–8:4. Indeed, the heart of Paul's sentence lies with the balanced
phrases on either side of the "in order that" introduction to the final
purpose clause, but the phrases themselves are nearly impossible to put
into equally balanced clauses in English that are at the same time still
meaningful English. Thus he says, "with respect to the law I died;
with respect to God I live." And our understanding of this (for us)
very dense sentence lies in fleshing out the intent of what is said here,
where "death and law" are deliberately contrasted with "life and
God."

The ultimate trouble with the law, it turns out, is not with the law
itself; the law, he will say in the later exposition, is good. But the good
thing brought about "my death" because it condemned me and had no
inherent power to give life; and this is why it must be replaced by
Christ and the Spirit. Because Christ has freely offered pardon to all
who have sinned by breaking the law's commands, his death brings the
time of the law to an end; and the Spirit is God's response to the end
of law, because the Spirit alone can do what the law could not do:
give life to the dead and empower a kind of life that bears God's
likeness and thus has no need of the law (see 3:2-5 and 5:13-26).

This understanding of the law and Christ's role in bringing it to an
end is what the rest of the present passage spells out in very (unusual
for Paul) personal terms. First, in the present sentence he articulates the
role of the law: "through the law I died to the law." This is simply a

terse way of putting the two primary realities regarding the law on this side of the cross. First, the law brought about his death, since transgressors of the law are under the sentence of death. But at the same time, second, his death, brought about by (his disobedience to) the law, had the effect thereby also of bringing the time of law to an end, since dead people cannot obey its commands. Hence, "through the law I died, and that means I also died with respect to the law's claims on my life." But this very terse clause is not the end of Paul's sentence. This twofold death (his own and his relationship to the law), had as its goal, just as in Rom 8:1-4, that "I might (now truly) live in terms of my relationship to God," the "how" of which Paul will go on to explain in the next sentence.

Verse 20. It is always difficult to write commentary on a well-known passage in Paul, in part because it is so well known that "who needs a commentary here?" but also in part because those who love this passage do so because it is (properly so) a very important part of their own personal relationship with God; and a commentary must insist on keeping it first within the context of Paul's argument in the present passage. What Paul sets out to do next is to explain how "living with respect to God" came about; and in so doing he picks up both sides of the preceding contrasting phrases: death and life.

Thus he first explains how he "died with respect to the law." It was in fact effected through the death of Christ, which Paul now expresses in a very personal way, by continuing his use of the first person pronoun that began in v. 18. Since Christ died in "my" behalf, that means in effect that "I have been crucified with Christ." One need only read on in Galatians to understand why Paul now turns to focus on Christ's death in his/the Galatians'/our behalf. It is Christ who brought the reign of the law to an end; and he did so through his crucifixion. So from this point forward the law drops out of this narrative altogether, and everything focuses on Christ and what he has done to effect life. With two very powerful, very personal clauses Paul sets forth the twin dimensions of the work of Christ, the first of which at the same time clearly presupposes the role of the Spirit. This is made clear in the very next paragraph, where Paul turns to apply all of this to the Galatians directly, and does so in terms of their experience of the indwelling Spirit, not in terms of the forgiveness of their sins.

The first explanatory clause that flows out of "with Christ, I myself was crucified" – which picks up the "death" motif from v. 19 – indicates the source of the new life. Since the crucified One is through his resurrection now the living One, so "I too live." Moreover, his

(Paul's)/our own new life is equally an expression of the resurrection, since in reality "it is no longer I" who is living, but "(the risen) Christ who is living in me." And we know from the next paragraph, as well as from other passages (esp. Rom 8:9-10), that Christ lives in us by his Spirit, the same Spirit who is also the Spirit of God. So in effect, Christian conversion is Trinitarian at its core, even though this language itself is not worked out until a later time. Whatever else, it is the living God, the Triune God, who indwells the believer, since it is the Spirit of God the Father who is at the same time the Spirit of Christ the Son who indwells the believer. The emphasis here, of course, is on the Son, since it was by his death and resurrection that he/we came to have life.

Paul goes on in the second explanatory clause to spell out the ultimate source of this new Christ-life that one who has died through the law now experiences. And here in ways that are quite unusual for Paul he lets us in on his personal life of devotion; in so doing, he has also momentarily lost sight of his Galatian friends, and the action of Peter in Antioch is but a memory. My present bodily life, he begins, is lived "in faith," thus picking up from v. 16 the main point of the entire passage. Paul's actual language for his present bodily life is "in the flesh," which some see as slightly pejorative, having to do with an abiding sinful nature. But that fails to take seriously Paul's own use of the term, and certainly does dishonor to the present sentence. To be "in the flesh" for Paul is not always pejorative; rather it is sometimes an emphatic way of speaking about our present existence, that it is still lived out in these very earthly bodies, which are subject to weakness and death.[87] Thus even though destined for final glory, we live out the life of the future by the Spirit in our present frail bodies.

Part of the power of the present rhetoric lies in its opening chiastic structure, "I live in flesh; in faith I live," which is almost certainly the reason for the unusual nature of the second phrase, "in faith." What Paul is positing by this deliberate contrast has to do with our two simultaneous spheres of existence. While we live in the present, we are "in flesh"; but at the same time we are already living the life of the future in our present bodies, thus we are living "in the sphere of faith in Christ Jesus." What comes to us "through faith" and thus "based on

---

[87] Dunn (146) makes the interesting observation that Paul often uses the word "flesh" in contexts where he emphasizes ethnic origin (e.g., Rom 1:3; 4:1; 9:3, 5, 8; 11:14), and thus it is most likely so in this context (Paul is thus identifying with Israel). But that seems highly unlikely here; how, one wonders, could the Galatians have so understood it, even if it was Paul's intention?

faith" (v. 16) is in fact the sphere in which we constantly live, which by its very nature excludes living on the basis of doing the law.

But what strikes one in this case is the very personal elaboration of the object of his faith, "the Son of God who loved me and gave himself for me." First, we should note that the way this is expressed in this instance is what gives possible credence to the view discussed but rejected on vv. 15 and 16. Here the word "faith" ($\pi\iota\sigma\tau\iota\varsigma$) is followed by the Greek article, which functions like a relative pronoun. Thus "faith, which is of/in the Son of God." If we did not have v. 16, where both the grammar and the context make such a meaning most highly unlikely, one could here make a good case that it refers to "the faithfulness of the Son of God." But since all other uses of this phrase, especially when it is without the genitive, indicate that he is the object of our faith, that is most likely its meaning here as well. The use of the article, therefore, is probably for emphasis: I live by trusting the One who is none other than the Son of God.

Thus at the end of this long narrative Paul returns to the language he had used about Christ in 1:16, that he is none other than the Son of God, the One whom the Father sent to redeem those enslaved to sin and the law and to give them "adoption" into God's own family (4:4-5). If what was striking in 1:16 was his emphasis that the Son was being revealed *in* Paul, here the surprising feature is the very personal way Paul speaks of the event of the cross. In fact it is nearly impossible to explain Paul's Christology without taking seriously his utter devotion to the Christ who saved him, expressed here in terms of the Son of God's loving *me* and thus giving himself up for *me* (by death on the cross). Ordinarily Paul speaks of our salvation in terms of (1) its being rooted in the love of God[88] and (2) of its being collectively for all of God's people. Here alone we find this expressed in terms of Paul personally, which in context of course is to be understood as also paradigmatic for the Galatians. One simply cannot easily get past Paul's own sense of being loved personally by God's Son in his crucifixion. It is this same love that "constrains" Paul in 2 Cor 5:14. And this is most likely "the law of Christ" that is being "fulfilled" (Gal 6:2) as one carries the burdens of others. It is this love of Christ for him personally that causes so much of what Paul says to be so christocentric.

But as always in Paul – and the rest of the New Testament – love is not to be thought of in terms of "warm feelings" toward another.

---

[88] See e.g., Rom 5:5-8; 2 Cor 13:13/14, which when expressed in terms of its relationship to Christ is referred to as "the love of God which is in Christ" (Rom 8:39).

Rather, love always expresses itself in action toward the one who is loved. So here the Son of God's love took the form of his "giving himself for me." Indeed, the second participle is probably best understood in a modal way; that is, "he loved me by giving himself for me," where the "giving himself up for me" is to be understood as the way the Son's love found specific expression. This is not to take away the personal dimension of his love for Paul – and thus for the Galatians and us – but it is to emphasize that in the New Testament love is not simply a "feeling" toward someone; rather it always finds expression in an action.

The action in this case is expressed by a very significant verb, "he gave himself up" (παραδόντος), which by the time this letter was written had become the primary language for what happened to Christ in his death. The verb in fact is a technical term used in the Roman legal system for "handing someone over in custody." It is thus the language that dominates the Gospel accounts as to what happened to Jesus at his trial and crucifixion, and therefore became the term of choice for the "words of institution" regarding the Lord's Supper. So Paul in 1 Cor 11:23, in repeating these "words" for the Corinthians, speaks of "the night he was handed over," which most English translations render with its obviously negative connotations, "the night he was betrayed." The point is that here Paul is using the standard technical language of the church, but in this case puts all the emphasis – the correct emphasis theologically – not on what others did to Christ, but on the reality that his death was in fact ultimately something he himself did for his people, which Paul here personalizes: he "handed himself over, gave himself up" for me. It has been much too easy for later Christians to think of Christ's death as a kind of "divine transaction" that secured our redemption. Not so Paul. The crucifixion was in fact a divine choice, predicated on the love of both the Father and the Son, to which the Son gave ultimate expression by "giving himself up" for me/us. It simply cannot get any better than that.

Verse 21. By the time one comes to the end of v. 20, it is easy to see that the "speech" that began in v. 14 has clearly "gotten away" from Paul. Nonetheless, and typical of the Apostle, the part that has "gotten away" turns out to be the truly important material. So Paul turns finally to wrap up the "speech" with a summary statement that recapitulates the main points, and does so by picking up, and thus juxtaposing, key language from what has preceded. "I do not set aside/invalidate the grace of God," he begins quite abruptly, now returning to what has been said in vv. 18 and 19. One simply cannot rebuild what Christ has torn down; to do so – to insist on Gentiles' obedience to aspects of Torah – would be to nullify the grace of God that found expression in the Son's "loving me by giving himself up for me." Everything is of grace; nothing can be "gained"; and to add Torah observance to grace is to negate grace. As noted above, the divine equation is not: Grace + works of law = righteousness; rather it is: Grace + nothing = righteousness. Otherwise one nullifies grace altogether.

But Paul in fact does not put it quite that way here; that will be the way the whole argument of Galatians plays itself out theologically. Rather, here he picks up language from vv. 15 and 16 and now expresses it in light of what he just said about the Son. "If righteousness (δικαιοσύνη) could be gained[89] through the law, then Christ died for nothing." And here especially the difficulty of translating into English emerges. The Galatians would not miss the connection with vv. 16 and 17, that "righteousness" here is the noun that expresses the "state of being" brought about by God's action expressed three times in the earlier sentences by the cognate verb "justify (= righteousize)." Whatever else, "righteousness" in terms of one's standing before God is freely given, not earned nor gained by doing law.

And with that Paul concludes the long narrative that had primarily to do with his own relationship with the "pillars" in Jerusalem – that his apostleship was totally independent of them, while at the same time fully accepted by them; and that his gospel was therefore also totally independent of them, but also in full agreement with them. But it was Paul, much more than they, who recognized the full implications of that gospel they held in common. The importance of the long recital, of course, has to do with the situation in Galatia, where some men have (presumably) put themselves forward as approved (if not authorized) by Jerusalem. Paul knows better; and his basic concern is to help the Galatians to recognize the true nature of those who are currently pushing them in a totally wrong, non-gospel direction. They have no authority at all; and their gospel is ultimately a false one at the very core of things. What Paul will do next is to appeal to the Galatians' own experience of grace and the Spirit, and then to take up the biblical arguments of the agitators and out-argue them on their own turf.

---

[89] Paul's clause is verbless in this case, which cannot be duplicated in English; the TNIV has rightly caught the sense of the argument by using "could be gained."

Reflection and Response – Part Two

Reflection

Reflecting on this passage is not easy for many reasons, in part because it covers so much ground, and in part because most of it is narrative, and listening to narrative in a reflective way takes special hermeneutical skill. So perhaps that is the place to start. How does one hear Paul's long narrative in which he both demonstrates that he and his gospel are totally independent of Jerusalem and yet were endorsed by Jerusalem and that Jerusalem in an apparently subtle way reneged on the agreement over the matter of food laws for the Gentiles?

The first point to make is that Paul is obviously appealing to his situation as a special case, and therefore none of us is in position to "emulate" him on these matters, even if we have had prophetic or visionary calls. Paul considers his calling to be unique and yet of the same order as the original apostles. What we are to learn about the apostle from this long narrative is that, by a calling that was uniquely Paul's own, we Gentiles owe an enormous debt of gratitude to God for our own existence, which was basically fought and won by the Apostle over the issues raised in Galatians 2.

But at one point in particular (1:10) we must show special care in following Paul's example. On the one hand, it is altogether too easy to water down the gospel to fit the tastes of the present generation. Being a "people pleaser" is an ever abiding danger for those in Christian ministry; after all, who wants to be brushed off as irrelevant or out of touch. On the other hand, perhaps the greater danger is the temptation to present the gospel in such a way that it unnecessarily turns people off, and then to use this passage as justification for one's own folly. We need to make sure it is the gospel itself that people are rejecting, not our own version of the Christian faith, which sometimes lacks the purity of the gospel that Paul is appealing for in this letter.

Our greater difficulty in appropriating to ourselves what God has done through Christ (and the Spirit) is that we have age-long tendencies to emulate Peter and Barnabas more than the Apostle, namely, to build up again what Christ has torn down on our behalf. How else does one explain the millennium-long tendencies in the church to turn grace into law, or to bring people to faith through their trusting in Christ and then to give them the law in the form of identifiable and quantifiable behavioral issues that give us identity as Christians from our non-Christian neighbors. Too often what identifies us is not our loving our neighbors by giving ourselves in their behalf, but by our not engaging in certain matters of food or drink or entertainment or dress that "they" do, with emphasis on the "they" as living quite different lives from us. These might indeed "identify" us vis-à-vis our neighbors (the new expression of "Gentiles" who live outside our boundaries); but they do not identify us at all as to our relationship to God.

It should surely be a cause of some wonder that some of the very people who feel most strongly about "justification by faith" and not "by works," turn about and create a new form of "law," defined by cultural standards and not by Scripture itself. One of my own striking examples in this regard had to do with a time when I was teaching in pastor's conference in former Yugoslavia and was publicly dressed down by a brother when I suggested that God did not care whether young people played soccer or not; yet that brother regularly drank wine with his meals and treated his wife as his slave, not as his sister in Christ. As with the believing Jews whom Paul is addressing through Peter in 2:15-18, he did not think of himself as being "saved" by not watching a soccer game; but in terms of attitude he was precisely where these "men from James" were with regard to Peter and Paul. And so with most of the young men who were forbidden to play soccer; they had put their faith in Christ and felt free to do so. But their problem then arose on the other side of things: How to do so in a way that was not divisive nor "in your face" with regard to the church. My instincts here are that the burden of love rests first with the older members of the congregation, even if they are not free themselves in this regard; and the young must learn to live lovingly in a context where they simply cannot understand where the old are coming from.

A final reflection is much more theological, having to do with a text that many Pentecostals find troublesome, and that has to do with Paul's saying that God "had set him apart from birth" (1:15). Here we are faced with biblical language around which much (to my mind, unnecessary) theological debate swirls; for whatever else is going on here, Paul, like the rest of Scripture, of necessity narrates God's visible activities within the framework of our human, time-bound experience. The eternal God by his very nature lives eternally outside this historical, time-bound framework. What should cause us never to lose our sense of wonder is that the eternal God, who is not time-bound, nonetheless accommodates himself to act within the framework of our historical existence as human beings. And to that degree God's own activities are narrated as within our time-bound existences, circumscribed by day following night and night following day, which are then numbered by us and given names.

Paul's emphasis is on God's grace; and his own experience of that grace was so unexpected and so outside his own choosing that he cannot imagine that God had not had him in mind for his unique mission from "time past." For Paul this was a cause for wonder and praise, not for explanation and debate. And so it should be for all of us who have experienced God's grace. If the lintel on the outside of the door reads, "whosoever will," the same lintel on the inside reads, "chosen from the foundation of the world." If this must finally be placed in the category of divine mystery, it also puts the emphasis in the right place – on God's calling us to himself, not on our accepting Christ as our Savior.

Response

In response we might ask the questions posed on page 29 one more time, and continue with some of these: How often have I imposed on others aspects of behavior that have to do with our own form of "law" and not with God's own word? Or how often have I stood aloof from people who do not share my own lifestyle on matters of food, drink, dress, etc.? Are there specific examples for which I should seek forgiveness? Am I guilty of coming to Christ through faith but not of living "in faith" on a constant basis? How much has the reality that "the Son of God loves me" freed me from the shackles of legalistic living and caused me to sit in constant wonder before him? Or do I secretly hold onto the notion that God is just a bit fortunate to have me on his side? Where else from this narrative might I learn to think about living "in faith" as the primary expression of my life in Christ?

1. Identify a specific individual or group from whom you may have stood aloof owing to differences in lifestyles in such matters as food, drink, or dress.
2. In prayer seek to hear the voice of the Lord in terms of what specific steps need to be taken.
3. Make a concrete commitment to meet or fellowship with those from whom you have been estranged. If this move involves asking for forgiveness look for the opportunities for such reconciliation during your time together.
4. Assess this experience with someone in you community in order to determine where this living out of the faith next leads.

Galatians 3:1–4:20

The Text

The First Argument from Scripture

The rest of this letter comes in three major parts: two arguments from Scripture (3:1–4:7 and 4:21-27) – both followed by immediate applications (4:8-11 and 4:28-31 plus 5:1-6) and personal appeals based on the Galatians' earlier relationship with him (4:12-20 and 5:7-12) – and a concluding argument, also based on Scripture, in which Paul demonstrates that the Spirit has superseded the law in both power and performance (5:13–6:10). It is of some interest, and therefore also an aid in interpretation, to note that Paul actually cites the Old Testament at only three points in the letter, in each case as crucial matter in its three major sections: seven times in 3:6-16; two times in 4:27-30, although this entire section is predicated on his readers' knowledge of the Old Testament story; and once (5:14) as the biblical basis for the argument that follows. All of this suggests that Scripture played a crucial role in the agitators' attempt to persuade the Galatians of the rightness of their case, and therefore that Paul's own use of Scripture is an attempt to outflank them, as it were, by showing that Scripture actually supports the inclusion of Gentiles by faith alone, apart from doing any aspect of the Law.

This first argument from Scripture tends to be complex for the modern reader, most likely because Paul is responding to the scriptural arguments presented by the interlopers/agitators. This also means that the Galatians are on a much more direct wave-length with the Apostle than we are, due to our own time and cultural distance from them. So good exegesis in this case requires us regularly to attempt to reconstruct the kinds of things the "Judaizers" would have argued that would have made a case so compelling as to have the Galatians on the verge of capitulating altogether. Thus much of Paul's strategy here is to show the Galatians a better understanding of Israel's Scriptures as to how they themselves fit into Israel's primary story, while at the same time appealing especially to their experience of the Spirit as the primary evidence that going the way of the law is utter folly.

Galatians 3:1–4:7 – The Argument from Scripture

In the argument to this point Paul has insisted, first, that his (law-free) gospel for the Gentiles came to him by direct revelation and therefore both his apostleship and understanding of the gospel are *quite independent of* Jerusalem; he needed no "credentials" such as the agitators apparently had – and in which they probably prided themselves (1:10-24). Second, although independent of them, Paul's understanding of the gospel was *not different from* those of "prominence" in Jerusalem (2:1-10); to the contrary, Jerusalem agreed that the gospel was law-free for the Gentiles. Hence, Paul uses Peter's betrayal of this agreement in the incident at Antioch (2:11-14) as the launching pad for his present argument with the Galatians as to the nature of the gospel itself, especially since the "betrayal" was over precisely the kind of thing that is now being urged on the Galatians by the agitators – allegedly with Jerusalem's blessing. But from Paul's perspective these interlopers cannot have Jerusalem's blessing, since he himself has it; and Peter serves as a prior example of one who allowed pressure from "some from Jerusalem" to cause him to capitulate on matters of observance, where at stake was the issue of forcing Gentiles' "to live like Jews." Hence Paul's reason for transforming the "speech" to Peter into his argument with the Galatians themselves (2:15-21).

That argument focused on three particulars, to be spelled out in the rest of the letter: that Christ's death and resurrection bring an end to the time of Torah (= "not by works of law"); that one's relationship to God is predicated altogether on God's grace, expressed in Christ's death and responded to by faith (= "by faith in Christ Jesus"); and that the one who has thus trusted in Christ has also thereby "died" with him and thus now "lives" because Christ (by his Spirit) indwells her or him (= "life in/by the Spirit"). This first argument from Scripture is about to pick up these threads and to demonstrate, especially from the combined evidence of Genesis and Deuteronomy, that the coming of Christ has meant the end of observance of the law, and therefore, as with Abraham himself, that the gift of righteousness rests on faith – for Jew and Gentile alike. The crucial *experiential* evidence that both of these are true is the indwelling, empowering presence of the Spirit.

The argument itself can be easily traced, even if some of its details are a bit obscure to the later reader. It begins with the rhetoric of vv. 1-5, where the three themes are woven together in an argument in which Paul urges that the Galatians' own experience of the Spirit plays the lie to their present wavering over the issue of Gentile circumcision. The Spirit is Exhibit A that relationship with God is *not* predicated on "works of law" but on "faith in Christ Jesus." Verse 6, which grammatically belongs to v. 5, serves as the transition to vv. 7-14, which pick up these two themes and argue from Scripture: first (vv. 7-9), righteousness comes to Jew and Gentile alike "by faith in Christ Jesus"; second (vv. 10-14), it cannot be "by works of law," inasmuch as Christ's having become a curse for us not only ended the time of the Torah but also made it possible for the blessing of Abraham now to come to the Gentiles, a promise that was fulfilled in their reception of the Spirit. This is followed in vv. 15-18 by yet another argument from Scripture – and from everyday life – that since a ratified will can neither be annulled nor added to, and since the "promise" to inherit *preceded* the advent of Torah (and circumcision), therefore the Torah could not annul the promise, which has in fact been fulfilled by the gift of the Spirit.

Since all of this sounds anti-Torah, Paul next (vv. 19-22) takes up the matter of the Torah itself: given what he has just argued about its relationship to the promise, then *why the Torah at all*? Indeed, *does not Torah itself stand over against the promise*? Paul's response to the first question is that Torah had a (necessary) temporary role – to "hem people in because of transgressions" – which in turn sets up the rest of the argument in 3:23–4:7. His response to the second question is typical, "God forbid!" The problem is not with Torah itself; it simply was not designed to do what the Spirit alone can do.

With the final two paragraphs (3:23-29 and 4:1-7) Paul ties together the various loose ends of the argument. The first deals with the role of Christ in freeing people from Torah observance. Picking up on the function of the Law to "imprison" people (from vv. 19-22), but shifting the analogy, Paul argues that being under Torah is in effect to be in slavery (vv. 23-24); however, the coming of Abraham's "true seed" (Christ [vv. 15-18]) has brought freedom from such slavery and has given "true sonship" to all who believe in him (cf. vv. 6-9 with 25-29). But even more (4:1-7), freedom from slavery and being Abraham's "children" means "sonship" of the highest order. Thus the Father sent his Son to redeem people from slavery and for adoption as children; and he sent the Spirit of his Son, whose cry of "Abba" (Jesus' own word of "sonship") from the heart of the believer is the certain evidence of such "adoption." All of this is then concluded in 4:8-11 by an appeal for the Galatian believers to apply all of this to their own situation, followed by a very personal appeal of loyalty to Paul himself (4:9-20).

Two further observations about this argument are pertinent. First, the "declarative" imperative in 3:7 ("know therefore that those who are by faith [not 'by the law' is implied], these are the children of Abraham") serves as a kind of thesis statement for the whole argument. Hence the double conclusion: in 3:29 ("Now if you are Christ's, you are therefore Abraham's seed, heirs according to promise") and 4:7 ("So then [because of Christ's redemption and the Spirit's indwelling], you are no longer a slave [under Torah] but a child, and if a child, then also an heir through God"). This suggests (a) that the question being addressed throughout is, "Who are Abraham's true children, thus heirs of the promise?" and (b) that the agitators themselves had argued, probably from Genesis 17, that the true children of Abraham (and by implication, children of God) are those who, as Abraham, seal their faith by circumcision. For Paul it was in the happy providence of God that in Genesis 15, before the covenant of circumcision, God had already both declared Abraham to be righteous by faith and included Gentiles in the promise made to Abraham. Thus both the *language* of Scripture and the *timing* of events are crucial for Paul's argument.

Second, one can scarcely miss the absolutely crucial role the Spirit plays in all of this.[1] In 3:1-5 *their own experience of the Spirit* had also *preceded* the coming of the law to them (in the form of the agitators' insistence on circumcision), thus absolutely destroying the agitators' arguments. Not only so, but the evidence of Scripture itself shows that both the declaration of righteousness and the promise of blessing for the Gentiles, which are predicated on faith, also precede Torah. What is crucial for Paul is his interpretation of the "fulfillment" of the "promised blessing" in terms of their experience of the Spirit (v. 14). This *double entendre* with regard to the "promise" – that the blessing of "sonship/inheritance" for Gentiles has been fulfilled by the gift of the Spirit – is probably also at work in varying degrees in the further references to the "promise" that follow (vv. 16, 17, 18, 21, 22, 29). The argument then concludes (4:6-7) with a final appeal to the indwelling Spirit as the ultimate evidence of "sonship" and thus of being heirs – of Abraham, but now especially of God himself.

Thus, in terms of the saving event itself, Christ is always and singularly the *focus* of the argument: redemption, freedom, adoption, and therefore righteousness itself have come through him, through his death and resurrection. Paul himself, as one "crucified with Christ"

---

[1] Although Lightfoot's otherwise helpful commentary is especially lacking at this point.

(2:19), so exhibited Christ in their midst (3:1). By hanging on a "pole"[2] Christ redeemed Jew and Gentile alike from Torah observance and made "sonship" possible (3:13; 4:5). But in terms of the certain evidence that life in Christ is by faith alone and quite apart from Torah, both at its beginnings and in its continuing expression, the Spirit plays the major role. Their own *experience* of the Spirit, both in conversion and in their present corporate life, is thus pressed on them as proof positive that the time of Torah is over and that the time of God's fulfillment of his promise to Abraham, including the blessing of the Gentiles, has come.

Galatians 3:1-6 – Appeal to Their Experience

> [1]*You foolish Galatians! Who has bewitched you? Before your very eyes Jesus Christ was clearly portrayed as crucified.* [2]*I would like to learn just one thing from you: Did you receive the Spirit by observing the law, or by believing what you heard?* [3]*Are you so foolish? After beginning with the Spirit, are you now trying to finish by human effort?* [4]*Have you experienced[a] so much in vain – if it really was in vain?* [5]*Does God give you his Spirit and work miracles among you by your observing the law, or by your believing what you heard?* [6]*So also Abraham "believed God, and it was credited to him as righteousness."*[b]

> [a] Or *suffered*   [b] Gen 15:6

The six rhetorical questions with which this argument begins start with the Galatians' experience of Paul's preaching of Christ (v. 1), then move to their own *initial reception* of the Spirit as proof positive that their new life in Christ is predicated on faith, not on "works of law" (v. 2). That in turn leads to the twofold question which is the primary urgency of the entire letter, that they cannot begin one way and come to completion another (v. 3), which leads to yet one more moment of pure rhetoric: Have they experienced so much (of the Spirit's activity among them, is implied) in vain (v. 4)? Which in turn leads to an appeal to their *present experience* of the Spirit and his miraculous activity in their midst, that this too is by faith and has nothing at all to do with the law (v. 5). Thus, before engaging them in a scriptural demonstration that Abraham himself – and therefore all his "genuine" children – received both the covenantal promise and the

---

[2] The TNIV has (correctly) translated the OT passage as referring to the pole on which the bodies of notorious people, especially conquered "kings," etc. were exposed to public shame after their deaths. See further the exposition of 3:14 below.

blessing of God (in this case God's gift of righteousness) by faith, he begins by reminding them of their own experience of the Spirit, which they received – and continue to experience – by faith.

Verse 1. From theologizing by way of personal testimony in 2:15-21, Paul turns to appeal directly to the Galatians themselves, and their own experience of Christ and the Spirit. The appeal is scarcely reasoned argumentation. Rather, he goes straight for the jugular – with the arresting vocative, "you foolish (ἀνόητοι)[3] Galatians." Equally arresting is the imagery of the rest of the sentence, surely designed to catch their attention: they are being deceived by "an evil eye," those before whose own "eyes"[4] Christ had been put on public display[5] as the crucified one. Perhaps alluding to his own physical condition noted in 4:13-14, Paul here describes his ministry among them as the public exhibition of the reality of the crucifixion, wherein Christ "loved (us) and gave himself for (us)" (2:20). If righteousness came by means of "works of law," then it is not of grace, and Christ's death was of no avail (v. 21).

Thus Paul's first question is remarkable for what it does not do – appeal to their own believing in Christ for salvation. Rather this is his way of tying the preceding narrative to the strong appeal that follows, an appeal to their experience of Christ and the Spirit, whose ultimate point will be that to submit to circumcision is to reject Christ himself.

Verse 2. But the appeal in v. 1, transitionally necessary as it is and having priority as it does, is not sufficient in the present situation to secure their allegiance to the gospel. Free people though they are in Christ, they are nonetheless freely submitting to the bondage of Jewish identity markers – as though Christ had died for nothing (2:21). Thus, to get at the argument of what Christ has done vis-à-vis the law (vv. 7-22), he must first appeal to their own experience of life in Christ – that it began, and continues, on the basis of faith alone quite apart from "works of law." And so he turns to further rhetoric, reminding them of the experienced nature of their entrance into Christian life – through the dynamic working of the Spirit: "I would like to learn just one thing from you: Did you receive the Spirit by observing the law, or by believing what you heard?"

---

[3] This adjective has to do with their lack of common good sense, rather than being simply witless or inane.

[4] Although there are not literal verbal correspondences between the Greek word for "deceived by an evil eye" (βασκαίνω; thus "bewitched") and the literal word "eye" (ὀφθαλμός), the "word play" is inherent in the ideas.

[5] This is the common word (προγράφω) for the posting of public notices.

In view of their present "bewitchment" and readiness to capitulate to "works of law" (at least circumcision and the observance of days), Paul wants to learn from them "this one thing only," a phrase which stands in emphatic first position in his sentence. And he can narrow everything to this one thing, because he himself had been present when in their response to his preaching of Christ crucified they had received the Spirit. Thus he begins his argument not with an appeal to theological truth or to Christ's saving work as such, but to the life of the Spirit, which he will use to demonstrate the truthfulness of his theology – and the wrongness of their present leanings.

Paul's own concern, of course, as both the context and the structure of the question itself make plain, is that their relationship with God is predicated entirely on their trust in Christ, not on their submission to "works of law." Again Paul's own word order, which does not make for very good English, helps one to see the emphases: "on the basis of works of law the Spirit did you receive, or on the basis of 'the hearing of faith'?" In so doing he picks up the two key prepositional phrases from 2:15-16, keeping them in their same order but changing the language of the one about "faith." More importantly he now inserts the new item, their reception of the Spirit; and by putting "the Spirit" before the verb "did you receive," Paul again displays his own emphasis – on the Spirit himself not on their reception of him. Some of these items need further elaboration.

First, he fronts the phrase "on the basis of works of law (= doing the law)," because that is the issue raised by the agitators. As before, and despite generations of Protestant interpretation to the contrary, the emphasis of this phrase is not on human effort to *obtain* salvation. Rather, as he will put it in v. 3, it is on believers' salvation "coming to *completion*" by their observing certain aspects of the law. Paul will make the theological point about "works" later, for now this is simply shorthand for the issue raised by the agitators.

Second, and more significant, is his altering the final phrase from "on the basis of faith in Christ" to the experienced dimension of entering into the new relationship with God through Christ. The new contrast, therefore, with "doing the law" is "the hearing of faith," which puts the emphasis on their putting their trust in Christ when they *heard* the good news proclaimed to them. Thus, "it was not your 'doing the law' that led to your reception of the Spirit, but your believing (thus putting your trust in) the one about whom you heard when the gospel was proclaimed," which incidentally also indicates that the earlier expression of the phrase is not about Christ's faithfulness (see on 2:15-16), but about the Galatians' putting their trust in him.

Third, along with many other passages throughout the corpus, this appeal to the "reception of the Spirit" as the evidence of entry into Christian life[6] demonstrates the crucial role the Spirit plays not only in Christian conversion itself but also as the singular "identity mark" of those who belong to Christ. After all, at issue throughout is proper evidence of identity. What uniquely distinguishes God's people, marks them off as inheritors of the promises made to Abraham? The agitators are urging circumcision, probably on the basis of Gentile inclusion in the covenant with Abraham in Gen 12:3 and 17:4-7, 12 (see on vv. 7-8 below). Paul argues for the Spirit. As this question makes certain, for Paul the Spirit alone functions as the seal of divine ownership,[7] the certain evidence that one has entered into the life of the new aeon. As such, even though Paul's expressed contrasts for his present purposes are between "hearing of faith" and "works of Law," the ultimate contrast in this argument is between life under law (= slavery) and life in the Spirit (= adoption as children), as 4:1-7 makes plain and as 5:13–6:10 will further amplify. The Spirit alone distinguishes God's people in the new covenant.

Fourth, the entire argument comes aground if this appeal is not also to a reception of the Spirit that was dynamically experienced. Even though Paul seldom mentions any of the visible evidences of the Spirit in such contexts as these,[8] here is the demonstration that the

[6] Interestingly, people with vested interests on both sides of the issue of the work of the Spirit in Christian life want to make this refer not to the Galatians' conversion as such, but to *subsequent* experiences of the Spirit. Some Pentecostals want this to refer to subsequent "Spirit baptism," while some Protestants see it as referring to subsequent gifts of the Spirit (e.g., Lightfoot).

[7] In light of the later church's penchant to tie the reception of the Spirit to water baptism, one is wont to add here, "and not water baptism." In the present case the idea that water baptism might have been involved with the reception of the Spirit is so foreign to the text, one would not even mention it negatively were it not so commonly assumed by some scholars in their discussion of this passage.

[8] The clear exceptions are 2 Cor 12:12 and Rom 15:18-19, where in sober matter-of-fact statements Paul notes what God had accomplished through him to bring about the obedience of the Gentiles, "by the power of signs and wonders, by the power of the Holy Spirit." If there are not more such statements in Paul, it is only because such evidences of the Spirit's presence were presuppositional for him and his churches; and he refused to appeal to them for the very reason that they might deflect from the essential message of the gospel of a crucified Messiah. Even so, these are references to extraordinary evidences of the Spirit that accompanied his ministry, which is not

experience of the Spirit in the Pauline churches was very much like
that described and understood by Luke – as visibly and experientially
accompanied by phenomena that gave certain evidence of the presence
of the Spirit of God. Not only is this the clear point of the rest of the
argument in vv. 4-5, but such an understanding alone makes the
present rhetoric possible at all. Not only so, but such an experienced
reality best accounts for the way Paul picks up the argument about life
in the Spirit in 5:13–6:10. Many of the difficulties moderns have with
the latter passage – and its promises – lie with the general lack of
appreciation for the dynamically experienced nature of life in the Spirit
in the early church.

Verse 3. With two further questions, full of sting, Paul ties together
and applies the rhetoric of the first two questions to the present scene
in Galatia, thus demonstrating their own self-contradiction. Indeed,
here is the heart of the matter – which drives the argument of the
entire letter: "So foolish are you [v. 1]? Having begun by the Spirit[9]
[v. 2], now by the flesh do you finish?"[10] This is the question to which
the entire argument of the letter is devoted as a response. Which in
turn means that the question is not, "How does one *gain* rightstanding
with God?" (meaning, "How are people saved?") but, "Once *given*
rightstanding with God, how is such a relationship sustained or
maintained?" The real question, finally, is whether Torah observance
has any role at all in Christian life. On this Paul is adamant: it has
none. As he will argue in 5:13-15, the whole of Torah is fulfilled in
the one command, "You shall love your neighbor as yourself," which
command is now fulfilled as the fruit of the Spirit.

This question is also the clear demonstration that the ultimate
contrast with which Paul deals in this letter is not between "faith" and
"works of Law," which have to do with a person's *entrance* into
Christian life, but between ongoing life in the Spirit – lived out always
by faith – and Torah observance. This is what makes 5:13–6:10 a
crucial part of the *argument* of Galatians, not simply a collection of
ethical instructions added at the end, after the theological argument is

---

precisely the same thing to which he is appealing here, namely to the Galatians' own
powerful experience of the Spirit in their lives.

[9] Paul's Greek here is the single word πνεύματι; on this usage see the discussion in
Fee, *GEP*, ch. 2 on Pauline usage. Given the usage with the article in v. 2, "*the* Spirit
did you receive," this passage is one of the clear evidences that the non-articular usage
in this dative formula can only mean "by *the* Spirit."

[10] See Phil 1:6, where Paul uses the same two verbs (ἐναρξάμενος and ἐπιτελεῖσθε)
to refer to the beginning of and eschatological conclusion to their life in Christ.

in place. The ethical result of life in the Spirit is part of the essential argument of the letter, since this is the burning question, "How do believers live?" And the answer given here is the surprising one, but fully in keeping with Paul's theology as it emerges elsewhere: not by "works of law," which he here describes as "coming to completion by means of the flesh"!

This is the second appearance in Paul's letters of a direct contrast between "flesh" and "Spirit" (cf. 1 Cor 3:1-2). In this instance an obvious word play is in process. The word "flesh" (σάρξ) first of all points to the literal cutting of the flesh in circumcision, as the usage in 6:12-13 would seem to make certain. But in Paul it is never quite so simple, since "flesh" is used by him as his primary description of life before and outside of Christ. To live "in the flesh" is to live according to the values and desires of life in the present age that stand in absolute contradiction to God and his ways.[11] Hence the ultimate contrasts in Paul are eschatological: life "according to the flesh," lived according to the present age that has been condemned through the cross and is passing away, or life "according to the Spirit," lived in keeping with the values and norms of the coming age inaugurated by Christ through his death and resurrection and empowered by the eschatological Spirit. The surprising dimension to this response is Paul's willingness to equate coming to completion "in the flesh" with submission to "works of law," a point that will be clarified later in ch. 5 and will be made again in Romans 7-8 and Phil 3:2-3. Since life before and outside of Christ is described as "flesh," and since compliance with the identity markers of the people of God under the former covenant is to revert to life before Christ, to submit to "works of Law" is therefore to revert to life in "the flesh." Not only so, but for Paul the issue is finally theological; to submit to circumcision is to put one's confidence before God in that which is merely an expression of "flesh," thus self-confidence, rather than trust in Christ and him alone for a proper relationship with God.

Thus Paul's frustration with the situation in Galatia. To yield to Jewish identity markers is neither an innocent reaching out to Jewish believers nor necessary for Gentile inclusion into the full privileges of the covenant with Abraham. This is not the way to become members of the people of God in the present age, inaugurated by Christ and the

---

[11] Thus "flesh" in Paul does not first of all refer to one's own "sinful nature," nor does it refer primarily to "what is merely human." While it sometimes obviously means the latter, when the usage is pejorative, it refers to what is "human and over against God in deliberate fallenness."

Spirit; rather it is to "rebuild" what Christ himself has dismantled (2:18), to try "to come to completion by means of the flesh."

Verse 4. Still reflecting on the absurdity of it all, Paul turns to rhetoric one more time – this time with yet another *ad hominem* question (cf. v. 1): "Did you experience so many things in vain?" This question has clear implications about the results of their following their present course and is the precursor of what is said with a plain indicative in 5:4, "you who are trying to be justified by the law have been alienated from Christ; you have fallen away from grace." To capitulate to "works of law" is to revert to life in the flesh; and to do that is to have experienced life in the Spirit "in vain"; it is to "cut themselves off from Christ," to "fall away from grace." In this first instance, of course, Paul is not suggesting that such has yet happened. The rhetoric expresses disbelief that people who had had "such remarkable experiences"[12] should even consider coming under Torah. To do so is tantamount to having experienced life in the Spirit "in vain." This, of course, is simply another way of reinforcing the previous question (v. 3).

The idea that people could have genuinely believed "in vain" has traditionally been a stone of theological stumbling. But the question needs to be kept within its Pauline context. He speaks earlier and later of the possibility of his having labored "in vain" (2:2; 4:11); and expresses similar concern elsewhere over his converts in 1 Cor 15:2 (cf. Phil 2:16). In the present case he is simply not ready to allow that such has really happened; thus his quick disclaimer: "If indeed it has been in vain." Whether or not such *might* happen is yet another question, to which Paul would certainly allow a "yes." But whenever he comes close to allowing as much about any of his own converts, he is quick to offer the disclaimer that he does not really believe that they have taken such a drastic step. And in this case, Paul has already said something similar about Christ in 2:21, that if the meddlers are correct then "Christ died for nothing," which he obviously cannot believe is true either really or hypothetically.

More significant still is to note that Paul is apparently appealing to their ongoing life in the Spirit, with his "so many things have you experienced?" It is true that the past tense of the verb might suggest a second reference to their conversion experience, with the plural referring to the experience of the entire community of believers. But

---

[12] This is the translation in BDAG (first entry under πάσχω, and entry 2b under τοσοῦτος).

what stands against such an understanding is his fronting the question with the word "so many things," which could also mean "such remarkable things," as the Bauer-Danker lexicon prefers. In either case, it seems much more likely to be picking up on their initial experiences of the Spirit and implying that such phenomena have been ongoing in their midst. What makes one think so is what he says next in v. 5, where by clear statement he brings the narrative into the present.

But in this case not all scholars think so, since the verb that Paul here uses for "experienced" elsewhere in his letters always refers to the experience of suffering.[13] Thus many English translations have followed the KJV: "Have ye suffered so many things in vain?"[14] However, Pauline usage, significant as this is in most circumstances, is in this case the *only* thing in favor of translating the verb "suffered." Against it is: (*a*) the verb itself has neither negative or positive connotations, which can only be determined by context; (*b*) the clear sense of the present context, in which the positive, and more traditional, meaning of the word makes such eminently good sense; (*c*) that in contrast to most of Paul's other letters there is not the slightest hint in this letter that the churches of Galatia are undergoing suffering of any kind, not to mention suffering "so many things"; and (*d*) that the word order puts the "so many things" in the emphatic first position, thus referring to what has just been said in vv. 2-3, not to "so many things in general." That v. 5 picks up on this question by putting their past experiences in light of their present experience of the Spirit seems to be the clincher. Otherwise the question sits in the middle of an appeal to their experience of the Spirit, past and present, as something of a rock, with no specific reference to the present context.

[13] The word traditionally meant simply "to experience, or be treated," referring to everything that can befall a person, whether good or ill. Eventually it came to be used predominantly of unfortunate experiences, although references to good experience still obtained. If indeed, as the context nearly demands, the present usage refers to the experience of the Spirit in vv. 2-3, then this is the only time in the NT it is used in this positive way.

[14] It should be noted that the house has long been divided on this one. For "suffering" see the NIV, NASB, Williams, Living Bible, Phillips; so also the commentaries by Calvin, Meyer, Lightfoot, Burton, Erdman, Duncan (*contra* Moffatt's translation), Bruce, Michaelis (*TDNT* 5.905), and others. For the TNIV rendering see, among others, RSV, NRSV, NAB, NEB, JB, Weymouth, Moffatt, and commentaries by Lietzmann, Ridderbos, Schlier, Hendriksen, Bligh, Mussner, Betz, Fung, Cole, and Longenecker.

Verse 5. If the Galatians' past experience of the Spirit is not enough to convince them that their relationship to God is based on faith alone, Paul will try one more time – this time appealing to their ongoing life in the Spirit as a community of worshipping believers: "Does God supply you with his Spirit and work miracles among you by your observing the law, or by your believing what you heard?" This question in fact is joined to the others, and especially to the disclaimer in v. 4b, by an inferential "therefore," whose sense the NRSV seems to capture best by translating, "well, then" (left untranslated by the TNIV). It follows, Paul seems to be arguing, that if indeed you began life in the Spirit (v. 2), and in light of *how much* of the Spirit's presence you have experienced (v. 4) – all by faith quite apart from Torah – then so too with your present experience of the Spirit. The rich supply of the Spirit in your midst, including the working of miracles, therefore, simply cannot be related to Torah; to the contrary, everything is based on faith in Christ. What follows, then, is yet another question that again has as its primary concern that life in Christ is based on faith, not on "works of law." But again, as in v. 2, what lies behind the question presuppositionally is of considerable importance to Paul's being able to make this appeal. Three matters are of significance.

First, Paul turns the appeal toward God himself, by reminding them that God is the one who continually and liberally "supplies[15] you with the Spirit." Thus their attention is once more drawn to God, as the one ultimately responsible both for the gift of the Spirit and thus for the work of the Spirit in their midst. Moreover, as with the similar passages in 1 Thess 4:8 and Phil 1:19, the clear implication is that even though they have already received the Spirit, there is another sense in which the Spirit is "given" again and again. However, in contrast to the other two passages, here the emphasis is on what happens in the community. Every "manifestation" of the Spirit among them "for their common good" (cf. 1 Cor 12:7) is to be understood as God's supply of the Spirit in their community life.

Second, the close tie between the two participles, "who supplies the Spirit and works miracles," suggests that these two ideas are to be held closely together. That is, God is present among them by his Spirit, and the fresh supply of the Spirit finds expression in miraculous deeds of various kinds. Thus Paul is obviously appealing once more to the

---

[15] The Greek word here (ἐπιχορηγέω) does not mean simply to "give," but to "furnish" or "supply" someone with something; cf. the same verb in Phil 1:19, which the TNIV correctly translates, "God's provision of the Spirit."

visible and experiential nature of the Spirit's presence in their midst, as the ongoing evidence that life in the Spirit,[16] predicated on faith in Christ Jesus, has no place at all for traditional "works of law."

Third, the thoroughly presuppositional nature of this final appeal serves as further evidence, along with 1 Cor 14 and 1 Thess 5:19-22 (cf. 2 Thess 2:2), of the genuinely "charismatic" nature of the Pauline churches. The evidence from 1 & 2 Thessalonians (and elsewhere) indicates that prophecy was a regular and expected phenomenon in these churches; the evidence from 1 Corinthians indicates that speaking in tongues was also a part of the broad experience of Spirit phenomena. This text makes it clear that what Paul elsewhere calls "signs and wonders" was also a regular and expected expression of their life in the Spirit. What we cannot know from this distance, of course, is all that Paul would have meant by the phrase, "works miracles among you." But usage elsewhere in the corpus suggests a variety of supernatural phenomena, including healings.

Those who tend to think otherwise about these texts do so much less on exegetical grounds than on existential ones. Many people's own experience of the church tends either to be unfamiliar or quite uncomfortable with such phenomena. Thus they would prefer to believe that the Pauline churches were more like ours and less like the Pauline (and rest of the NT) evidence suggests they really were. But the evidence in this case seems incontrovertible: The Spirit stood near the center of Pauline theology precisely because the experience of the Spirit in the life of the believer and the church was such a central feature of their experience and existence as believers.

Verse 6. By choosing to put this verse in the present paragraph the TNIV translators (cf. UBS[4], NAB) recognize that grammatically it belongs to v. 5, even though it clearly serves as the transition to the scriptural argument that begins in v. 7. Thus (literally), Paul asks, ". . . or by believing what you heard, just as Abraham 'believed God, and it was credited to him as righteousness.'" The problem lies with the word "just as" (καθώς) with which the clause begins. In Paul this adverb is normally used as a conjunction signalling that some kind of comparison is in view. If it begins a sentence, it is accompanied by a "so also" (οὕτως); if it concludes a sentence, as here, it offers a comparative illustration. Those who make it begin the next paragraph invariably resort to some kind of tinkering with Paul's sentence to make

---

[16] Some commentators entertain the option that "miracles" have to do with the "moral world" (Lightfoot); but that flies full in the face of the argument itself, not to mention the meaning of this word in Paul.

it work: either as a stand alone sentence, making "just as" a pure adverb, as the NASB's "even so"; or as the NRSV, changing the grammar of v. 7, so as to make v. 6 function as the beginning of that sentence, which option has neither grammatical nor lexical warrant.

Paul's comparison seems clear enough. The clause modifies the phrase "by believing what you heard," and should grammatically be included in the question itself. Paul's final question is therefore not intended to conclude with the repeated prepositional phrase (from v. 2), but with a comparison that leads him directly into the scriptural argument that follows. Thus his sentence ends on a note one is not quite expecting, but which makes perfectly good sense: "Does God supply you with the Spirit and work miracles among you by your observing the law, or by *believing* what you heard, just as 'Abraham *believed* God, and it was credited to him as righteousness'?"

One may assume he ends his sentence/question this way for at least two reasons, and probably a third. First, the citation deals with Abraham, the recognized "father" of the Jewish nation, to whom the agitators had almost certainly appealed by citing from the covenant of circumcision in Genesis 17, with its key language of an "everlasting covenant" (v. 7) and "those born in your household or bought with money from a foreigner" (v. 12). Second, it also had in it the key words "*believed*" and "it was credited to him as *righteousness*,"[17] words, third, which were fortuitously spoken to Abraham *before* he was circumcised. So one can be sure that by ending his final rhetorical question with this citation, Paul was intending a kind of *coup* over his opponents' use of the Genesis account of Abraham and his circumcision. So with this question-ending citation Paul launched directly into his own argument from Scripture regarding Abraham, raising the question, "Who are Abraham's 'legitimate' children?"

Galatians 3:7-14 – Who are Abraham's True Children?

> [7]*Understand, then, that those who have faith are children of Abraham.* [8]*Scripture foresaw that God would justify the Gentiles by faith, and announced the gospel in advance to Abraham: "All nations will be blessed through you."*ᵃ [9]*So those who rely on faith are blessed along with Abraham, the man of faith.*
>
> [10]*All who rely on observing the law are under a curse, for it is written: "Cursed is everyone who does not continue to do everything*

---

[17] While this phrase could mean, "as an act of righteousness," context demands that "it was attributed to him by God as grounds for acceptance."

written in the Book of the Law."[b] [11]*Clearly no one is justified before
God by the law, because "the righteous will live by faith."*[c] [12]*The law is
not based on faith; on the contrary, it says: "The one who does these
things will live by them."*[d] [13]*Christ redeemed us from the curse of the
law by becoming a curse for us, for it is written: "Cursed is everyone
who is hung on a pole."*[e] [14]*He redeemed us in order that the blessing
given to Abraham might come to the Gentiles through Christ Jesus, so
that by faith we might receive the promise of the Spirit.*

[a] Gen 12:3; 18:18; 22:18 [b] Deut 27:26 [c] Hab 2:4 [d] Lev 18:5 [e] Deut 21:23

With these two paragraphs Paul offers his basic arguments from Scripture that support the rhetorical questions of the opening paragraph.
The argument itself is in two parts, vv. 7-9 and 10-14, each in turn
picking up the key phrases from Paul's "speech" in 2:16, which in
turn have been repeated (and the second rephrased) in 3:2 and 5. Thus
the main subject in the first paragraph is about "those based on faith"
(οἱ ἐκ πίστεως; vv. 7 and 9), while v. 10, in deliberate contrast with
v. 9, begins "as many as are based on works of law" (ὅσοι ἐξ ἔργων
νόμου). The way the two paragraphs are constructed, both of them
based on scriptural citation, suggests that Paul is here responding
directly to the scriptural arguments of the interlopers. This seems
especially to be so in light of Paul's way of dealing with the issue,
which is to answer the question, "Who are Abraham's (true) children?"

On the basis of how Paul constructs his argument, one can
reconstruct the position of the agitators with a fair degree of
confidence. They would have argued, "believe in Christ for salvation,
to be sure, but:

(a) to inherit the blessings (promise) of God's covenant with Abraham,
(b) which includes the Gentiles,
(c) one must also seal the covenant by circumcision
(d) just as Abraham himself did (Gen 17);
(e) and thus the circumcised are the true heirs of the covenant."

Paul responds by way of rebuttal: "Believe in Christ for salvation, *and that
alone*, since:

(a) to inherit the blessings (promise) of God's covenant with Abraham,
(b) which includes the Gentiles,
(c) one must have faith
(d) just as Abraham himself did (Gen 15);
(e) and thus those with faith are the true heirs of the covenant."

The opponents' argument apparently rested on the narrative of Genesis 17,[18] where God said to Abraham (v. 4): "This is my 'covenant' (διαθήκη) with you: you will be the father of many 'nations' (ἔθνη)," about which (v. 7) God promises it to be an "everlasting covenant between me and you and your seed (σπέρμα) after you." Abraham is then required to seal the covenant (v. 10), by having "every male among you … circumcised." Although Paul does not make a point of it here, it should be noted that this covenant had especially to do with the land, not with Abraham's relationship with God per se.

Paul's argument in turn rests on the narrative in Genesis 15, which not only precedes theirs, but also (especially) has to do with Abraham's special relationship with God, although it also picks up the promise of the land. Crucial for Paul is the fact that in this prior covenant God promised Abraham an *heir*, to which Abraham responded by having *"faith* in the Lord," who in turn *"credited it to him as righteousness"* (v. 6). Only *after* this does the narrative conclude: "the Lord made a covenant with Abraham" (v. 18).[19] Thus Paul, having cited Gen 15:6 at the end of his opening set of questions (v. 6 above), now picks up that citation and spells out its implications for Gentile believers. In his second paragraph (vv. 10-14) Paul goes on to spell out on the basis of Scripture why being "based on faith" absolutely excludes being "based on the law," since Scripture in effect demonstrates that these are mutually exclusive options.

Verse 7. In many ways this sentence serves as a kind of thesis statement for the rest of the argument through 4:7. Having concluded the final rhetorical question (vv. 5-6) by citing Gen 15:6, with its key words "believed (had faith)[20] in God," Paul now moves on to draw the proper inferences from the citation, and does so by picking the key phrase from vv. 2 and 5 in the preceding paragraph. "Therefore," he says, "know/understand that those who are based on faith, these are the 'sons' [= children] of Abraham." The choice of "sons" here, rather than the more general word for "children," as for example in Rom 8:16-21 and elsewhere, is that this is the one word that makes the following argument work right through to its conclusion in 4:7. Its

[18]That this is so is demonstrated not only by the language and nature of the present argument itself, but also by the presuppositional way the word "covenant" appears suddenly in vv. 15-18, as something to be argued *from.*

[19] It should be noted further that in the paragraph that follows (vv. 15-18) Paul picks up the language "and to your seed," which occurs in chs. 12 and 13, but not in ch. 17. Thus the promise to Abraham's "seed" precedes the covenant of circumcision.

[20] For this verb see the discussion on 2:15-16 above.

next occurrence will be in 3:26, where Paul is already anticipating *our* "sonship" in relation to that of Christ, the Eternal Son, which is then spelled out in detail in 4:4-7. Thus Paul draws the proper inferences from the combination of realities presented in vv. 1-6: their own experience of the *Spirit* on the basis of faith, and Abraham's having been reckoned as *righteous* on the basis of faith. What follows spells out the implications for the Galatians.

Verse 8. Given the thesis statement of v. 7, Paul now moves on to demonstrate from the Genesis narrative how the Gentiles are included among those who are Abraham's (true) children. First, he points out that "God's justifying *the Gentiles* 'by faith'" was "foreseen" in the Scripture itself. In doing so Paul picks up his verb "proclaim the good news" that he had used five times in 1:8-16, but now prefixed with the preposition "beforehand." Thus the gospel as "good news for the Gentiles" was already in view when God promised his blessing to Abraham at the very beginning. Citing Gen 12:3 as the crucial "Scripture," but in the language of Gen 18:18 (where "nations = Gentiles" is used in place of "tribes of the earth"), Paul now traces the inclusion of the Gentiles to the very beginning – in the "blessing of Abraham" ("all nations will be blessed through you").

Crucial to his point is the fact that for the more general word for "nations" in Hebrew, the Septuagint translators had (correctly) used a Greek word that had become fixed during the intertestamental period as a technical term for "Gentiles (ἔθνη)." It is this combination of citations from Genesis 12 (here) and 15 (in v. 6) – which happily for Paul precede his opponents' texts about circumcision in Genesis 17 – that allows him to argue with his opponents on their own grounds, and hopefully to win this first (basic) round in favor of the non-necessity of circumcision for his Galatian converts.

Verse 9. With the "so then" that begins this final clause Paul wraps up the first part of the current argument by drawing together all the necessary particulars: "those who rely on faith are blessed along with Abraham, the man of faith." Thus, he first picks up the crucial prepositional phrase "those based on faith (οἱ ἐκ πίστεως)," a phrase that goes back to its twofold use in 2:16. This is now its fifth occurrence in the present narrative (see vv. 2, 5, 7 and 8) and here it not only concludes the present paragraph, but is once more set out in deliberate contrast to "those based on works of law," with which the next sentence (and thus next paragraph) begins.

Paul then picks up the language of "blessing" from the immediately preceding citation of Gen 12:3/18:18 and ties it to the citation of Gen

15:6 (in v. 6 above). But in this latter instance he does so with a kind of word play on the Greek word "faith" (πίστις) that is impossible to put into English in quite the same way, since the Greek word can also mean "faithful = constantly living by faith." Thus the TNIV (correctly) puts the emphasis where Paul intends it, "the man of faith," but at the same time leaves one without the further sense of Abraham's enduring faith, thus of his remaining "faithful" in his trusting God.[21]

Verse 10. With another explanatory "for" (not in the TNIV), Paul now presents the logical opposite consequence of what he has just argued on the basis of Abraham's faith – what it means for the Galatians if they submit to doing the law. The beginning of the sentence ("all who rely on observing the law are under a curse") stands in clear contrast to v. 9 in two ways. The primary contrast goes back to 2:16, picked up in 3:2-5, between living on the basis of "the hearing of faith" (v. 9) and living on the basis of "works of law" = doing the law (v. 10). The second, equally important, contrast is between "the blessing" that rests on those who have faith (v. 9), and "the curse" that rests on those who go the way of "doing the law" (v. 10). Paul thereby moves from the blessing of Abraham in Genesis (vv. 7-9) to the curses of Deuteronomy 27-28 on those who do not obey the law (vv. 10-13). He does so by citing the final, summarizing curse in Deut 27:26 – as it appears in the Septuagint, but with some verbal modifications (in italics) from 29:19-20: "Cursed is anyone who does not abide in *all the things written in the book of* the law, to do them."

Paul has chosen his citation carefully, as the addition from Deut 29:20 and the citation of Lev 18:5 in v. 12 make certain. At issue for Paul is the Judaizer's *selectivity* with regard to the law. It is therefore doubtful whether Paul's substituting language from the second Deuteronomy passage has any further significance; at least he does not pick up on it anywhere in what follows. After all, both Deuteronomy passages have the key word "all." The borrowed language simply spells out "the words of this law" in 27:26 in terms of "the things written in the Book of the Law" from 29:20, so that it is the *written* legal code found in the Book of the Law that is in view. What Paul has done here is similar to what he did in v. 8 – include *language* from a second

---

[21] It is not surprising to find a variety of renderings in the tradition of English translations. The KJV rendered it literally, as "faithful Abraham"; in this they were followed by the REB. Most contemporary translations do something similar to NIV/TNIV, including the ESV, which breaks ranks with its tradition at this point, since the RSV/NRSV revert to "who believed," while the NASU and NET Bible render it, "Abraham the believer"!

text so that everything he wants to emphasize is found in the one citation.

Paul's point is that those who choose to live by the law thereby exclude themselves from the blessing, because they must now "*abide* in the *whole* law, to *do it*," and they are cursed if they do not so "abide." What Paul is thus setting out to demonstrate is the *total incompatibility* of living on the basis of faith while also trying to live on the basis of doing the law. Thus the three key words (besides "cursed") for Paul's argument have been italicized. First, if the Galatian men allow themselves to be circumcised, they are making a choice "to live by the law"; and because people must "*abide in* [continue to live in] everything written in the law," they are thereby excluding themselves from living by the Spirit, based on faith in Christ Jesus. What the Galatians must recognize is that these two ways of living are mutually exclusive; one lives one way (by faith) or the other (by law); and to live by the other (the law) only partially is to be under a curse. Therefore, second, they cannot be partial in their obedience: to choose to live by the law means of necessity to live by the *whole law*; partial obedience (just circumcision, food laws, and sabbath observance) is not permissible. So this too is part of the curse; it is either no law or the whole law. Third, to abide in the law carries with it the necessity of "*doing* the law," which automatically means that one is not *trusting* Christ for salvation. The logical consequence of all this is that the one who chooses to live by the law is thereby excluded from Christ, cut off from salvation altogether; and this is the real concern for Paul in all of this argumentation. The plain assumption in all of this, one should note at the end, is that people *can* do "the righteousness" found in the law, understood as observable behavior, as Paul claims that he himself did (Phil 3:6). The curse is that they *must* do so, and thus they are excluded from Christ.

That these three concerns are Paul's point becomes clear from the supporting Scripture in vv. 11 to 13. Nonetheless here is a text that has had a long history of misinterpretation, especially within Protestantism, where all kinds of ideas from other Pauline texts are brought in from the outside as "guides" through the paragraph.[22] But

---

[22] It is most often read in light of Rom 7:13-25, where Paul accuses the law of bringing about his death, since he was not aware of his sin until the law pointed it out. The issue there, however, is indwelling sin; thus it is not by accident that the one text Paul cites in that passage has little to do with "behavior" as such, namely the tenth commandment and its prohibition of covetousness. Here the issue is with "*doing* the law," about which Paul says in Phil 3:6 he was blameless.

that is quite unnecessary, since all the clues rest within the present argument itself. Moreover, the common interpretations have Paul saying things that are not only not said here, but are in fact foreign to the present argument.[23] For example, Paul does not say, nor does he imply, that anyone who disobeys one point of the law is guilty of breaking the whole (a point made by James [Jas 2:10] but not Paul), and that any single infraction puts one under God's curse.[24] Nor does he even remotely hint at people's *inability* to keep the whole law, which is the most common Protestant interpretation.[25]

Not only are these things not said, but not a single word in this passage points in these directions.

If we stay closely with what Paul actually says, and read it in light of the later explanation in 5:3 of this same letter ("every man who lets himself be circumcised is *obligated to obey the whole law*"), then the point is clear enough: Paul's Gentile converts in Galatia cannot pick and choose what they will obey from the law. Rather, to go the way of the Torah is to go the whole way; there is no provision for *partial* obedience. Here, then, is the paragraph that puts all of this in its starkest form; and it is this point that Paul sets out to explain from Scripture. The rest of the paragraph is thus made up of three further explanations from Scripture of the key ideas in this first citation ("faith, living by law, curse"), before Paul in v. 14 brings it to climactic conclusion in favor of Gentiles' being included in the "blessing" through Christ and the Spirit, accessed by faith alone.

Verses 11-12. These two verses must be kept together precisely because Paul now spells out on the basis of Scripture that these two ways of living – by faith or by doing law – are mutually exclusive options. First (v. 11), he repeats the point already made in the preceding paragraph, that "justification/righteousness" has nothing to

---

[23] For example, it is common to read in the literature that "on the surface, Deut 27:26 says the opposite of what he claims it says" (Betz, 145). But that is only because scholars have predetermined on the basis of their reading of Romans 7 that this is what Paul is saying here.

[24] See, e.g., Burton (p. 164), "The unexpressed premise of the argument, necessary to make this passage prove the preceding proposition, is that no one does, in fact, continue in all the things that are written in the book of the law to do them." There simply is no unexpressed premise in this argument; what Paul says is what he means. The curse lies in the necessity of doing the whole law, which automatically excludes living by faith.

[25] See, e.g., Lightfoot (137): "It is impossible to fulfill the requirements of the Law, and the non-fulfillment lays us under a curse." That is simply not Paul's view, as Phil 3:6 makes clear.

do with the law. Rather it not only comes about on the basis of faith (as it did with Abraham, vv. 7-9) – now of course meaning "by faith in Christ Jesus" – but all of life must also be lived on the same basis. In fact there is a considerable word play going on here that is nearly impossible to bring off in English. One will note that the citation of Hab 2:4 at the end of v. 11 responds directly to Paul's introductory clause in the same sentence ("clearly no one is justified before God in the law"); thus "the righteous person (= the one who is justified)," "by faith" (as over against living by the law), and "shall live" (= "before God"). But Paul's concern now is not with how one *begins* Christian faith, but with how one *lives it out* – which is precisely the same way as one came in, "by faith [in Christ Jesus]."

In the context of the issue in Galatians, this is clearly Paul's concern – not with how they *became* believers, but with how they *live* as believers. Thus "being justified before God *in* the law" refers not to how one *enters* the newly formed people of God, but with how such "righteousness" before God is maintained: what must one *do* to be pleasing to God? Paul's word here is that they do not need to add "works of law" to faith in order to be brought to "completion."

That much seems clear enough. The problems arise with the next citation (in v. 12), which has regularly had the misfortune of being interpreted as having to do with people's *inability* to live fully in keeping with the law. But Paul has chosen his text carefully, and it says nothing about inability. Rather it says exactly the opposite. His concern, after all, is expressed in the introductory clause, "the law is not based *on faith*." Here Paul picks up the phrase that has driven the argument since 2:16 and has been repeated throughout (3:2, 5, 7, 9), and which has been brought in again to stand in contrast to living "based on works of law." His point now is, and it is the crucial point in his entire argument with the Galatians, that one cannot *add* "works of law" to faith as a basis of "living" before God. To the contrary, the law itself is quite plain on this matter.

Thus, picking up both the final phrase of the opening citation "to do them (ποιῆσαι αὐτά)" and the verb "to live" from Hab 2:4, he cites Lev 18:5: "the one who *does* them (ὁ ποιήσας αὐτά) *shall live* (ζήσεται) by (or 'in') them." The verb in this case does not mean "come to life" but "to live in an ongoing way," and the preposition is not a form of agency (= *by means of*) but locative (= the sphere in which one must live). And this is the "curse": the one who does the law is condemned not only to doing the *whole* law, but must live *altogether* within the context of doing Torah, which thus automatically excludes living by faith.

The "logic" is thus certain and forceful, and Paul's point is clear: You Galatians cannot have it both ways; it is an either/or situation. One either comes to life, and continues to live, on the basis of faith, or one is condemned to living by the law and that alone, and that quite excludes living by faith. To make this mean something else theologically is not only to do injustice to what Paul actually says, but takes the argument out of Paul's context in order to make it fit another concern altogether. That is both misguided and unnecessary; there is plenty of contemporary application of what Paul actually says without resorting to what he does not say at this point.

Verse 13. As his final argument from Scripture, and still expounding the introductory passage from Deuteronomy, Paul now picks up the language of "curse" and turns it completely on its head. As it turns out on this side of the cross and the gift of the Spirit, the "curse of the law" has to do with the necessity of living under the law and thus of being excluded from living by faith, wherein alone righteousness is to be found. What Christ has done, Paul now argues, is thus to deliver us from this "curse of the law," this necessity of living by law *at all*, and especially in light of vv. 10–11, living by law *alone* with the companion necessity of doing the "whole law." This is precisely what he will state with an "again" in 5:3, and what he accuses the agitators of not doing (6:13). There is not the remotest hint here that the curse rests on us because we are *incapable* of doing the law, something that Paul could easily have said. But in fact "inability" is *not* the issue anywhere in this letter; rather it is *necessity* that is the issue, the "adding" of law to faith in Christ Jesus that Paul inveighs against.

Christ did this, Paul goes on to explain, "by becoming a curse for us," that is, "in our behalf" or "in our place" (as in 1:4). But before he goes on (in v. 14) to express the ultimate twofold purpose of Christ's becoming a curse for us, he pauses to offer the biblical grounds for what he has just said. Indeed, Paul can bring Christ back into the picture at this point precisely because he has yet another Old Testament text that has the concept of "curse" in it, this time in conjunction with language of being "impaled." Moreover, this is not a random citation that just happens to have these two words in conjunction; rather here is yet another citation in Paul where the whole Old Testament context is in purview, and which he assumes his readers will know. Standing at the head of a series of "random laws" as it does, Deut 21:23 concludes a passage that begins in v. 22 regarding what Israel is to do with people *guilty of a capital crime*. Such a person is to be "put to death and their body . . . exposed on a pole." The curse comes in the next clause, which has to do with burial on the same day, since "anyone who is hung on a pole is under God's curse." While Paul can make theological capital of this idea elsewhere,[26] here he is satisfied just to apply the text to the present situation. Christ, who was crucified on the alleged basis of the "crime" of insurrection, through his death in fact became "a curse *for us*." But in this case the "curse" is no longer for a capital crime; rather Christ took on himself the "curse" of anyone's – especially Gentiles' – having to do law, so that, as Paul will go on to conclude in v. 14, they might get in on "the blessing" of Abraham.

Verse 14. With the twin purpose clauses that constitute our v. 14 Paul does three things at once. First, he concludes *the sentence* that began in v. 13, thus offering the twofold aim of Christ's having become a curse for us: that the blessing of Abraham might come to the Gentiles; and that we (he and the Gentile Galatians together) might receive the promise of the Spirit. At the same time, second, this obviously also concludes *the entire section* that began in v. 1, so that in chiastic order he picks up the concern of vv. 7-9 and vv. 1-6 and brings them to conclusion together with these twin clauses. This means, third, that he also thereby concludes *the present paragraph*, whose passion has been singularly that "justification" is not based on works of law in any possible way, since that means to live under the curse of having to do the entire law and apart from grace and faith. In passing we should note that these twin concluding clauses also play havoc with the idea that the present paragraph has to do with our inability to keep the law, since they have nothing at all to do with such an idea.

We begin our analysis with a word about the nature of v. 14 itself, which is made up of two identically structured "in order that" clauses:

> in order that the blessing given to Abraham
> > might come to the Gentiles by faith;
> in order that by faith
> > we might receive the promise of the Spirit.

Since there is no "and" joining the two clauses, it is not immediately clear whether the second is intended to modify the first in some way or whether they are intended to stand in apposition to each other,

[26] See esp. 1 Cor 1:21-25, where a crucified Messiah, a scandal to Jews seeking signs and folly to Gentiles seeking wisdom, is in fact God's own wisdom and power at work in the world, thus overturning the world's views on such matters.

both of them together modifying the main clause, "Christ redeemed us from the curse of the law." While this cannot be decided definitively, the latter seems to be by far the better option, especially since in the second one Paul abandons the third person pronoun for the first person plural, and it is hard to imagine how he could have conceived of his own reception of the Spirit as in some way dependent on the blessing of Abraham as coming to the Gentiles. Thus Paul is about to spell out for his Gentile readers the two major conclusions to the argument to this point, the first picking up how Christ's becoming a curse "for *us*" affects what was argued in vv. 7-9, while the second picks up the emphasis on the reception of the Spirit in vv. 2-5 and thus includes Paul as well.

The first purpose of Christ's becoming a curse "for *us*" (v. 13) is best seen by a literal rendition of Paul's Greek so as to keep his own emphases. His clause begins, "in order that *unto the Gentiles* the blessing of Abraham might come in Christ Jesus." Thus the primary emphasis is on the point of the argument from the beginning: how the work of Christ affects the Galatians, themselves Gentiles. What has come to the Gentiles through Christ is the promised "blessing of Abraham," as noted and thus argued for in v. 8. Christ's taking "the curse of the law" on himself in his crucifixion eliminates altogether the need for Gentiles to observe any aspect of the Torah. And finally all of this has happened "in Christ Jesus," meaning here not as they exist in Christ – although that would be true as well – but that God himself fulfilled his promise to Abraham in and through the work of Christ's death on the cross.

The second purpose is the one that catches the reader by surprise, but which on further reflection should not do so. Again, in order to catch Paul's own emphases we render it much more "literally": "in order that the promise of the Spirit we might receive through faith." Thus this concluding clause takes us back to where the argument began, with the Galatians' own reception of the Spirit. But Paul does far more than simply repeat what had been said in vv. 2 to 5. First of all, picking up the "for us" from the main clause (v. 13), he includes himself and other Jews in the reception of the Spirit by faith.[27] Not just

---

[27] In this final phrase Paul shifts prepositions from ἐκ ("on the basis of") to διά ("through") and at the same time adds the definite article "the." It is doubtful whether this has any "meaning" other than to call specific attention at the very end of the sentence (and present paragraph) to "*the* faith" (= trust in Christ) he has been arguing for right along. That is, he is not here emphasizing personal "faith" in Christ but speaking of it more in the abstract, as the means of appropriating Christ's redemption.

you Galatian Gentiles, but all of us have received the Spirit by faith. The truly new element (at least for the letter itself) is his referring to the Spirit's coming as "the *promise* of the Spirit." Here is one of those moments where one may rightly conjecture that when Paul first came among the Galatians he had spoken of the Spirit in terms of his fulfilling the long-awaited coming day of Yahweh, when God's Spirit would himself rest upon and indwell his people, including the Gentiles. This is especially relevant in the present context because the promise of the Spirit in Ezekiel 36 and 37 – where Ezekiel has re-worked the promised new covenant in Jer 31:31-34 – involves the Spirit's "fulfilling" *the law* by writing it on people's hearts. Thus the Galatians' common reception of the Spirit has in effect brought Torah observance to an end, since the aim of the law is now written on the heart and thus fulfilled through the gift of the Spirit.

Thus with these concluding clauses, Paul's present argument has come full circle, in two ways. First he has appealed to their reception of the Spirit at the beginning of their life in Christ, that it was an experienced reality that came to them quite apart from doing the law. Second, taking up the arguments of the agitators themselves, he has shown that there is a better way to read the story of Abraham with its promise of Gentile inclusion, which has nothing to do with their being circumcised in order to belong to the newly-formed people of God. All of this happened through the death of Christ who redeemed them so that the blessing of Abraham and the gift of the Spirit might be theirs *in Christ Jesus*, and therefore quite apart from the law.

Galatians 3:15-18 – The law does not Void the Promise; plus Who is Abraham's "Seed"?

> [15]*Brothers and sisters, let me take an example from everyday life. Just as no one can set aside or add to a human covenant that has been duly established, so it is in this case.* [16]*The promises were spoken to Abraham and to his seed. The scripture does not say "and to seeds," meaning many people, but "and to your seed,"[h] meaning one person, who is Christ.* [17]*What I mean is this: The law, introduced 430 years later, does not set aside the covenant previously established by God and thus do away with the promise.* [18]*For if the inheritance depends on the law, then it no longer depends on the promise; but God in his grace gave it to Abraham through a promise.*

> [h] Gen 12:7; 13:15; 24:7

With this paragraph Paul sets out to reinforce the conclusions just made regarding the role of Gentiles in the plan of God, as promised to Abraham and fulfilled in Christ. He does so by yet one more argument from Scripture, where his concerns are twofold: (*a*) to demonstrate from the human sphere, that a ratified "will"/covenant can neither be annulled nor added to; and since the promise preceded the coming of the law by centuries, the latter could therefore not annul the promise; and (*b*) that Christ himself is the true heir of the promise, which is ultimately the way all others are included. Keeping with the argument of vv. 7-9, the "promises" refer explicitly to Genesis 12 and 15, which Paul has heretofore carefully avoided calling a "covenant." The rest of the argument, taken up in the next four sections, will speak to both of these matters still further.

The present argument can be easily traced. Verse 15 simply states the analogy from the human sphere, which in v. 17 Paul will argue also works in the divine sphere: no one can set aside or add a codicil to a ratified covenant/will (διαθήκη). But before that, in v. 16 Paul turns to the promise(s), which v. 17 makes clear refers to the former covenant that cannot be annulled at a later time. Those promises were spoken and that covenant/will was made by God to Abraham *and to his seed* (singular), which Paul now explains is a meaningful singular. Thus the "seed" is argued first to refer to Christ, before it is expanded later in v. 29 to refer to God's true people, including especially the Gentiles, who become Abraham's "seed" through Christ the "seed." Therefore, after demonstrating (v. 17) that the Torah cannot annul the prior covenant (of promise made to Abraham and his seed [Christ]), he concludes in v. 18 by simply reinforcing all of this by bringing in the final motif, the inheritance, which was what the promise was all about in the first place. If the inheritance were in fact "based on law," then it is no longer "based on the promise"; but the simple fact is that God promised it to Abraham, quite apart from his obeying the law.

Verse 15. With the use of his first vocative ("brothers and sisters") since 1:11, Paul turns now to apply what he has argued from Scripture in vv. 6-14. The application itself is taken "from everyday life,"[28] since the Gentiles by birth and culture lie outside the story of Israel, even though they have been brought in by Paul through the promise made to Abraham. Paul needs to do this – and can do so – because the translator of Genesis into Greek (the Septuagint) chose the word for

---

[28] This is an idiomatic rendering of Paul's own idiom that says literally, "I speak according to 'man' (= at the human level). In the TNIV the "I speak" has been absorbed in the phrase "let me take."

"will" or "testament" (διαθήκη) to render the Hebrew word for "covenant" (*berith*). Although there is some overlap between the words "will" and "covenant," there is also some significant difference between them; and Paul now sets out to demonstrate the *secondary* nature of the law on the basis of these differences, namely its primary meaning in Greek as a "will."

The function of a covenant was to establish a binding relationship between two parties, agreed on by both, and therefore based on a strong element of trust. Thus at the human level Jacob and Laban made a covenant between them, in which both men agreed on the "boundaries" and expectations of their future relationships (Gen 31:44-54). The same is true for David and Jonathan regarding each others' descendants (1 Sam 18:3; 20:42). But the primary kind of "covenant" in the Old Testament is that between Yahweh and his people, which is more unilateral. God promises to bless them; they in turn are expected to be loyal to him alone, which included scorning other "deities" and had inherent in it that they would obey Yahweh. It is this latter kind of "covenant" that Paul has in mind at the one level. But to make this point he picks up the other dimension of the word, the aspect of a "will," which in this sense is made unilaterally by the testator. This is the kind of "covenant" (διαθήκη) that cannot be set aside or added to by the initiative of another.

Verse 16. However, before Paul goes on to spell out the implications of such a "will," he chooses first to establish who the real recipient of the "will" was. He does so because what concerns him is not simply the significance of the promise as antecedent to the law, but because this is also the way the Gentiles will finally be included in the promise. So he notes that "the promises were spoken to Abraham *and to his seed*," which he then elaborates by pointing out that the word "seed" is a (grammatically) singular noun, not plural; and thus the true *seed* of Abraham is ultimately Christ himself.

For those who tend to read texts in isolation from one another, this has been a troublesome clause, since it appears to be making texts say what one wants them to say, rather than what the divinely inspired author of Genesis intended. But trying to understand this in isolation is precisely what one may not do, since this designation is part of a deliberate messianic understanding of Christ as Son of God that pervades this letter.[29]

---

[29] On this matter see, Fee, *Christology*, pp. 209-23.

Thus, in order to understand what Paul is doing here one needs to keep this sentence in the context of the larger argument. At issue, it must be remembered, is the question, "Who are Abraham's true *children*, his 'seed' who will inherit the promise that includes the blessing of the Gentiles?" The ultimate answer to this question is given in 3:29; "those who are of Christ" are Abraham's true descendants ("seed") and thus "heirs in keeping with the promise." This conclusion is then elaborated in 4:4-7. In the process of getting to this point, Paul here first identifies *Christ*, the Son of God, as the true "seed" of Abraham, so that those who are "of Christ" in turn are Abraham's true descendants and thus God's "sons" (= children). This momentary "aside," therefore, is a purely anticipatory moment for what comes shortly in vv. 26-29 and 4:4-7.

So this present passage is not Paul playing theological word games in order to score his present point. Rather, he is picking up on his "Son of God Christology" already expressed in 1:16 and 2:20, and which will be further explicated in 4:4-7. Such Christology is emphasized in this letter for two reasons: first, because it is ultimately related to Abraham and his "seed" in the biblical narrative – the passage that is being explicated throughout – and, second, because it is through God's true "Seed/Son" that the Galatians themselves are included as Abraham's seed, and thus as "sons/children" of the living God.

Verse 17. That the second sentence in the preceding verse was parenthetical – and thus intentionally anticipatory – becomes evident when we come to this crucial explanatory sentence. As in v. 14 above, Paul's emphases can be found especially in his word order. First, he starts in similar fashion with a "but this I say," which deliberately picks up the "I say" in v. 15 (see n. 28 above). He then immediately echoes his opening language from the same earlier sentence, with a deliberate contrast between "a will (διαθήκη) ratified by a human being" (v. 15) and "the covenant (διαθήκη) *previously* ratified by God." Thus the sentence (in cumbersome literalness; cf. KJV) reads: "This I say: the covenant previously ratified by God, the after-430-years-enacted law does not 'de-ratify' (= annul)." And with that "the law," which has been the focus of attention since v. 2 is now back in the picture. What is of special interest is that Paul now places the covenant of circumcision in the context of the Mosaic law, and thus no longer in the Abrahamic covenant – rightly so, since it is *codified* by Moses (Lev 12:3), along with the observance of days and the food laws.

Paul's sentence ends with a result clause, repeating what the law cannot do, since, as he will go on to explain in the next sentence, it was never intended either to abolish the promise, or to set it aside. Thus Paul returns to his repeated emphasis regarding God's promise to Abraham, that his "seed" (offspring) would be as numerous as the stars in the sky, and would also include the Gentiles in the benefits of his people. This is the promise that Abraham "believed" – so that his "faith" was counted to him as righteousness – which could not possibly be set aside by the law that came over four centuries later.

Verse 18. Paul concludes the paragraph with an explanatory clause that picks up the final clause in the preceding sentence and sets the two options in sharp negative contrast. "For," he begins, if it were the other way about, that is, "if the inheritance was indeed based on the law, then it is no longer based on the promise." That is, if what was at one time based on the promise is now based on the law that came 430 years later, then it is "no longer" related to the promise at all. That truism is then followed by the affirmation that has been both assumed and argued for since v. 7: "But in fact God 'graced' Abraham through a promise." The verb in this case is not the ordinary word for "give"; rather it means to bestow something graciously on a recipient that is otherwise undeserved. Thus Paul ends the current argument by picking up the theme of "grace" from chs. 1 and 2 (1:6, 15; 2:21).

Galatians 3:19-22 – The Role of the law

> [19] *What, then, was the purpose of the law? It was added because of transgressions until the Seed to whom the promise referred had come. The law was given through angels and entrusted to a mediator.* [20] *A mediator, however, implies more than one party; but God is one.* [21] *Is the law, therefore, opposed to the promises of God? Absolutely not! For if a law had been given that could impart life, then righteousness would certainly have come by the law.* [22] *But the Scripture has locked up everything under the control of sin, so that what was promised, being given through faith in Jesus Christ, might be given to those who believe.*

Paul has now made his basic arguments from Scripture, demonstrating that the blessing of Abraham embraces the Gentiles by faith in Jesus Christ and not by works of Torah. But once he has established the link between (*a*) faith, (*b*) righteousness, (*c*) the blessing of Abraham, and (*d*) the promise (of the Spirit), and at the same time has broken the link between the law and any and all of these, he feels the need to explain what role the law did have. That is, having established the link between doing the whole law and the curse (if the *whole* law is not done, vv. 10-14) and the temporary nature of the law (vv. 15-18),

Paul turns now to explain *why* the law was given at all. The law itself is not a bad thing; it simply was not intended to replace, or do the work of, the promise.

In this paragraph, then, Paul takes up two matters about the law. First, why the law was given at all, if the inheritance promised to Abraham is based on that promise alone. To this he will respond in two ways, one (v. 19a) that sets up the rest of the argument in 3:23–4:7, and the other (vv. 19b-20) that adds one more point about its secondary role. Second, in light of the negative press Torah has received to this point, he raises the further question, "Is Torah over against the promise?" To which the answer is, "God forbid!" If a life-giving Torah were possible, then righteousness would have come that way; but as it is, Scripture (= the law) existed rather to hem in all people who are now under sin's rule, with the ultimate goal that they might get in on the promises through faith.

Verse 19. The sentences that make up this verse start out easily enough, but end on a more difficult note, at least from this distance. Paul begins by setting forth the question which he feels compelled to answer in light of what he has said previously about the law. The question is brief and to the point: "Why, then, the law?" which the TNIV has interpreted to mean, "what is the purpose of the law?" While that gets at the ultimate point of the question, what Paul is raising here has more to do with its existence at all, not its purpose as such. One can almost hear the question from Galatia: "If in fact the inheritance promised to Abraham has *always* been based on believing the *promise*, then why did God bother to give Israel the law at all?"

Paul's answer to this question picks up on what he has just argued about the *temporary* role of the law between the giving and fulfillment of the promise. In two clauses Paul offers first the *reason* for the law ("added because of the transgressions"), while the second ("until the Seed should come") speaks to the question of its limited *time*. Thus "it was added," Paul now explains, "because of transgressions," returning to language used in 2:18. But our difficulties with understanding also begin here, starting with the preposition "because of" (χάριν). This word evolved from the accusative of the word "grace" (χάρις) into a preposition that means either "for the sake of" or "because of." It can therefore have either positive or negative connotations in this sentence. Does it mean, because of their sinfulness this was God's way of "hemming his people in," as it were, "until the promised 'seed' should come," as in vv. 22 and 23-24 following? Or is it more negative, meaning, "it was added to bring about (or bring into the open) the people's *sinfulness*," thus to produce transgressions in order to lead people to Christ?[30] Most likely, in light of the follow-up argument in v. 23, it is the former. One will note how easily Paul could have gone from the present answer straight to v. 23: "The law was added because of the transgressions, until the Seed should come to whom the promise had been made.... Now before faith came, we were kept in custody under the law, locked up until the faith that was to come would be revealed."

But Paul does not in fact go straight to v. 23; rather he adds another item about Torah that offers still further explanation as to its secondary character, thus going back to vv. 15-18. Although the clause itself is full of difficulties, its point in the context of the argument seems reasonably clear. His present concern, based on what was just said, is that *the promise* was made to Abraham, and thus to Israel, directly by God himself. But it was different with *the law*. Using the passive voice, Paul says "it was added," a verb which in itself, as well as its passive voice,[31] points to its secondary character. Moreover, the "addition" came by way of a twofold mediation – angels and Moses – thus offering further evidence of its secondary character. All of this is easy enough to follow as argument. Our problems with understanding, therefore, lie not with the overall argument, but with two of the particulars within it: the role of the angels, and the reason for Paul's asserting (in v. 20) the basic tenet of Judaism, that God is One.

Regarding the first matter, Paul here gives evidence that he is a man of his own time within the Jewish tradition. Based on the blessing of Moses in Deut 33:2, where Moses tells Israel that "Yahweh . . . came from Sinai . . . with myriads of holy ones [= angels] . . . from his mountain slopes," an understanding arose in intertestamental Judaism that the law itself had been given to Moses by angels, a point picked up elsewhere in the New Testament in Acts 7:53 and Heb 2:2. Both here and in Acts 7:53, however, it is not "mediation" itself that is emphasized, but the fact that angels "ordered" Moses to write the law, a point simply asserted as a commonly held understanding. Paul's real concern is with the second reality, that it was "mediated" to Israel by the hand of Moses.[32]

---

[30] The latter is the position taken, inter alia, by Lightfoot, Burton, and Danker (BDAG*a*); but this seems less likely in view of the follow up explanation in v. 23.

[31] That is, Paul does not say directly that "God added it," as he had said in v. 18, "God by his grace gave it"; rather that is only implied by way of the passive.

[32] For a list of Jewish texts that make a considerable point of this, see Lightfoot, 196.

Verse 20. With this short, and to many, enigmatic sentence Paul explains how the "mediation" of the law through Moses, as ordered by angels, points to its secondary character. There is no such thing as a mediator for only one party, he points out; and since "God is one," and God gave the promise directly to Abraham, God's "oneness" adds support to the superiority of the *promise* over the law. The *law*, on the other hand, was mediated to Israel by way of Moses (and the angels). With this statement, of course, Paul is appealing to the core reality of all Jewish faith, the *Shema* of Deut 6:4: "Hear, Israel, Yahweh our God, Yahweh is One" (cf. 1 Cor 8:6; 1 Tim 2:5; Eph 4:6). Thus "God's oneness" – meaning that the one God is the only God there is; there are no others – serves as the theological grounding of Paul's conviction that the one God's promise to Abraham is not set aside by the law, which came later to serve other purposes, and was mediated with angelic help through "the hand of Moses."

Verse 21. The argument to this point (from v. 15), especially that of vv. 19-20 as to the secondary character of the law vis-à-vis the promise, leads Paul to ask yet another question. Does all of this mean, then, that "the law is *opposed to* the promises of God?" The only surprise here is the unexpected plural, "the promises of God," which most likely is a recognition that God made his promise to Abraham on more than one occasion,[33] since Paul has no interest in any other promise that was made to Abraham and "his seed." The resounding response is the second "Absolutely not!" in the letter (μὴ γένοιτο, traditionally "God forbid!"; cf. 2:17). This is rhetoric, pure and simple, intended to point out the absurdity of the suggestion. Thus the question itself is simply a circuitous way of saying that even though the law is related to the transgressions, not to the giving of life, it is not itself evil. It was a good thing, which was never intended to bring life or to fulfill the promise to Abraham.

The more striking moment comes in the explanatory sentence that follows, which starts a movement back to where the argument began in 3:2, and thus toward the conclusion in 4:6-7.[34] With a "contrary-to-fact" conditional sentence, Paul in the protasis ("if-clause") establishes what the law was *incapable* of doing, and which therefore points to its intermediate character (i.e., its place between the promise and its fulfillment in Christ and the Spirit; v. 19): "if a law had been given" – or indeed *could* have been given – "that was able to impart life

---

[33] This is also the considered opinion of most interpreters.

[34] At the same time, of course, it points forward to the final major argument in 5:13-25.

(ζωοποιῆσαι)." With this final verb, "impart life," Paul moves to the very heart of things, because this is precisely what Christ and the Spirit have done.

With this language Paul is reflecting a contrast made a few years earlier in 2 Corinthians, where a similar situation had arisen in Corinth from some itinerant "super-apostles" (11:3-5). By advocating adherence to the law, they ended up preaching "another Jesus, another Spirit, and another gospel." In his earlier argument in 2 Cor 2:16–4:6, where he took up the substance of his opponents' arguments, Paul contrasted the new covenant with the former one in terms of "the letter [= doing the law] kills, but the Spirit gives life [the same verb as in our present text]" (2 Cor 3:6), which the rest of that argument through 4:6 spells out in some detail.

In the present verse, as in vv. 10-14 of the preceding paragraph, Paul's statement has nothing to do with the Galatians' inability to keep the law; rather it is for him the simple undeniable fact that the law cannot, because it was not intended to, give life to those who are dead in their trespasses and sins. It is not by accident, therefore, that this language also reflects Ezekiel's vision of the resurrection of God's people from their death in exile, where twice Yahweh says (in the LXX): "I will give my Spirit 'into you' and you will live" (Ezek 37:6 and 14). Significantly, this promise appears in a context where Yahweh has just said to exiled Israel: "I will give you a new heart and put a new Spirit within you; . . . I will put my Spirit in you and move you to follow my decrees" (36:26-27). This, then, is how "the law" is fulfilled and thus superseded. Thus by speaking of the law as unable to give life, Paul anticipates that which the Spirit does and which the law could never do.

That this is the larger context in which to understand our v. 21b is made the more sure by the apodosis ("then-clause") in the present sentence, "then righteousness would certainly come by the law." As with the language of the protasis, Paul is again reaching back to the beginning of the argument, in this case back to 2:21 ("if righteousness could be gained through the law, then Christ died for nothing") by way of the citation of Gen 15:6 in 3:6 above ("Abraham believed God and it was credited to him as righteousness"). This is why the law cannot be thought of as standing in opposition to "the promises of God"; it simply has nothing at all to do with the Spirit's giving life to God's people (including Gentiles) and thus giving them righteousness.

Verse 22. With the two clauses that make up this sentence Paul at once contrasts what the law does do (negatively), since it does not –

because it cannot – give life, and then what the positive outcome of the law's "imprisonment" will be when its purpose is actualized through Christ (3:23-24). In doing so, Paul introduces yet another striking metaphor regarding the intermediate role of the law, which resulted in a positive purpose for its existence.

In the main clause, which stands in bold contrast to the final sentence in v. 21, Paul says "the Scripture has locked up everything under the control of sin," a clause that is not immediately transparent, given what has been said to this point. The problems for interpretation are three: (*a*) the meaning of "the Scripture," (*b*) what Paul intends by the metaphor of imprisonment, and (*c*) how "the Scripture" imprisons people (literally) "under sin."

The first problem, the meaning of the term "the Scripture" is more difficult in this case because Paul's usage elsewhere seems to stand in some tension with what is said here. Elsewhere when Paul uses the singular noun "Scripture" (γραφή) with the definite article "the," he is referring to a single passage from the Old Testament. That has happened already in 3:8 and will happen again in 4:30; it is then picked up several times in Romans (4:3; 9:17; 10:11; 11:2) and one further time in 1 Tim 5:18. At the same time, and on the other hand, when he uses this word to refer to all of Israel's Scripture he uses the plural.[35] But it is also possible to make too much of this point, since we have such limited evidence. In any case if Paul had a given text in mind, it is difficult to imagine which it might be;[36] and since when Paul picks up this idea in the next sentences he refers to the law in general, it seems most likely that he was generalizing with the present usage as well.

Second, as to the meaning of the metaphor itself in this case, it must also finally be understood in light of the elaboration Paul himself gives it in the immediately following sentences. Moreover, it is clear from what follows that Paul is less than comfortable with this metaphor, so that he gradually changes it to the role the "slave/pedagogue" plays in the Greco-Roman household, which suits his immediate concerns in a much better way. So with that proviso, one should not consider the verb translated "locked up" in the TNIV to be a metaphor for a prison as such. Rather, it most likely is intended here to convey the idea of

---

[35] See Rom 1:2; 15:4; 16:26; 1 Cor 15:3, 4.

[36] Burton, e.g., thinks it refers back to Deut 27:26, cited in v. 10 above; but that is based on a quite misleading interpretation of Paul's sentence (see the discussion above), and what is said here is scarcely hinted at there. Paul simply does not use Scripture so thoughtlessly.

"being hemmed in," so as not to run loose; and thus in a certain sense, as will be explained in what follows, its serves a useful purpose – very much like ":the law" in one's home is intended to "hem in" the children until they are able to internalize the value of the "law" for themselves.

Therefore, third, the real difficulty with the sentence is *how* the Scripture "confines" people *under sin*. Here is a clause that has often been taken out of context and made much more theological than Paul himself probably intended. A certain sector of the evangelical community, for example, wants this to mean that "the Scripture *has declared* the whole world as a prisoner of sin" (NIV), or that "the Scripture *pictures* all mankind as sinner" (AmpNT); thus the purpose of "Scripture" is seen as first of all pointing out that all human beings are sinful and thus accountable before God. The problem with such a view in this instance, of course, is that it is so unrelated to the present argument. Moreover, it usually involves an incorrect understanding of vv. 10-14, and in so doing, makes this sentence stand out like an aberration, rather than as a part of what Paul is presently arguing.

The best solution would seem to be one that sees the prepositional phrase "under sin," in combination with the metaphor for "confinement," as a kind of shorthand attempt to express the ultimate reason for the confinement: to "hem people in" while they themselves are "under sin," that is, under the dominion of sin. Paul is thus picturing "all things" (= all people) as "confined" by the law because they are at the same time under (the sway of) sin. That is, as Paul expresses clearly elsewhere, both Jew and Gentile alike (which is almost certainly what the "everything" means here) have sinned and thus come short of the glory God intended for humanity when they were created (Rom 2:1–3:23, esp. 3:23). Thus they live "under sin." Enter the law, and it does *not do away with* this primary reality, sin, since it is incapable of doing so; rather it was given to "confine" people ("hem them in," as it were), during this period of their being "under sin." Such an understanding accents the point of the entire argument of Galatians, namely that Christ and the Spirit are sufficient to do what the law does not, because it cannot, do: take care of the problem of sin.

That this interpretation moves in the right direction seems to be supported by the rest of Paul's sentence, which gives the ultimate purpose of the law's "hemming people in," namely "so that what was promised, based on faith in Jesus Christ, might be given to those who believe." That is, the law's purpose for those (all people, in this case) who are under the sway of sin was to keep them "confined" (that is, to keep them from "overt" sin) until God's promise to Abraham could be realized through his Seed, namely Christ. Thus Paul at the end of this part of the argument brings all of its crucial themes together: "the promise"; "given (freely)"; "based on faith in Jesus Christ"[37]; and offered "to those who have such faith."

Not much more needs to be said by way of comment. "The promise" takes us back to the initial scriptural argument in vv. 7-9, as articulated in vv. 14-18. The word "given (freely)" stands in immediate contrast to what could not be given by any form of law (v. 21), while "based on faith in Jesus Christ" takes us back to the way the whole argument began in Paul's speech to Peter in 2:16-17. And the phrase "to those who believe" takes us back to the same "redundancy" one finds in 2:16 (based on faith for those who believe). This recapitulation by Paul is clear evidence that the argument that began in v. 15 is now brought to conclusion. At the same time, however, it also launches him into the elaboration that comes next (vv. 23-25), which in turn points to the ultimate twofold conclusion to the entire argument in vv. 26-29 and 4:4-7, having in turn to do with the Galatians as belonging to "Abraham's true seed " (v. 29) and thus to be "God's true children" (4:4-7).

Galatians 3:23-29 – First Conclusion: Those in Christ are Abraham's Seed

> [23]*Before the coming of this faith,*[1] *we were held in custody under the law, locked up until the faith that was to come would be revealed.* [24]*So the law was put in charge of us until Christ came that we might be justified by faith.* [25]*Now that this faith has come, we are no longer under the supervision of the law.*
>
> [26]*So in Christ Jesus you are all children of God through faith,* [27]*for all of you who were baptized into Christ have clothed yourselves with Christ.* [28]*There is neither Jew nor Gentile, neither slave nor free, neither male nor female, for you are all one in Christ Jesus.* [29]*If you belong to Christ, then you are Abraham's seed, and heirs according to the promise.*

[1]*22-23 Or* through the faithfulness of Jesus ... [23]*Before faith*

With this section and the next (4:1-7) Paul brings this first argument from Scripture (3:1–4:7) to its twofold conclusion. It will be useful at this point, therefore, to recap where the argument has been going that brings us to these two concluding moments, as well as to point out the relationship between the two sections as they together bring closure to

---

[37] On this phrase (see the note on v. 23 in the TNIV), see the discussion in 2:16.

what began in 3:1. Having established on the basis of their experience
of the Spirit that righteousness is based on faith, not on doing the law
(vv. 1-5), Paul concluded that appeal (v. 6) by citing Gen 15:6, that
Abraham also "believed God and that was credited to him as
righteousness." Paul then argued through a series of steps that
Abraham's true heirs are those who have faith like Abraham (vv. 7-9),
and that it has nothing to do with the law, since these are mutually
exclusive options (vv. 10-14). He then turns to say some things about
the law itself, since this is the crucial issue. First he argues that a
covenant of promise cannot be annulled or added to, and that the law
is quite unrelated to the promise (vv. 15-18). This leads, second, to the
crucial question of "why the law at all," since it was incapable of
giving life. The answer is that it served the useful function of
"hemming people in" while they were under sin's power, until the
promise was fulfilled in Abraham's true seed, Jesus Christ (vv. 19-22).

Paul now sets out to tie together all the loose ends with these two
final sections, which themselves have several points of similarity. Both
of them begin with the imagery of the law as our pedagogue; both
conclude with our being "heirs"; and the key imagery in both is
"sonship" as opposed to slavery. Verses 4:1-7 in fact are the
elaboration (or explanation) of the present section. Thus this section
asserts that the law is a pedagogue, the next spells out what that means;
this one asserts that "you are all 'sons' of God," the second explains
how that happens. Nonetheless, their function is different in terms of
the whole argument. The present section, which begins as an
elaboration of vv. 19-22, at the same time ends by tying several earlier
points together: that (*a*) *Christ* is the key to present salvation, (*b*)
salvation is by *faith* in Christ, and (*c*) through him Jew and Gentile
together are Abraham's *seed* and therefore *heirs* of the promise. Thus,
vv. 23-29, by way of vv. 19-22, tie together all the matters taken up in
vv. 6-18, that Gentile believers are among Abraham's *heirs*. Verses 4:1-
7, also by way of vv. 19-22, then tie the issue of *sonship* to the
redemptive work of the Son and to the experience of the Spirit of the
Son, thus bringing the argument full circle by going back to vv. 1-5.
The net result is two passages that are among the more significant in
the Pauline corpus and therefore require careful attention.

Verses 23-25. These two (Greek) sentences function together as a
transition between the preceding paragraph and vv. 26-29, which
bring the argument to its first conclusion. Paul begins (v. 23) with an
elaboration of the points made in vv. 21 and 22; but with a result
clause in v. 24 he shifts the imagery from "imprisonment" to

"pedagogue," which serves his present purposes better. All of this, he concludes (at the end of the first sentence [v. 24]), had as its ultimate purpose that "we might be justified on the basis of faith," a clause which at first glance does not seem to follow well with what has preceded. But in fact it has been the goal of the entire argument right along. Thus the shift is from the basic pre-Christ role of the law (to "hem people in") to its penultimate purpose now revealed in the present age ("to serve as a pedagogue for Christ"), all of which has as its final goal "that we might be justified by faith." Then in v. 25 this is all summed up, while partly repeated.

Paul begins the sentence (v. 23) by repeating the basic content of v. 22 and spelling it out more clearly; in doing so he also picks up the more abstract way of speaking about "faith" from v. 14.[38] Before the coming of "this faith" (just referred to),[39] meaning before this present time when "faith" is the rule, we were detained under the law. The imagery in this case refers to the basic use of prisons by the Romans: to hold people in custody until their case could be disposed of. All of this is then said again by way of a participial construction that repeats the verb from v. 22, "being 'locked up' until 'the faith' that was to come had been revealed." With this latter word he echoes the theme of "revelation," one of Paul's more important ways of speaking about the coming of Christ and the Spirit, which he had used earlier regarding his own experience of Christ (1:16). It is also important to note his return to the pronoun "we" (see v. 14), which continues through v. 25. In this case, however, it is not the inclusive "we" (Jew and Gentile together) of v. 14, to which he will return in 4:3-5; rather he is here speaking from the perspective of a Jewish believer in Christ (= we Jews), anticipating the inclusion of the Gentiles with the "you" in v. 26.

Thus with a "so that," Paul in v. 24 repeats for the third time the theme of the law as custodial until the coming of Christ; but he does so now with a deliberate change of images that fits much better the actual relationship of the law to Christ – an image he will capitalize on further in 4:1-3. The "imprisonment" of the law is now pictured as (literally) "the law became our pedagogue [παιδαγωγός[40]] unto[41]

[38] See n. 27 above.

[39] Thus the TNIV (correctly) sees the definite article here as anaphoric (= referring back to the word "faith" in v. 22). Lightfoot (148) sees it as referring to "the objective teaching" found in the Gospel, as in 1:24; but this seems much less likely here.

[40] This Greek word expresses its basic content quite literally, being a construction of "child" (παιδός [gen. of παῖς]) and the verb "to lead" (ἀγώ).

Christ." The pedagogue in the Greco-Roman world was a trusted slave, usually better educated than the majority of free men, whose primary function was the care of the son in the family who would eventually become heir. Thus he was responsible to guide the son to and from school, and to watch over his conduct in general so that the son would be well equipped someday to take over the duties of the household. For Paul the role of the law as pedagogue was to "guide" God's people, and thus to watch over them, until the coming of Christ. Thus it served as a "pedagogue unto Christ."

The final purpose clause in v. 24 serves together with v. 25 as a kind of summary that brings the current discussion (from v. 21) to its proper conclusion. The short clause itself picks up the final phrase from the preceding clause ("unto Christ") and ties it by way of contrast to the end of v. 21: if there were such a thing as a life-giving law, then "justification would be based on the law." But as it is, Paul says, the law served a different function, as a pedagogue to guide us to Christ, "in order that we might in fact be justified on the basis of faith." This in turn takes us back to the sharp contrasts that began in Paul's "Peter speech" in 2:16, that were picked up again in the present argument in verses 2 through 14.

Verse 25 then simply summarizes the present discussion: (literally) "Now that this faith has come, we are no longer under a pedagogue." For the sake of the contemporary reader, the TNIV chose to eliminate the metaphor altogether ("no longer under the supervision of the law"), which of course is what Paul intends with the metaphor. But there are three further things to note as well: (*a*) the language "this faith" recognizes the use of the definite article as anaphoric (picking up and referring to preceding usage in v. 23); (*b*) Paul is once more using the inclusive "we," and again it refers to himself and his fellow Jewish Christians; and (*c*) the phrase "no longer under the pedagogue" simply brings v. 24 to its logical conclusion. As a pedagogue the law served to lead us to Christ, which means that with the coming of "faith" the pedagogue has no further function. The clear implication of this sentence is that the law has absolutely no further role in the lives of those who are in Christ, and therefore that the Galatian Gentiles are under no obligation to the law whatsoever. So here he makes it plain that Christ brings an *end* to the law; in 5:14 he will go to argue that the Spirit fulfills the *purpose* of the law.

---

[41] Danker lists this preposition (εἰς) as a time referent, thus "until the time of Christ" (BDAG 2aα); but it could just as well have a directional meaning, hence playing on the theme of the pedagogue's role in the home.

Verse 26. The paragraph that begins with this sentence is made up of three explanatory clauses, with a final result clause (v. 29). Verse 26 is the first explanatory clause, where Paul finally applies all of the preceding argument directly to the Galatians, and where the shift from "we" in v. 25 to the present "you (plural)" should be noticeable to any careful reader. At the same time this verse functions as the "thesis sentence" for the rest of the paragraph, so that the second and third explanatory clauses (vv. 27 and 28b) serve to explain further the implications of this one.

As with some earlier sentences (e.g., 3:14), Paul's emphases lie at the beginning and the end of his sentence: "you all" and "in Christ Jesus." But if in fact we were to translate in Paul's own word order[42] ("You all are 'sons' of God through faith in Christ Jesus"), no English-speaking person could catch what Paul is actually saying. It is not that such a "translation" says something that is not otherwise true; it simply misses the point Paul is making, namely, that as you are "*in Christ Jesus* you are 'sons' of God through faith." Two considerations make this certain. First, Paul never uses the preposition "in" (ἐν) to refer to someone's putting their trust *in* something or someone.[43] That is English, but not Greek; so Paul's word order would not cause the Galatians to read it incorrectly. As with John in his Gospel, Paul's ordinary idiom for this is "to put one's faith 'into' (εἰς) someone" (cf. 2:16 above). Second, as in v. 28 below, Paul's emphasis is on the believer's new position (being "in Christ") that has come about "through the (= this)[44] faith" that he has been talking about right along. Thus it comes at the end of the sentence both for emphasis and as the lead in to what he goes on to explain in v. 27. So the only way one can get to Paul's meaning is to follow the lead of most contemporary English translations: keep Paul's emphasis by putting this phrase in first position in the English sentence. Thus, by being "in Christ Jesus" you are "'sons' of God," and this comes about by faith, by trusting Christ, not by doing the law.

But these two prepositional phrases, important as they are in expressing the source and means of the Galatians' new life, enclose the much more important subject and predicate of the sentence: "You *all* are 'sons' of God," where the "all" and its further definition in v. 28

---

[42] As was done, for example, by the KJV, followed by NASB, NAB, and NIV.

[43] See the discussion of 2:20 above, for the most likely meaning of this phrase there, which some would see as a possible exception to Paul's standard usage.

[44] The phrase has the definite article again, as in the three previous uses in vv. 23 and 25.

make clear that he means all the believers in Galatia, both men and women. The reason for his choice of "sons" here is that he intends a double word play on this word. On the one hand, he is picking up the language that first appears in v. 7, where Abraham's true progeny, his "sons" if you will, are those who live by faith in Christ Jesus. On the other hand, we ourselves become "sons" because the ultimate "son" of Abraham's lineage is Christ himself (4:4 and 6), who as in 1:16 and 2:20 has already been referred to as "*God's* Son." What is of ultimate significance in this sentence is that Paul is here addressing Gentiles, who by being in Christ Jesus through faith are thus among the true heirs of Abraham, the man of faith – and this quite apart from any adherence to the law. Here, then, is where the long argument (from v. 6) has been heading right along.

Verses 27-28a. With another "for," Paul goes on to explain simultaneously what it means for them to be "in Christ" and how it is that all of them can thus know with full surety that they are part of God's children without going backwards – by doing (parts of) the law. How Paul does this looks from our distance like a stroke of genius, but for Paul it would have been as natural as breathing: he reminds them of their point of entry into the Christian community, namely, their baptism in water. Thus he begins, "as many of you as were baptized into Christ," meaning "all of you who were" so baptized.[45] What makes this such a significant moment in the argument is twofold, both of which are matters of considerable importance in the argument. First, their baptism has served for them precisely the role circumcision served for the Jewish community, as the "rite of passage" – in the Galatians' case into the Christian community. Thus, those who by faith are now "in Christ" have by their baptism "into Christ" thus "put on Christ."[46] Christ himself is the center of their new identity as the children of God.

Second, whereas the Jewish "rite of passage" was reserved for males only, in the new community of God's people, entered into by faith in Christ Jesus and experienced by the coming of the Spirit, the "rite of entry" was available to all. This is quite the point of the clause that follows (v. 28), where Paul singles out the three most obvious ways

[45] At least that is what the majority of interpreters think Paul's ὅσοι means here; but Dunn (202) suggests that Paul is indeed here referring to the Christian norm, but also making allowance for visitors present at the reading of the letter.

[46] The verb "put on" is that used for putting on clothing; it seems very likely, but not fully certain, that this alludes to believers' having a new garment to wear after coming up out of the waters of baptism.

people are "distinguished," and thus separated, from each other –
ethnicity (Jew and Greek), social status (slave and free), and gender
(male and female) – but who have now been made "one" in Christ
Jesus. It is especially true of the last designation, where Paul does not
use the more traditional, case specific, language of "man and woman"
(cf. Gen 2:22), but the language which puts emphasis on gender as
such (from Gen 1:27). Thus the very thing that excluded women from
full participation in Israel, the fact that they were "female" and could
not be circumcised, has been set aside in Christ, since "all of you"
were baptized into Christ. Now *all* of you have had the same "rite of
passage."

It needs to be emphasized that this alone is what the passage is all
about; but because of later concerns that have surrounded it, much
more needs to be said. We begin with the reference to baptism in
v. 27. This is often read as having to do either with the *necessity* of
baptism or with baptismal regeneration; but that is to read later ideas
back into Paul's text. The "for" does not here explain how they *became*
"sons = children" or how they were regenerated, but what they have
in common with all other brothers and sisters in Christ that makes
circumcision for men in the Christian community so anathema for
Paul. Circumcision does not take one forward, but backward; it is not
a "fulfillment" of the promise to Abraham, but a denial of the work of
Christ and the Spirit. For above all, it excludes women as full members
of the community of faith.

The point is that Paul is not trying to make any point at all about
baptism other than the one he makes: it is the common entry point
into the Christian community for everyone, irrespective of race, social
status, or gender. Does Paul assume that all have been baptized? Yes.
Does he understand baptism to be the identifiable rite of entry into the
believing community? Yes. He simply would have no categories in
which to understand the concept of an "unbaptized Christian"; such a
thing would not have existed in his churches. Did he assume
immersion in water? Yes, since there was no other kind of "baptism"
known to him. Did he believe that the one so baptized had been
uniquely identified with Christ so as symbolically to "die" and "come
to life" in so doing? Yes. But did he also believe that people were
actually regenerated through their baptism? Hardly, since that for Paul
is distinctly the work of the Spirit, which is never explicitly associated
with water baptism in his letters.[47] None of this is to minimize either

---

[47] On this matter see Fee, *GEP*, 860–63.

baptism itself or its importance; but it is to try to keep its importance and significance within Paul's own parameters, what he himself apparently believed by what he actually said.

Second, more needs to be said about the "equalizing" force of v. 28, since at this point it has little or nothing to do with any "role" people play in the Christian community except the "role" they all have in common in God's story as believers in Christ. But what this passage does do is to put the major *human-made* barriers to one side with regard to people's being "in Christ." What is seldom seen clearly in contemporary western and westernized cultures is the truly radical nature of this sentence with regard to the context in which it was written. Here is the ultimate Christian "Magna Carta" for those who by cultural definition were not only seen as unequals, but were treated as such. It should be noted that these categories do not deal with three different kinds of people as such – since every human being is some combination of the three – but with people who by cultural definition are "different." In Paul's day the top of the ladder belonged exclusively to a "free Gentile male," while a "Jewish female slave" would be at the bottom. It should be noted further that in the culture into which Paul is speaking, position and status prevailed in every way, so that one's existence was totally identified with, and circumscribed by, these realities. By the very nature of things, position and status gave advantage to some over others; and in Greco-Roman culture, by and large, there was very little chance of changing status.

Thus Gentiles had all the advantages over Jews, so Jews took refuge in their relationship with God, which they believed advantaged them before God over the Gentiles. The hatreds were deep and mutual. Likewise, masters and slaves were consigned to roles where all the advantages went to masters;[48] and the same was true for men and women, where women were dominated by men and basically consigned to childbearing. In fact, according to Diogenes Laertius, Socrates used to say every day: "There were three blessings for which he was grateful to Fortune: first, that I was born a human being, and not one of the brutes; next that I was born a man and not a woman; thirdly, a Greek and not a barbarian."[49] The Jewish version of this,

---

[48] This is one place, it should be pointed out, where change could take place in that culture, because slavery was not based on race as it was in the tragic history of the United States. Rather, it was based primarily on war, captivity and economics, so that people could change status; e.g., in economically hard times people could sell themselves into slavery, and masters often manumitted slaves.

[49] 1.33 (Loeb Classical Library).

obviously influenced by the Greco-Roman worldview, is the rabbi who says that "everyday you should say, 'Blessed are you, O God, … , that I'm not a brute creature, nor a Gentile, nor a woman'."[50]

It is therefore especially difficult for most of us to imagine the effect of Paul's words in a culture where position and status preserved order through basically uncrossable boundaries. Paul asserts that when people come into the fellowship of Christ Jesus, significance is no longer to be found in being Jew or Greek, slave or free, male or female. The all-embracing nature of this affirmation, its counter-cultural significance, the fact that it equally *disadvantages* all by equally *advantaging* all – these stab at the very heart of a culture sustained by people's maintaining the right position and status. But in Christ Jesus, the One whose death and resurrection inaugurated the new creation, all things have become new; the new era has dawned.

What Paul is asserting here is not that people cease to be any of these in combination, but that in Christ the old *significance* of these distinctions – and the *values based on them* – no longer maintain. Paul's point, of course, is that through the work of Christ, no one of these has any advantages over the other. Thus in the context of this letter and its present argument, here is why circumcision is such an anathema to Paul, the Christian apostle – because circumcision kept the old boundaries intact at two crucial places regarding who people are in Christ, namely ethnicity and gender. Gentiles were thus being forced to become Jews, while women were excluded from privilege altogether. For Paul Christ and the Spirit have transcended, and thus eradicated, all such nonsense.

Verse 28b. With a final explanatory clause Paul now puts the capstone on what he has just argued on the basis of their common baptism. And again, Paul's emphases can be seen in the word order: "All of you one are in Christ Jesus." His emphasis lies with all three points. First, "all of you" picks up the preceding emphasis, "there is neither Jew nor Greek, neither slave nor free, neither male nor female." Now he concludes by starting his sentence with "all of you," whichever combination of the three you may happen to be.

Second, "all of you are one." As pointed out above, this does not mean that Christ has effected a kind of homogenization of his people, so that the distinctions are obliterated as such. Rather, just as in 1 Corinthians, when he says the "body is one," his point is its unity, not its uniformity. In Christ Jesus we no longer find our basic values in

---

[50] Talmudic tractate *Menahoth* 43b (Epstein translation).

what differentiates people from one another, but in the unity that Christ alone can bring into our continuing diversity. It is one of the sad realities in the history of the church that so few of God's people have ever really caught on to what Paul is here asserting to be true: We are *one people* together, united in our common life *in Christ*.

Third, and not surprisingly, Paul ends the sentence precisely as he ended v. 26, the "topic" sentence of which vv. 27 and 28 are the explanation. There he asserted "all of you" are God's children because you are "in Christ." So now at the end of the explanations as to what that entails, he reminds them that they are one people, because what they have in common is that they exist together "in Christ Jesus."

Verse 29. In one sense the immediately preceding sentences say it all. They absolutely exclude the necessity of these male Galatian believers' being circumcised; they put the emphasis on the fact that the common denominator to their new existence is the same "faith" (v. 26) and the same "baptism" (v. 27); and they do so in such a way that women and slaves are equally included in what God has done in Christ Jesus. Nonetheless, Paul's argument with his opponents has not yet come to an end, since everything for them goes back to Abraham and the covenant of circumcision. So Paul brings the entire argument from v. 6 to its first conclusion with these words: "Therefore, you are Abraham's 'seed,' 'heirs' in keeping with the promise."

What is of immediate significance for the argument of the entire passage is his return to the language of "seed," which in v. 16 he had narrowed to the singular so as to point to Christ. Now he expands that to include these Gentile believers. Since they are *"in* Christ," Abraham's seed, that means they also *are* Abraham's "seed." Not only so, they are his true "heirs" in keeping with the promise God made to Abraham. And with that the argument is brought to its first point of conclusion. But the argument is not finished, because what has been left hanging right along, which was momentarily brought back into the argument at v. 26, is the reality that they are "heirs" because they are in fact "sons." This is the concern to which Paul will now turn in order to bring the whole issue to its ultimate conclusion, where the concepts of "sonship" and of being "heirs" are brought together and where Paul expresses it in terms of divine ultimates. Thus the argument will end by Paul's affirming the role that each of "persons" of the "three-personed" God – Father, Son, and Spirit – has in bringing all of this off.

Galatians 4:1-7 – Second Conclusion: Those in Christ are God's True "Sons"

> [1]*What I am saying is that as long as heirs are underage, they are no different from slaves, although they own the whole estate.* [2]*They are subject to guardians and trustees until the time set by their fathers.* [3]*So also, when we were underage, we were in slavery under the elemental spiritual forces*[a] *of the world.* [4]*But when the set time had fully come, God sent his Son, born of a woman, born under the law,* [5]*to redeem those under the law, that we might receive adoption to sonship.*[b] [6]*Because you are his sons, God sent the Spirit of his Son into our hearts, the Spirit who calls out, Abba,*[c] *Father.* [7]*So you are no longer slaves, but God's children; and since you are his children, he has made you also heirs.*

[a]3 Or *under the basic principles*
[b]5 The Greek word for *adoption to sonship* is a term referring to the full legal standing of an adopted male heir in Roman culture. [c]6 Aramaic for *Father*

Paul now sets out to bring this first argument from Scripture to its final conclusion. As pointed out above (pp. 135-36), it follows hard on the heels of the first conclusion, which ended on the note of Gentiles' being part of Abraham's true "seed," and thus heirs in keeping with the promise God made to Abraham in Genesis 12 and 15. This is the point presupposed by and elaborated in the present paragraph. The paragraph begins and ends with the motif of "heirs"; and since only "sons" are heirs in Greco-Roman culture, the heart of the paragraph spells out how the Galatian Gentiles have become "sons" so as to become heirs. Thus vv. 1-3 elaborate and reapply the theme of the law as a pedagogue leading us to Christ (3:24); while vv. 4-7, still using the pedagogue imagery but now with an extraordinarily powerful application of it, spell out how it is that "we" became "sons" and thus "heirs."

Verses 1-2. When Paul first used the "pedagogue" imagery in 3:23-24, his emphasis was on the historic role of the law, which was to serve as Israel's custodian until the time that faith would be revealed. That argument then concluded with the affirmation that through Christ the Galatian Gentiles themselves became part of "Abraham's seed," and thus "heirs in keeping with the promise." In picking up the "pedagogue" imagery once more (in v. 2), Paul's emphasis is now altogether on the "heir-in-waiting" – the one who has all the privileges, but has not yet entered into those privileges while still a minor. Thus with this new twist to the imagery he sets up the climactic conclusion to the argument, by showing how all people – Jew and Gentile alike – who under the law are merely potential "sons" and heirs, are brought into the family through Christ and the Spirit. In doing so, Paul at the same time picks up the "slave/free" contrast from 3:28, which in that case was an actual cultural reality, but is now used metaphorically to refer to those under the law. The son-heir is no better off than a slave as long as he is under the tutelage of the slave-tutor.

The sentence that makes up these two verses thus spells out these cultural realities, but without making specific application – even though it lies right under the surface, and his Galatian readers could hardly have missed it. The Jewish community, who until the coming of Christ had lived all their lives under the law, are like a son who is heir of the whole estate; nonetheless, until the son reaches his majority (the time appointed by his father), he is de facto no better off than a slave. Lord of the whole estate as he ultimately is, in fact he is presently "subject to guardians and trustees."

Verse 3. All of that is easy enough to follow; the shocker comes in this applicational sentence, which makes perfectly good sense until the final prepositional phrase. But there are also several difficult exegetical choices along the way before we come to that final phrase. The "so" or "thus" with which the sentence begins makes it certain that Paul intends now to apply the preceding analogy; moreover the third word in the sentence, the (unnecessary) pronoun "we," is intentionally emphatic, thus suggesting that Paul is here, as elsewhere in this letter, speaking especially in the context of his being part of the Jewish community.[51] At issue, therefore, is the adverb (καί) that comes between them, as to whether it means simply "also" or something more emphatic like "even." The context seems to suggest the latter: "thus even we (Jews), when we were underage, were 'enslaved'." The words "underage" and "enslaved" thus pick up the two crucial words from v. 1 regarding the young heir.

But right at the place where one might legitimately expect "enslaved under the law," Paul in fact uses language that comes from the Greco-Roman world regarding their "enslavement" to the "elemental spiritual forces of the world" (τὰ στοιχεῖα τοῦ κόσμου). While the precise meaning of this phrase is a matter of considerable debate, there can be little question that Paul is herewith equating Jewish "bondage" to the law with pagan bondage to the "powers," whatever the nature

---

[51] See esp. 2:15, 16; the earlier occurrences (1:8; 2:9) have to do with Paul's own ministry.

of these enslaving "powers" might actually be.[52] What is clear is that, given the coming of Christ and the Spirit, Paul is ready to lump Jew and Gentile together as "enslaved," like a minor who is an heir but still under tutelage by a slave. All alike await the freedom that only Christ and the Spirit could bring.

Verses 4-5. In one of the great "Trinitarian" passages in the New Testament, Paul proceeds to explain in two brief, but pregnant, sentences (vv. 4-5 and 6) how God – Father, Son and Spirit – effectively delivered people from their former bondage and made them "sons," that is, God's own children. In so doing Paul brings the entire argument from 3:1 to a splendid climax. And since this is the "second conclusion" to the argument, one needs especially to note the new elements in this final elaboration: (*a*) the explicit contrasts between being "slaves" and "sons," thus "slave" and "free" – the motifs that become operative in the rest of the argument (4:21-31; 5:1, 13); and (*b*) the re-entry of the Spirit (v. 6), last mentioned in 3:14, now as the experiential evidence of "sonship" – and the key to living godlike (= bearing the divine image) when the law is no longer in place (5:13–6:10).

This present sentence thus offers the christological-soteriological basis for Paul's singular interest throughout – that because they are in Christ, the Galatian Gentiles do not need to come "under Torah." The sentence begins with language that ties what is about to be said to the preceding analogy (vv. 1-2) and its application (v. 3). In contrast to a former time when God's people were no better off than "a minor," still under the tutelage of a slave-pedagogue, "the fullness of time" came for them to reach their maturity. As Paul has argued in a variety of ways throughout, God's time came with Christ, especially through his redemptive work on the cross. And as he argued at the beginning (3:2-5), this has been evidenced experientially through the gift of the Spirit (v. 6).

Thus, as with 3:5, the emphasis is on the activity of God; what God himself has done is reason enough for the Galatians to cease to listen to those who would bring them "under Torah." But in this case, it is

[52] This word occurs 4x in Paul, here and in v. 9; and in Col 2:8 and 20. For the basic matters of the debate see BDAG, plus the bibliography there. Given the usage in Colossians, it seems most likely that it means something like entry 2: "transcendent powers that are in control over events in the world." But given the ambiguity of things, and esp. that Paul is willing to place Jewish law-keeping under this same umbrella, one should be necessarily cautious in trying to fine tune the meaning more than this.

even more. What God has accomplished, he has done as the eternal Trinity.[53] As always God the Father is the subject of the saving verbs; but his saving activity has been carried out through the redemptive activity of the Son, who has inaugurated God's eschatological salvation, with its inclusion of Jew and Gentile alike as his own children; and that saving activity has been made effective by the Spirit of the Son whom the Father sent "into our hearts."

In the rest of the present sentence (vv. 4-5), four points are made about Christ and his saving activity, which can be seen most easily by noting the chiastic structure of the whole:

(A)   God sent his Son,
        (a)   born of a woman
                (b)   born under the law,
                (b★)   to redeem those under the law,
        (a★)   that we might be adopted as "sons"
                                    [and to effect this]
(B)   God sent the Spirit of his Son

First, in language that seems deliberately chosen so as to tie together the work of Christ and the Spirit, Paul says that "God sent forth (ἐξαπέστειλεν) his Son." Despite a few voices to the contrary,[54] two matters combine to indicate that this is an assertion of Christ's preexistence, that Christ is himself divine and came from the Father to effect redemption: (*a*) the otherwise unnecessary clause "born of a woman"; and (*b*) the parallel in v. 6 about God's sending forth the Spirit. Thus even though the verb by itself does not necessarily imply

---

[53] I use this language guardedly, knowing full well that the spelling out of the doctrine does not happen until after the NT is in place. At issue in the doctrine itself is the question of "being," the Three in One and One in Three. These issues are not raised in the NT; but this passage is one of those that plays a major role in the later formulations, since it asserts the preexistence of the Son and the Spirit, and the Spirit is explicitly called "the Spirit of [God's] Son."

[54] See esp. J.D.G. Dunn, *Christology in the Making* (2nd ed.; Grand Rapids: Eerdmans, 1989), 38-44, whose case builds on a series of (correct) observations that on its own this verb neither argues for (which is certainly true) nor necessarily presupposes preexistence. Thus he points to messenger and commissioning formulae which use this word, including, e.g., Jesus' use of it in his parable of the wicked tenants. But this is a case of "divide and conquer," which fails to take into account the cumulative effect of what is here said, and neglects altogether the significance of the parallel language of the Spirit in v. 6. It is certainly true that the concern for Paul is not in fact Jesus' origins; but the cumulative weight of the evidence and the way all of this is expressed certainly presupposes preexistence. See further, Fee, *Christology*, 212-20; cf. Walter Kasper, *Jesus the Christ* (New York: Paulist, 1976), 173.

preexistence, in the parallel sentence in v. 6 Paul uses the same verb to refer to the sending of the Spirit; and it would take a considerable amount of exegetical courage to argue that the Spirit was not pre-existent.

Second, Paul's emphasis with the (otherwise unnecessary) phrase "born of a woman," in passing though it seems to be, is on Christ's Incarnation, who thereby stands in stark contrast to the ahistorical, atemporal "elemental spiritual forces of the world" (v. 3) to which these former pagans had been subject. That is, if this clause makes certain that the main clause "God sent his Son at the right time in history" implies his preexistence, then in its own way it puts special emphasis on his genuine humanity[55] – that "the Son of God" was no docetic Christ, but shared fully in our humanity, preexistent Son of God though he was. At a given point in time, he was "born of a woman."

Third, the two middle members of the sentence ("born under Torah, in order to redeem those who are under Torah") reiterate the primary point of the whole argument. The Galatians must not be circumcised – because that means to "come under Torah," and Christ himself came "under Torah" so that no others would need to. Thus in the interest of his argument to this point – that Gentiles by the Spirit have become God's people through faith in Christ Jesus and are thus *not obligated to observe Torah* – Paul at the same time emphasizes that they nonetheless fit into God's ongoing story. In becoming God's children through Christ and the Spirit they are thereby also Abraham's children and thus heirs to the promise God made with Abraham. And here is the reason for emphasis on the Incarnation. It was precisely because Christ himself entered history within the context of Israel's story that he eliminated for historical Israel "the curse" of having to live by the law, which thus excludes living by faith (3:12-14). Thus the twofold focus of the two "was born" clauses: God's Son was both truly human and born within the context of Israel.

Fourth, with a striking turn of images in the final clause Paul draws all sorts of things together: "in order that we[56] might receive 'the

---

[55] So most interpreters; e.g., Betz (207-08): "This anthropological definition [born of a woman, born under the law] is given a christological purpose, indicating that Christ's appearance was that of a human being in the full sense of the term"; cf. Longenecker (171): "As a qualitative expression 'born of a woman' speaks of Jesus' true humanity and representative quality – i.e., that he was truly one with us."

[56] Note the similar shift from Israel under law ("those under law") to "we" – both Jews and Gentiles who believe – as in 3:13-14.

adoption as sons' (τὴν υἱοθεσίαν)." As pointed out in the TNIV footnote, this is a technical term, used especially in Roman culture, that refers to the full legal standing of an adopted male heir. In its most immediate context this word picks up the analogy of vv. 1-2 and refers to the time when the "son" enters "maturity." But far more is going on with this choice of words. Although the word itself does not appear in the Septuagint, it is clear from Rom 9:4 that Paul understands God's election of Israel in terms of their "adoption as a son."[57] Thus with this word Paul wraps up the argument from 3:6. The promised blessing of inheritance, which included Gentiles, has been effected by Christ, through the same act of redemption that also set people forever free from Torah observance. Thus Abraham's true "sons," including Gentiles who through Christ share in the promised blessing, are none other than *God's* "sons," having become so through the adoption that God's own Son effected for them. It is this relationship – "sonship" with God himself, thus taking up the "sonship" of Israel through Abraham's true seed – that is the point of everything for Paul's argument. Through Christ Gentiles are not simply freed from their own form of slavery to beings that are not gods; they are also thereby freed from that form of slavery to which Jews had been enslaved, under which the agitators would now bring them. Through Christ believers are not slaves; they are free children, "with all the rights and privileges that pertain thereto."

Verse 6. But just as in 3:13-14, and in keeping with how the argument began in 3:1-5, the assertion of their "adoption as 'sons'" does not bring the argument to conclusion. That is what Christ effected indeed; nothing can add to or take away from that. But for Paul – and for them, if they will but pay attention – the certain evidence of such adoption is the gift of the Spirit. To put that in another way, for Paul the work of Christ is a historical and objective reality. At one point in human history, when God's appointed time had arrived, Christ entered our human history (born of a woman) within the context of God's own people (born under law), so as to free people from Torah observance by giving them "adoption as 'sons'." But this historical and objective reality becomes realized (a "subjective reality" in this sense only) by the work of the Spirit. It is this twofold reality, both its historical objectivity and its experienced realization, that makes his present argument work, since it is their actualizing the "sonship" Christ provided through the experienced life

---

[57] Cf. Exod 4:22; Isa 1:2; Hos 11:2; Jer 31:9.

of the Spirit that serves for Paul as the certain evidence that he is right
and the agitators are wrong. Hence Paul has yet one more word.

The present sentence further certifies that the primary issue of this
letter is not "justification by faith," but Gentile inclusion as Abraham's
– and therefore God's – true children and thus rightful heirs of the
final inheritance. Paul now concludes the argument by bringing back
into focus the Galatians' – and his and others' – experience of the
Spirit (from 3:1-5), thus showing how that relates to what he has just
said about Christ. But here is a case where Paul simply cannot keep
himself out of the story, which accounts for some of the awkwardness
of the sentence. Thus it begins, "because *you* are 'sons'," but concludes
"in *our*[58] hearts."

More importantly, Paul makes several assertions and reveals several
presuppositions vital for our understanding the role of the Spirit in
Paul's understanding of the gospel. Two matters are crucial. First, Paul
deliberately ties together the work of the Son and the Spirit – in two
ways: (*a*) by means of the identical "sending formula." In a historically
particular moment for the Galatians themselves – and others – "God
sent forth [ἐξαπέστειλεν ὁ θεός] the Spirit of his Son" (v. 6), exactly
as previously "God sent forth [ἐξαπέστειλεν ὁ θεός] his Son" (v. 4) at
the right historical moment so as to redeem. This symmetry is unde-
niably deliberate, even though the locus of the sending is considerably
different.[59] (*b*) by use of the (rare) designation, "the Spirit of his Son" –
the same Son whom he had sent to redeem. This precise language in
fact occurs nowhere else in Paul, although it is quite in keeping with
that of Rom 8:9 ("the Spirit of Christ") and Phil 1:19 ("the Spirit of
Jesus Christ"). These three passages, besides saying something rather
significant in terms of Christology (it is no small thing that the Spirit of
God can so easily also be called the Spirit of Christ), also say something
rather significant about the Spirit: that the indwelling Spirit, whom
believers know as an experienced reality, is the way both the Father
and the Son are currently present in the believer's life.

[58] There is textual variation here, between "our" (ἡμῶν) and "your" (ὑμῶν); indeed,
the latter eventually became the majority text and thus made its way into the KJV. But
all the rules of textual criticism favor "our" in this case: it has by far the better
evidence; and it is almost impossible to imagine a scribe changing a perfectly
meaningful "your" into the very awkward "our," while the reverse is especially easy to
account for.

[59] Within the context of human history and among the Jews, in the case of Jesus;
within the hearts of believers, in the case of the Spirit.

Second, what lies behind this designation is in fact the point of everything in terms of holding the present argument together. In one sense, Paul could have made his overall point had he simply said, "God sent forth his Spirit." But Paul's present interest is not simply in the Spirit as such, a concern given plenty of airing in 3:1-14. His interest now is to make sure that the Galatians understand *who* the Spirit is: none other than the Spirit of Christ – the same Christ who "loved [them] and gave himself for [them]," who now by his Spirit indwells them. But his point goes further yet. For the Spirit is not called "the Spirit of Christ" in that direct way, but "the Spirit of [God's] Son." This is the linchpin. The same Son whose death effected redemption and secured "sonship" for them (v. 5), now indwells them by his Spirit, "the Spirit of the Son," whom God sent forth as he had the Son himself. The ultimate evidence of this "sonship" is their use of the Son's own address to the Father in prayer: *Abba.* With this sentence and this word the "sonship" motif that goes back as far as 3:7 is brought to its ringing climax.

Thus in sum: Paul's concern right along has had to do with Gentile believers as true "sons" of Abraham. That was made possible because of the redemptive work of Abraham's one "seed," Christ, who thereby made it possible for all who trust in him to share in his inheritance as fellow "sons." But quite beyond that, such "sons of Abraham" are in fact "sons of God," made so through Christ (v. 5). The certain evidence of such shared "sonship" is the presence of the Spirit of the Son, who by crying out "*Abba*" from within the believer bears witness to the presence of the Son who made us "sons," since this is the Son's own distinctive term of address to God his Father.[60] Thus: "Because you have received 'sonship' through Christ's redemption, God's own confirmation of that for you experientially stems from God's also having sent forth the Spirit of his Son himself into your hearts, evidenced by the fact that the Spirit of the Son cries out to God in the Son's own word of intimacy, '*Abba*,' which means, 'Father'."

That these are Paul's present concerns seem to be made certain by a comparison with the companion passage from Romans 8. Four matters are of moment: (*a*) Even though the language "adoption as sons" recurs in Rom 8:15, when the application is picked up in vv. 16-17 Paul shifts from the term "sons" (υἱοί) to the broader term "children" (τέκνα); thus the word play on "son (υἱός) is unique to Galatians; (*b*)

---

[60] As Mark's Gospel makes clear (see Mark 14:36), written to a Greek audience, but keeping Jesus' own Aramaic word intact, while also translating it into Greek.

rather than "the Spirit of *his Son*," in Rom 8:14-15 the Spirit is simply "the Spirit *of God*," who is also "the Spirit of 'sonship'" (= the Spirit who effects 'sonship'); (*c*) rather than the Spirit himself crying out "*Abba*," in Rom 8:15 "we cry out by means of the Spirit" (which obviously for Paul means the same thing, but the present passage ties the cry more directly to the Spirit of the Son); and (*d*) although "becoming heirs" is the net result in both passages, in the present passage the connection of being a "son" with being "an heir" is the main thrust, as v. 7 makes clear, whereas in Rom 8:17 the main thrust has become eschatological and focuses on our shared "heirship" with Christ himself.

It should be noted further that this interest in tying together as closely as possible the historic work of Christ with the Galatians' experience of the Spirit is almost certainly the cause of the somewhat awkward, and for us unusual, way by which these two sentences are joined: "Because you are 'sons'." At first blush, that looks as though Paul considered the experience of the Spirit (v. 6) as subsequent to conversion (v. 5) and the one (conversion) as the cause of the other (the coming of the Spirit).[61] But that is to read this passage in terms of individual conversion experience, whereas Paul is concerned altogether with "the history of salvation" as that was effected first by the work of Christ and then made effective by the coming of the Spirit. Individual conversion history is simply not in view here nor throughout the passage – even though the experienced reality of the Spirit is still the primary reality of any single person's conversion.

Such an understanding is thus the way forward through our sense of awkwardness in Paul's sentence, in which the entry clause implies that the coming of the Spirit is the *result* of the prior work of Christ, whereas the content of the sentence itself indicates that the Spirit is the *evidence* of "sonship." Both are true, in the sense outlined above: the Spirit's indwelling gives evidence to the "sonship" that Christ's redemption has brought about. In that sense, Christ is the "cause" and the Spirit the "effect" as far as "sonship" is concerned.[62] To make more of this text than that tends to miss Paul by too much.

---

[61] This is indeed the position taken by very diverse writers; but in every case vested interests appear to precede a concern for discovering Paul's own interests in this passage.

[62] One should perhaps also point out, therefore, that the discussion on the tenses of the verbs "you are" and "God sent," as though that says something significant about the "chronology" of conversion, is almost totally irrelevant. Paul's usage is dictated by the realities he is trying to affirm, not their order of occurrence.

But a bit more needs to be said about the "*Abba*-cry" itself. First, the use of the verb "cry,"[63] with the Spirit as the subject, has led some scholars to see the *Abba*-cry as a form of "ecstasy." Although "ecstasy" itself is one of those elastic terms that tends to mean whatever the user wants it to mean in a given moment, usually it refers to an experience in which "there is no involvement of the 'ego,' except as an 'onlooker'."[64] Our problems may be semantic, but since the language of "ecstasy" so often carries such a connotation of the "Spirit's takeover," as it were, a less loaded term such as "Spirit-inspired prayer" is much to be preferred. Such "crying out" by the Spirit would scarcely presuppose wild and uncontrolled utterance, given Paul's argument for "order" in 1 Cor 14:26-33 as reflecting God's own "shalom." Nonetheless, we need to take seriously that believers "cried out" to God within the assembly, and did so with full awareness that the Spirit was moving them so to do, and that they were thus using Jesus' own word of intimate relationship with the Father.[65]

Second, as to the language "*Abba*" itself, a considerable amount of literature has grown up around this word. The landmark study in this regard was that of Joachim Jeremias,[66] who among other things concluded (*a*) that this was the address of intimacy, originating with small children, in an Aramaic home, (*b*) that Jesus' use of this term to address God was unique to him in all of known Jewish literature, (*c*) that the prayer thus revealed the uniqueness of his own self-understanding as Son of the Father, and (*d*) that he invited his disciples to use this term as his own extension of grace to them. As with all such "landmarks" in New Testament scholarship, some correctives and advances are eventually made. But when the dust has finally settled, and even if one were to assume an extreme minimalist position,[67] much of this still remains. Indeed, it is this usage in Paul as much as

---

[63] Gk. χράζον, a word that implies loud speech, but not necessarily inarticulate or ecstatic speech. See W. Grundmann, TDNT 3.898–903.

[64] This is the definition found in D.J. Lull, *The Spirit in Galatia: Paul's Interpretation of Pneuma as Divine Power* (Chico: Scholars Press, 1980).

[65] The best analogy in the Pauline corpus is probably to be found in the confession "Jesus is Lord" in 1 Cor 12:3, which no one can make except by the Spirit. In both cases, it is not ecstasy that is in view, but the presence of the Spirit, to whom such basic prayer and confession is ultimately attributable – as certain evidence that one is truly Christ's.

[66] As ch. 1 in *The Prayers of Jesus* (SBT 2/6; London: SCM, 1967), 11-65.

[67] As in James Barr, "'Abba' isn't 'Daddy'," *Journal of Theological Studies*, 39 (1988), 28-47.

anything that tends to verify the basic soundness of Jeremias's conclusions.

For our purposes, several matters are of significance:

1. This usage by Paul both here and in Romans – a church that Paul has never visited! – presupposes the widespread usage of this prayer language in the Gentile churches.[68] Furthermore, these two passages together and the argument of this one in particular serve as primary evidence for its significance both in the life of Jesus and the early church. Such widespread, presuppositional usage of this prayer language – in its Aramaic original – is most easily accounted for historically on the grounds that this was Jesus' own term and that he in fact invited his disciples to use his language after him. Indeed, in the case of the present argument, everything hinges on the fact that believers now, by the Spirit of the Son, are using the language of the Son. To deny the origin of such usage to Jesus himself, and through him to the early church, is to push historical skepticism to its outer limits.

2. The jury still seems to be out on the precise meaning, and therefore significance, of the term *Abba* itself. Most likely the word was in fact an expression of intimacy, used by children first as infants and later as adults, reflecting what is true in many such cultures where the terms of endearment for one's parents are used lifelong – which is generally not true in English-speaking homes. The fact that it was used by adult children as well as small children is surely irrelevant. What is relevant is that it was most likely the language of intimacy and endearment. If "Daddy" is not a very good equivalent – and it almost certainly is not – the basic thrust of the term, and the significance of Jesus' use of it in addressing God, still carries considerable theological weight. If the term cannot be demonstrated to be unique to Jesus, it can surely be argued to be distinctively his form of address; and for Jesus it is best understood as a term denoting his own sense of unique Sonship – by his addressing God consistently in the language of the home. That he should invite his disciples to use his word after him was almost certainly an expression of grace on his part.

3. Both the meaning of the term itself, and the fact that such a cry comes from the heart, suggest that for Paul a form of intimacy with God is involved. Here is the ultimate evidence that we are God's own children, in that we address God with the same term of intimate

---

[68] This is evidenced all the more by Paul's switch to "our hearts" in this clause, which implies that for Paul this is the common experience of believers in all of his churches.

relationship Jesus himself used. We are not slaves, but children. The Spirit has taken us far beyond mere conformity to religious obligations. God himself, in the person of his Spirit, has come to indwell us; and he has sealed that relationship by giving to us the language of his Son, the language of personal relationship. For Paul – and for us – this is the ultimate expression of grace. No wonder Paul was such an enemy of Torah observance, because it invariably breaks this relationship of child to parent in favor of one that can only be expressed in terms of slavery – performance on the basis of duty and obligation, in which one "slaves" for God, rather than being recreated in God's own likeness (cf. 4:20), resulting in loving servanthood toward all others (5:13). Christ has effected such a relationship; the Spirit makes it work. All attempts to destroy it by Torah observance should be cursed, as though one were related to God on the basis of religious obligation!

Verse 7. With the "so then" (ὥστε) that begins this sentence, Paul in effect brings closure to three matters at once: most obviously, (*a*) the present paragraph itself; but also (*b*) the argument from the experience of the Spirit with which the present passage began in 3:1-5; and finally (*c*) the argument from Scripture that began in 3:7 and has been sustained in some form throughout – although not as visibly so in this final conclusion. Thus, "you are no longer slaves, but God's children; and since you are his children, he has made you also heirs." The key words in the sentence are "son," "slave," and "heir,"[69] Through the work of Christ and the Spirit the Galatian believers are no longer "slaves": first of all to "the elemental spiritual forces of the world," but also now especially to the need to keep Torah. Second, that slavery has ended because through Christ and the Spirit they have become God's own children ("sons"). And that means, third, that they are not just Abraham's "heir," but heirs of God himself through his Son, Christ Jesus.

However, we should note the final prepositional phrase in the passage is not "through Christ," but the totally surprising, "through God," which brings the whole passage full circle to its theocentric starting point.[70] As significant as Paul's statements about Christ and the

---

[69] Interestingly, Paul puts this conclusion all in the second person singular; thus he has moved from the first person plural (vv. 3-5) to the second plural (v. 6a), back to the first plural (v. 6b), and now to the second singular.

[70] The Greek text reads εἰ δὲ υἱός, καὶ κληρονόμος διὰ θεοῦ ("if a son, also an heir through God"), which is almost certainly the original text. Because of what was perceived to be a latent theological difficulty, a whole variety of modifications were made, with the later majority text finally reading, "heirs of God through Christ." The

Spirit are for Christology and pneumatology, Paul will frequently bring us back to his basic monotheistic roots – that all of this, the work of the Son and the Spirit which effect and make effective our salvation, are ultimately attributed to God the Father. In this case, therefore, the whole passage is enclosed by the phrases "God sent forth" and "through God." What needs to be noted further about the concluding expression of this framing device is that God is now seen as the "agent," language that is usually reserved for Christ. Thus the "interchange" in this case goes the other direction; what the Son ordinarily does, the Father also does. So with this phrase the long argument from 3:1 comes to its proper conclusion. What remains is for Paul to apply it directly to their situation, which is what 4:8-11 is all about.

Galatians 4:8-11 – The Application: Do not Return to Slavery

> [8]*Formerly, when you did not know God, you were slaves to those who by nature are not gods.* [9]*But now that you know God – or rather are known by God – how is it that you are turning back to those weak and miserable forces*[d]*? Do you wish to be enslaved by them all over again?* [10]*You are observing special days and months and seasons and years!* [11]*I fear for you, that somehow I have wasted my efforts on you.*

[b]9 Or *principles*

In the preceding paragraph Paul brought to conclusion the basic biblical argument that began in 3:1; in the present paragraph he applies this argument to the Galatians' situation in a very direct way. In that sense, therefore, and especially in light of the strong "but" with which the sentence begins,[71] this paragraph brings the argument full circle, and thus to its proper conclusion. Up to this point, beginning with 3:26 ("for *you* are *all* children of God"), carrying through v. 29 ("if *you* are Christ's, then *you* are Abraham's seed"), and picked up in 4:6-7 ("because *you* are children"), Paul has already applied the biblical argument itself to the Galatians *as Gentiles*, in terms of their relationship to God's covenant with Abraham. But now he applies all of this in a directly personal way to their present situation vis-à-vis the agitators and himself.

TNIV has rightly put this into more straightforward English, "he [God] has made you also heirs."

[71] Gk. ἀλλά, left out in most contemporary English translations (the REB a notable exception), since the adversative sense is inherent in the clause itself.

One should thus note that none of the special language from the preceding argument is found here (faith, works, righteousness, Christ, Spirit, Torah, Abraham, sonship), although "Torah" is obviously implied in vv. 9-10. Rather, this application is all about the Galatians themselves – they are, after all, the subject of all seven verbs in vv. 8-10 – while at the end (v. 9) Paul returns once more to his relationship with them ("*I* fear for *you*, lest *I* have labored in vain for *you*"). As with preceding moments when the Galatians themselves and their relationship with Paul and the agitators are in view, the passage is full of emotional language. Paul can hardly believe what is happening in Galatia. The new matter here is that the observance of Torah in this case is not the issue of "circumcision," which apparently has not yet happened (see on 5:2-3 below), but the observance of the Jewish calendar, which has in fact already begun. Paul is rightly perplexed.

Verse 8. With the combination of the strong "but" and the adverb "formerly" Paul sets out to apply the preceding argument to the Galatians' present situation, by contrasting their former way of life (v. 8) with what has come to them in Christ (in v. 9). The contrast itself takes a very Jewish turn, while at the same time returning to the theme of bondage to the powers which he used of himself and fellow Jews in v. 3 above. At the same time the sentence proceeds directly out of what was said in vv. 6 and 7, now by way of contrast. The issue is now put in terms of "knowing God," whom these former pagans by the very nature of things could not have known. Such knowledge comes by revelation alone, a revelation that has taken place in Israel's special history, especially to Moses on Mount Sinai. Even though the law given to Moses has now been superseded by Christ and the Spirit, what remains within the context of Jewish faith is the revealed "knowledge of God."

By way of contrast, these former pagans not only did not know God, but were themselves "enslaved" to "those who by nature are not gods." This is a typical Jewish condemnation of idolatry in any and every form. And while some translations suggest that these slave masters are "beings" of some kind (NRSV, NET), it is doubtful whether Paul himself thought of them as such,[72] since he goes on in v. 9 to refer to them as "those weak and miserable 'forces'" to whom he has already referred in v. 3, with regard to the law. The important connection between what is said here and what has preceded, of

---

[72] Although see 1 Cor 8:4-7; on the one hand, he adamantly denies their existence, but then, on the other hand, allows that such "gods" and "lords" exist as demonic powers (10:19-22).

course, lies with the language of "enslavement," which immediately picks up the "you are no longer slaves" in v. 7. What Paul is about to do, therefore, is to tie their readiness to submit to the "bondage" of Torah-observance with their former bondage to "the powers" – a bold stroke indeed for a Jew well-trained in the law.

Verse 9. This sentence stands in purposeful contrast to v. 8 in two ways: first, by the "but" (δέ; lit. "on the other hand"), which in Paul's Greek sentence stands as the follow-up to the "on the one hand" (μέν) that preceded in v. 8 – although English translations will not use such stilted language where the contrast is so obvious without it; and second, by asserting that these particular Gentiles have indeed now come to "know God." But since putting it that way also puts the emphasis at the wrong place, Paul immediately – and typically[73] – qualifies himself: "or rather are known by God." In a letter in which everything that Paul has to say to his friends is predicated on grace, he will not allow even the truth that these former pagans who did not know God have now come to know God through Christ and the Spirit to become for them a form of "works." And in this case it is not so much that they would have done so, but that by this little interruption he can make sure they keep their focus on God and not on themselves.

But the surprising element is the way the sentence ends. Where one might well have expected it to end on a note that balances with v. 8 (i.e., "now that you know God you have been set free from your former slavery to those who by nature are not gods"), Paul instead resorts to a rhetorical question: "how is it that you are turning back to those weak and miserable forces?" Although this tends to catch one by surprise, in fact it takes one back to v. 3, where Paul has identified his (and others') prior life as a Jew living under the law with these same "elemental spiritual forces of the world." While it is not difficult to imagine what a fellow-Jew might have thought of this cross-pollination of "bondages," Paul is in fact not writing for fellow-Jews but for his former pagan converts, who need to recognize the similarity between "bondages." After all, his whole point is that for them now to revert to "law-keeping" is to put themselves under a bondage *equal to* that of their former way of life as pagans.

This is rhetoric, it should be noted, not careful and precise logical reasoning. So intense is the rhetoric that Paul falls into a moment of

---

[73] See how he does a similar thing in 1 Cor 5:7: "Cleanse out the old leaven so that you might become an unleavened loaf – as you really are (through Christ)."

redundancy, that merely highlights the agitation: "how is it that *you are returning again*," he begins, and then ends with their "wishing to be enslaved *all over again*." At issue for Paul is enslavement; they formerly knew one kind, and are now willingly submitting to another. While it may be difficult to imagine a more "unJewish" sentiment than this, it has similar moments when Paul asserts that "neither circumcision nor uncircumcision is anything" (5:6; cf. 1 Cor 7:19), or when elsewhere he calls such Judaizers who insist on Gentile circumcision "dogs" and "mutilators of the flesh" (Phil 3:2-3). Indeed, all those in every age who insist on some form of law-keeping for God's people need to hear the rhetoric, since they will continually try to justify through their own reasoning an insistence on law-keeping for themselves and others.

Verse 10. Paul turns now from his rhetorical interrogative to an indicative that is equally full of rhetoric. "How is it that you can return to slavery?" he has asked. Now, full of disgust, he reminds them of the slavery to which they have already turned, namely, the observance of the Jewish calendar ("you are observing special days and months and seasons and years"). While the language itself is not precise, as one finds for example in Col 2:16 ("feasts" [ἑορτῆς], "new moons" [νεομηνίας], and "sabbaths" [σαββάτων]),[74] there can be little question that this is his own language for the weekly, monthly, and annual feasts that gave rhythm to the Jewish way of life. The ambiguity itself is probably part of the rhetoric, since the word "days" that appears first in Paul's sentence almost certainly refers to the one item to which they have already capitulated, namely keeping minimal regulations for the Jewish sabbath.[75] The TNIV has rightly caught the rhetoric by concluding the sentence with an exclamation point.

Verse 11. With this sentence Paul brings the whole issue back to them and him, and his former ministry among them, the same note on which the argument began in 3:1. Here he expresses it first in terms of "fearing for you," which, as often in Paul, expresses a degree of anxiety at the personal level. The fact that they have already capitulated on the matter of "days" gives him good reason for concern, as to whether they will have taken the ultimate – and incredibly

---

[74] These three words are found esp. in Exodus and Numbers; see, inter alia, Exod 34:18-25; Num 28:11-15.

[75] One should note that at issue is not sabbath as *gift* (the OT view), but sabbath as though it were given for God's sake and not ours – and thus it had to be regulated to get it right!

painful – step of succumbing to circumcision. His letter was written precisely to stop them from such an act.

But that is on the Galatians' side. From Paul's own perspective at issue is "whether I have labored among you in vain." Picking up language he has already used regarding the Corinthians' own faith (1 Cor 15:1-2), and especially at the beginning of the present argument in 3:4, he is hoping still that it is not true regarding the Galatians. In so doing Paul echoes language that appears first in the mouth of Isaiah's Servant of the Lord (49:4), which is then transferred to Yahweh's "chosen ones" in 65:23. And while the TNIV's idiomatic, "I have wasted my efforts on you," gets at the point Paul is making, it nonetheless fails to capture the echo from Isaiah that Paul is almost certainly intending, that if they capitulate to circumcision he will indeed "have labored in vain" among them – because they will have severed themselves from Christ (5:4). Here is the certain evidence that one cannot add a plus factor to grace and still be under grace (see on 2:19 above). Rather, one thereby chooses to be related to God on the basis of obedience to some form of law – and that eliminates grace altogether, not to mention any relationship with God!

Thus this application is basically an appeal for them not to return to slavery (v. 9). With that in hand he will now make a flat-out personal appeal that they return instead to their earthly brother (v. 12) and parent (v. 20). In each case, one can scarcely miss both the pathos and the chagrin. What perplexes Paul the most is not simply that such a thing has happened, but how was it possible for it to have happened at all – a perplexity that becomes especially evident in what follows.

Galatians 4:12-20 – The Appeal: Return to Your Earthly Brother/Parent

> [12]*I plead with you, brothers and sisters, become like me, for I became like you. You have done me no wrong.* [13]*As you know, it was because of an illness that I first preached the gospel to you.* [14]*Even though my illness was a trial to you, you did not treat me with contempt or scorn. Instead, you welcomed me as if I were an angel of God, as if I were Christ Jesus himself.* [15]*What has happened to all your joy? I can testify that, if you could have done so, you would have torn out your eyes and given them to me.* [16]*Have I now become your enemy by telling you the truth?* [17]*Those people are zealous to win you over, but for no good. What they want is to alienate you from us, so that you may have zeal for them.* [18]*It is fine to be zealous, provided the purpose is good, and to be so always, not just when I am with you.* [19]*My dear children, for whom I am again in the pains of childbirth until Christ is formed in*

you, ²⁰how I wish I could be with you now and change my tone, because I am perplexed about you!

Although Paul's argument with the Galatians is not yet finished (he will return to one further argument from Scripture [4:21-31] and then show how the Spirit has replaced the law [5:13–6:10]), the final, personal words of the preceding paragraph cause him to launch into a considerable personal appeal to the Galatians – based on their former relationship. In effect he says: If the argument itself is not enough, remember how things really were between us, when I was there among you; whereas the agitators, by way of contrast, have only the basest of motives in trying to curry your favor. Thus the overall argument of this paragraph is generally easy to trace – at least the point of it is – but as is often the case in such very personal material, where the highest level of understanding between a writer and his readers exists, there are several details that are not at all easy. Here is a clear case where we are on one end of a highly personal conversation, and can only guess at what is being said on the other end.

Here also is the proper place to note how often this kind of personal appeal happens in this letter:

1:10	Am I now trying to persuade people?
1:11	I remind you, brothers and sisters, about the gospel I preach
1:13	For you know about my former way of life in Judaism
1:13–2:14	The long *apologia* regarding his (basically non-)relationship with Jerusalem
3:1	Who has bewitched you, before whose eyes Christ was portrayed as crucified?
4:12-20	A recital of his time with them in Galatia
5:2-12	The application of 4:21-31 is full of personal appeals
6:11-16	The letter ends with more of the same

It seems clear from all of this that the apostle is especially sensitive about three related matters: (*a*) the fact that the Galatian Gentiles are *his* converts; (*b*) that they are being wooed by people who are clearly *his opponents*; and (*c*) that the Galatians are in process of abandoning *him* for *them*. Under anyone's view of life, that obviously smarts; and Paul's sensitivity to it comes through nowhere more clearly than here. Nonetheless, even here he reminds them that they had received him as "Christ Jesus" himself (v. 14), and at the end he appeals to their being "formed by Christ." But in fact the very paucity of such appeals, in comparison with the appeal to his and their former relationship, probably tells us much about the personal struggle Paul himself is going through on their behalf. Here is a Paul we are simply not used to; nonetheless here also is evidence that the great apostle to the Gentiles was a man with very deep personal feelings toward those he had come to know and love.

Despite the intensity and personal nature of this appeal, one can easily see how it proceeds. Paul begins (v. 12a) with a general appeal for them to "become as I am" with regard to Torah observance. That launches him into recalling for them how they had accepted him when he was with them (vv. 12b-14), which was far better than one might have humanly expected, given the nature of his bodily weakness. This in turn leads to a pair of rhetorical questions, asking what has happened in the meantime to their former attitude toward him (vv. 15-16). Then after a vigorous denunciation of his opponents in terms of their motive – to alienate the Galatians from Paul (vv. 17-18) – he concludes by assuming the role of a mother, while admitting his utter perplexity at what they are currently doing (vv. 19-20).

Verse 12a. The intensity of Paul's feelings emerges in this first brief sentence. The word order itself tells us much: "Become as I am; because I also [am/became][76] as you are, brothers and sisters, I beg you." Thus, up first in the sentence is the appeal itself, not his own verb of appeal ("I beg you"), which stands in last place. And in Paul's own dictated sentences (without spacing or punctuation breaks), the opening imperative "become" immediately follows the final preposi-tional phrase, "for you," in the preceding sentence.

The appeal itself is almost certainly related to the whole of the preceding argument (3:1–4:7), especially with its frequent interchange between "we" and "you," meaning "we Jews" and "you Gentiles." Thus "become as I am" means "become as one who through Christ has been redeemed from the bondage of Torah"; that is, given that the apostle who led you to Christ has himself abandoned "keeping Torah," you should follow his example on this matter. The reason for their doing so is that "I am as you are"; meaning that in following Christ I abandoned life under Torah, thus putting myself on the same level as you Gentiles with regard to the law.

Verses 12b-14. Paul's next appeal begins with a brief sentence (v. 12b) that sets the tone for the whole. This is followed by a very long

---

[76] The absence of the verb in this second clause leaves us with some guess work. Did Paul intend his readers to pick up the verb from the first clause, as most English translations, or did he intend "as I am" (cf. GNB). One might also note that the close relationship between vv. 11 and 12 has caused at least two English translations (GNB, NET) to see v. 12 as the conclusion to the preceding paragraph.

sentence (vv. 13-14) reminding them that, despite an illness whose loathsome nature had all the possibilities of putting them off, they in fact treated him far better than one might normally have expected under such circumstances. That much is easy enough; it is some of the details that leave us guessing. Thus he begins, "you did me no wrong." There has in fact been a strong tendency among English translators to turn Paul's aorist (simple past tense) into a perfect ("you have done me no wrong");[77] however; this is not about something more recent, but a reminder of how the Galatians treated him when he was among them. After all, this is the lead sentence to the explanation that follows in vv. 13-14, regarding how they were toward him when he was there.

Thus he begins by reminding them of the physical ailment that caused him to come to them in the first place. And Paul's sentence can hardly mean anything else. That is, his understanding of his mission to Galatia was not that it had been planned by him – or even directed by the Holy Spirit. Rather he came and preached the gospel to them precisely "because of a weakness of the flesh," meaning a physical illness. And because he is simply recalling what they both knew, there is no elaboration as to details. Since in v. 15 he speaks of their readiness "to tear out your eyes and give them to me," it seems altogether likely that he was suffering from some kind of eye malady. But beyond that, we know nothing, nor is there any real value in speculating. The only other question might be whether, or how, this is related to his "thorn in the flesh" mentioned earlier in 2 Cor 12:7; and while I personally tend to think it is so related, good sense causes one to recognize that this is guesswork, and therefore nothing bordering on certainty.

Both the severe nature of Paul's malady, and its obvious and repulsive appearance, can be rightly deduced from the way Paul describes their (non-)reaction to it at the beginning of v. 14. Indeed, the word order and the awkward way he put it ("your trial in my flesh you did not scorn or despise") are certain evidence that the malady was both visible and, from Paul's own perspective, loathsome. What he is therefore reminding them is not how ill he had been among them, but that their own reaction to him far exceeded what might have been common expectation. Thus, from Paul's own perspective (from previous experience?) his illness should have put people off. What happened rather was that "you received me," he tells them from

---

[77] See among others: RSV, NRSV, NASB, NIV, TNIV, NET, GNB, NJB. Not so: NAB, ESV; cf. NLT ("You did not mistreat me when I first preached to you"), which is precisely what Paul intended.

his perspective, "as the angel of God, as Christ Jesus." And with this analogy Paul has opened up what for us is a very difficult exegetical moment indeed.

Two matters need discussion: (*a*) whether the first phrase is generic and means "*an* angel *from* God," or whether it is specific, wherein Paul is picking up a common septuagintal phrase and intends "*the* angel *of* God"[78]; and (*b*) what is the relationship between the two "as"-phrases, whether they are appositional (the second clarifying the first) or progressive and ascensive (one phrase leading to the next that is higher). It should be noted also that the second issue exists only if one decides that the phrase is specific. If it is generic, then it automatically means the two phrases are progressive (and ascensive).

On the first matter, despite the fact that English translations have been loathe to go this way, the evidence seems strongly to favor Paul's having picked up a common phrase from the Septuagint. Several things favor this choice. First, this is quite in keeping with Paul's regular habits. He simply eats and breathes the language of the Greek Bible, so that it emerges in ever so many ways and in all kinds of contexts. Here the Septuagint evidence is both striking and a bit confusing. In the first place, one called "*the* angel of the LORD (or God)" regularly serves as the divine messenger in several Old Testament narratives; and in some of these narratives the "angel" turns out to be the Lord himself. This is especially true of the crucial narratives in Genesis 18 and Exodus 3-4, plus the Gideon narrative in Judges 6. In each case the first occurrence is anarthrous (without the definite article) as here, although it is certainly intended to be understood in an articular way.[79] That is, this "angel" is not "an angel," but is "*the* angel of the Lord." Paul's anarthrous use in this instance seems to point in the same direction, since "an angel of God" has no certain Septuagint background. Given the likelihood of its Old Testament roots, scholarly distaste for what seems to be the natural sense of the phrase is difficult to fathom, especially since Paul next speaks even more boldly, that they accepted him as Christ Jesus himself. Thus it seems altogether likely that Paul is here reaching high as he

[78] For advocacy of the latter, see Wallace, *Grammar*, 252 n. 97, following N. Turner, *Syntax*, 180. For further discussion see also W.G. MacDonald, "Christology and 'The Angel of the Lord'," in *Current Issues in Biblical and Patristic Studies* (Grand Rapids: Eerdmans, 1975), 324-35; D. Hannah, *Michael and Christ: Michael Traditions and Angel Christology in Early Christianity* (WUNT 2/109; J.C.B. Mohr, 1999), 19-20.

[79] In the Genesis and Judges narrative, the subsequent occurrence have the article as an anaphora (= *the* angel referred to at the beginning).

acknowledges the level of acceptance that he received from them. "You received me as the angel of God."

But whether Paul's next phrase, "as Christ Jesus," is intended to stand in apposition to, and thus to identify, the angel of God is a different matter. That is, Christ may very well assume the role of the Old Testament "angel of the Lord/God," but in light of the rest of the Pauline corpus, it seems unlikely that Paul is intending an absolute identification. In any case, what is of interest here is the ease with which Paul can bring Christ into the picture as a divine presence in Galatia, as the ultimate kudo he can offer them as the way they received him in his visible weaknesses. Thus we seem in fact to be dealing with progression here rather than identification, which would mean that Christ is a full rung higher than the angelic theophanies of the Old Testament.

Verses 15-16. This former acceptance of him leads to two rhetorical questions, which surround yet another reminder of how much they accepted him on that first mission. Thus, in light of their former attitude toward Paul, he turns to direct appeal: "Where then is your blessing?" Or at least that is what he appears to say. But this brief question has had a long history of being tampered with, so that in the late majority text it reads, "What then was your blessedness?" The difficulty lies with the word "blessing" (μακαρισμός), which the TNIV and others have rendered as "joy," taking it as the Galatians' own experience of blessedness when Paul was with them. But it seems far more likely in context that Paul is reminding them of the blessing they experienced in "blessing" Paul the way they did, receiving him and accepting him despite his physical condition. Otherwise the question sits like a rock in the middle of his recalling their former attitude toward him. This, then, as the context makes certain, has not to do with their own experience of "joy," but with their acceptance of Paul.

This is confirmed by a momentary return to the narrative of their acceptance of him, this time reminding them specifically how they would like to have "blessed" him when he was there. And a remarkable bit of testimony it is indeed. Had such a thing been humanly possible, he reminds them, some of you would have torn out your own eyes and given them to me. His point is that their empathy with Paul in his physical weakness was total, their readiness to bless him complete. This, of course is also the sentence that makes it quite clear that his malady was some kind of eye problem, which the context implies was not only a burden to him but also to those who had to look at him. But the Galatians were not repelled by it; rather they would gladly have exchanged eyes with him.

With yet one more rhetorical question Paul asks in effect, "what has gone wrong?" How is it that after all your acceptance and affection you have now turned your back so totally on me as your apostle, as the one whose ministry among you led you to Christ? Indeed, he puts it starkly, "Have I now become your enemy by telling you the truth?" That is, am I presently to be seen as your enemy because I told you the truth when I originally preached Christ to you? This question now moves him out of a recital of their past relationship into the present scene. At issue for him at the personal level is how this could possibly have happened, this present readiness of theirs to reject him and his gospel in favor of these outsiders who care nothing for them at all, but only for their own gaining trophies of foreskins among Paul's Gentile converts.[80]

Verses 17-18. These two (Greek) sentences make it clear that this whole appeal is to be understood in light of what Paul's opponents are doing. In fact, they are specifically mentioned only in v. 17 in this entire passage; but it is their "zeal" to make law-keeping converts of Paul's converts that has driven the entire passage. Thus these two sentences are driven by the verb "zeal" (ζηλόω), a word that has just enough elasticity to allow Paul to confront his opponents directly by a bit of a word play. The verb itself can have either positive value or negative, depending on context; when it moves in a totally negative direction, it comes very close to the sense of "jealousy."

So Paul begins by condemning his opponents' "zeal" for the Galatians, which here does not mean to have a deep concern for them as people, but exists (from Paul's perspective) for the sole purpose of "excluding you," which is just ambiguous enough to cause one to use caution here. Does Paul mean that their zeal for the Galatians has as its ultimate aim "shutting you out from the freedom that is yours in Christ," or "excluding you from the promises made to Abraham that include you, apart from circumcision," or as the TNIV has (perhaps rightly) rendered it, "to alienate you from us." The follow-on purpose clause ("so that you may have zeal for them") would seem to point to the latter as Paul's basic intent. This is the kind of exclusive "zeal" that borders on "jealousy." Such "zeal" is "for no good" precisely because

---

[80] While this may seem a bit harsh, it is in fact exactly what Paul finally accuses them of in 6:12-13.

it does not have the Galatians' interests at heart but only his opponents' own.

But Paul is well aware that "zeal" in itself is not a negative value, so he elaborates, in part so as not totally to condemn the Galatians themselves, and in part to redirect a proper "zeal" back toward himself. Using the passive form of the verb, he asserts that "it is a good thing to be zealously sought after," but then adds the proviso, "in a good way" (lit. "with good"; ἐν καλῷ). His point is that "zeal" with regard to others is not in fact a bad thing; after all, this is what he is obviously currently exhibiting toward them. But it all has to do with motive, whether it is for the Galatians' sakes ("provided the purpose is good"), or for his opponents' own sakes, which Paul feels is obviously the case with regard to the agitators. From his point of view they care nothing for you Galatians as people, and will not think of you again once they are gone. They are only interested in "trophies."

Thus Paul concludes his sentence by bringing the two parts of this narrative together: their former "zeal" for him in light of the misguided "zeal" for them on the part of the agitators. The kind of "zeal" the Galatians had for Paul when he was with them is what he wants rekindled in their hearts; thus "zeal for what is good" is always appropriate, and not just (as in the past) when "I was present with you." In doing so, Paul is not trying just to be clever; rather he is bringing the focus back to where it belongs – on the Galatians and their own proper zeal for the gospel, which has currently gone astray under the influence of Paul's opponents. And this in turn leads to the final, concluding appeal.

Verses 19-20. With a second vocative in this brief narrative Paul turns at the end to appeal directly to them. The narrative began with a plea to his "brothers and sisters"; it now concludes on the more tender parental note, "my dear children." Indeed, the passion is so intense that instead of following it up with a sentence on its own, what follows is grammatically simply part of the vocative. But at the end it is equally clear that the long vocative has itself become the sentence. With a considerable mixing of metaphors, he sees himself in this letter as taking on the role of a mother giving birth. His agony over them is like the "birth pangs" of such a mother (which, of course, he can only know by observation or by having been told). But the goal of his "birth pangs" is where the metaphor gets mixed. His "giving birth" will be realized only when "Christ is formed in you," which should take them back to the argument of 3:26–4:7. But even if the metaphor gets a bit of a workout, Paul's point is clear. He is presently in great agony over those for whose "birth" in Christ he had basically served as midwife. And whereas their original "birth" was not a cause of agony, but of joy and delight, now the entrance of the agitators is about to cause them to be "stillborn"; and that is cause for agony of a kind that only a birthing mother has known.

The narrative is then brought to its (presently unfulfilled) conclusion with Paul's expressing his desire to be currently present with them and thus to change his tone. The first part of this final sentence is fully understandable; face to face is infinitely better than writing a letter, precisely because "the tone"[81] can never be the same when someone else reads his letter aloud in the Galatian churches. They need to "hear" Paul himself; instead they get only a letter. Indeed, the very fact that he himself suggests "a change of tone" indicates his own uncertainty about how strongly he has written to them. In any case, as a way of justifying his present "tone," he concludes on a note of uncertainty with regard to the Galatians themselves. His "tone of voice" is due altogether to the fact that "I am perplexed about you." Given their past history, he is simply at a total loss because of what they are now doing.

And with that Paul brings his first argument from Scripture to a conclusion. He surely hopes that the argument itself will suffice to get the Galatians back on course; but the closing application and this final appeal make it clear that he is less that certain. Thus he will try one more time to convince them from Scripture (4:21-31) and by way of further appeal (5:1-12) to return to the gospel by which they were saved.

Reflection and Response – Part Three

Reflection

How does one legitimately reflect on this long argument, that begins with the Galatian believers' *experience* of Christ and the Spirit but is then dominated by a *scriptural argument* whose primary interests are so different from anything we ourselves know from experience? Indeed, it occurred to me as I was contemplating this dilemma that I have never heard a series of sermons on Galatians – and for twenty years I have attended a church that preaches through Scripture expositionally as a matter of course. Almost certainly the reason we have avoided Galatians is that, first of all, we got bogged down in a long series on Romans(!) a few years back, but mostly because it is difficult to imagine how to preach through this material section by section in a

---

[81] The Greek word here is "voice" (φωνή); our ordinary idiom for this would be "tone of voice," hence "tone."

contemporary university setting. So how, then, does one respond to this extremely important passage?

The place to begin, it seems to me, is by acknowledging at the outset that the issue Paul is dealing with here – whether Gentile believers must also adopt certain aspects of the Jewish law – is simply not an issue for most of us. It is not that Paul's issue cannot be understood to transfer into our setting in some way, but that Paul's issue as such is foreign to us. Furthermore, part of the problem in bringing it into the twenty-first century is that the makeup of the church as we know it is so radically different from that addressed in this letter. This letter was written to Gentile believers, who were in effect the "outsiders" with regard to the first generation of followers of Christ; whereas our situation is radically different in every way: Gentiles make up the vast majority of most Christian communities and Jews who become believers in effect often feel constrained to "become like Gentiles" in order to belong. So one needs to think through what "application" means for several of these texts.

Moreover, one needs to be especially careful about using this passage as a "model" for how to read and preach from the Old Testament – because here is a case where Paul's agenda has been set for him by his opponents, and he is using their texts to outflank them with regard to what Christ and the Spirit have done. Nor should what he does here be thought of, as some in fact have, as an illegitimate use of Scripture; Paul is simply able to work with Scripture better than his opponents. But the fact is that they have set the agenda, both for the use of Scripture as such and for the texts that come under purview. Therefore, what Paul does here should be for us a cause for wonder at the divine providence that brought Paul to the church for such a time as this; for if Paul had lost this battle, then we would simply never have come into existence as believers. A church that tried to believe in Christ for salvation, but was still strapped with certain aspects of the Jewish law – aspects that gave Jews their special identity as Jews in a Gentile world – would have had a very short lifespan in the Greco-Roman world. And God in his grace raised up Paul, himself a diaspora Jew trained in the "law of the rabbis," as the one uniquely gifted person who could fight the battle of grace for Gentiles, and be able to do it on Jewish turf against Jewish opponents and still win the day.

But what about some of the specifics in this passage, how do they "translate" into today's world? We should begin, I think, by acknowledging that one of our greatest challenges is to try to read the text as if the Reformation had never happened; that is, to try to read the text on Paul's own terms and not in terms of the agendas of Luther and Calvin. At issue for Paul was not whether people are "justified by faith" or "justified by works of law," that is, with how a person "gets saved" or comes into a right relationship with God – even though in a different setting one might well raise the issue in those terms. Rather at issue for Paul is whether people who had believed in Christ, evidenced by a dynamic reception of the Spirit, must also keep certain aspects of the Jewish law in order to be "completed" as believers. What Paul recognizes clearly is that one cannot add a "plus factor" of any kind to grace, since the "plus factor" in effect eliminates grace and puts the emphasis on what one does, rather than on the gift of the Spirit and the life that one has received. That is, the agitator's formula read: "Grace + aspects of law = rightstanding with God." To which Paul responds with a loud "No!" (at least any good reading of Galatians should be able to hear his "no"); rather it is "Grace + nothing = rightstanding with God."

So far so good, and most contemporary Christians can either relate to, or at least understand, such a way of putting the issue. But the breakdown for many also occurs right at this point, in one of two ways. Either one has enormous difficulty accepting grace, meaning to accept the fact that God simply accepts me, warts and all; so a bit of law-keeping is added "just in case God cannot be trusted" (even though, of course, no one would ever put it so crassly). Or one hears the "plus nothing" part and thinks that God cares little or nothing for the way I live my life as a believer; he has already accepted me freely by his grace, so why sweat the small stuff in terms of how I live. And the traditional response of the church to the latter has been to oblige such people with a minimal expression of law-keeping; whereas, as we will see when we come to 5:13–6:10, Paul has a radically different way of handling this issue, which has altogether to do with "walking by" or "living in" the Spirit, which makes all forms of even "minimal law-keeping" utterly irrelevant.

If one learns nothing else from this passage, two matters are absolutely central. First, for the believer in Christ, who is at the same time a person of the Spirit, there is absolutely no form of "abiding in the law" that is relevant. And this includes such a small matter as tithing, which was always justified in my historic context on the basis of Matt 23:23-24: "you should have practiced the latter (justice, mercy, and faithfulness), without neglecting the former (tithing mint, dill, and cummin)." But that actually works very poorly, since Jesus is speaking to Pharisees, not to disciples; and no one I know ever tithed of their spices (which was a pharisaic way of not caring for the poor!). My experience with the tithe is that it is imposed as law precisely because pastors cannot bring themselves to trust people to become true followers of Christ, and thus to live by the "rule of generosity" (2 Cor 9:6-11), which is the only teaching on "giving" in the New Testament. In some ways it is extremely difficult to make disciples (true Spirit-people) of Christians, because they have been well taught to be keepers of the law, rather than to be people overflowing with gratitude to God for his abundant grace and mercy. Furthermore, tithing gives one a false sense of ownership, as though the ninety per cent were really mine, when in fact everything belongs to God, and it is "ours" only as gift. To limit one's giving to the tithe is a clear indication that one has never truly *experienced* grace.

Second, and the way forward as a corrective to the previous issue, God's people need to be helped to understand that their true relationship with God is that of a child, at once totally free to grow into family likeness through the power of the Spirit and totally dependent on the God who by his Spirit has invited us to address him as "Abba." Much of this has to do with perspective. Many believers think that the goal of "getting saved" is to make it to heaven; whereas God's goal in redeeming us and making us his children is to recreate us back into the divine image, so that we who call him "Abba" are continually by his Spirit being transformed into children who bear family likeness. It is for this, Paul says, that we have been predestined: "For those God foreknew he also predestined to be conformed to the image of his Son, that he might be the firstborn among many brothers and sisters" (Rom 8:29). This is the text that needs to be emblazoned on every believer's forehead, that the goal of everything is the restoration in us of divine image that was lost in the garden. And the way forward for us here is a rebirth of freedom, which ironically means a childlike dependency on God as our heavenly *Abba*, who can be utterly trusted with our lives – both now and forever.

Perhaps the most difficult aspect of this argument for those of us in churches of the northern hemisphere to come to terms with – Pentecostal and evangelical alike – is the way it all begins. Who of us would ever think of starting an argument against those who pressure believers to adopt certain aspect of "biblical law" as Paul does in 3:1-5, by appealing to the dynamic experience of the Spirit, both at the beginning and as an ongoing feature of Christian life. There are certain places in southern hemisphere churches where this would work, but hardly anywhere in the north. So what do we do, act as if the text is not there? or do we find a place of repentance and of committing ourselves to becoming much more the kind of Spirit-people that is exemplified in this passage? And perhaps we Pentecostals are partly to blame here, by emphasizing the work and empowerment of the Spirit as a kind of "add-on," rather than an essential feature of Christian life as a whole?

One final aspect of Paul's argument that especially needs to be renewed within Pentecostal circles in the present day, where we have tended to become more "evangelical" than Pentecostal, is the way we listen to what Paul affirms in 3:28: that in Christ the old distinctions no longer prevail, as having any bearing on who or what one is in Christ. In an earlier day, Pentecostalism (rightly) understood Spirit-gifting to precede gender in terms of ministry within the church. But now that this has become such a hot issue among evangelicals – many of whom believe that women in ministry is the direct result of the women's liberation movement! – Pentecostals will do well to re-examine their roots, which in this case are thoroughly biblical roots. The only question worth considering on this issue is, "What came first, Spirit-gifting or church offices?" And since the answer is obviously "Spirit-gifting," then one needs to hold "lightly" to the concept of office and let those truly gifted of the Spirit minister widely in the church. Here is where some who think otherwise need a good dose of historical and biblical reality so as to let the Spirit guide the church and its ministry and not present-day fear of the women's liberation movement.

Response

In response to all of this, and to the passage itself, we may need to think through questions like these: How might I more consciously become a Spirit-person, both in my relationship with God as my heavenly *Abba* and with others? Do I really believe that the Spirit is the absolutely central "ingredient" of life in Christ, or is he merely an "add-on"? Is my life truly characterized by trusting Christ wholly and only, or am I a closet "Judaizer," who hopes God looks kindly on my "works" as having some merit? What aspects of law-keeping might be lurking within my thinking that give me secret hope of special favor with God? Or perhaps even more damning, what forms of failure to keep the law do I see in others that keeps me from accepting them without reservation? So what, in fact and practice, does it mean for me to be a Spirit-person, both in the church and in the world?

1. Assess your life "in the Spirit" beginning with your conversion and identifying your first conscious awareness of the Spirit's presence in your life as well as significant later moments.
2. Write the story of your life in the Spirit in the form of a narrative in order to discern more fully the presence of the Spirit in your life and those times when you failed to allow him to guide you fully.
3. Share your testimony in oral or written form with others in the community in order to assess your life more fully and honestly.
4. Identify and attend to those practices and disciplines that enable such Spirit empowered living.

Galatians 4:21–5:12

The Text

The Second Argument from Scripture

Given Paul's application and appeal in 4:8-20 following the argument from Scripture in 3:1–4:7, one is not quite prepared for what begins in 4:21: yet another argument from Scripture. Moreover, its unique nature has served as difficult terrain for many readers to negotiate. Nonetheless one misses too much of the argument of Galatians as a whole to toss it aside as an afterthought before turning to the final biblical argument that Paul takes up in 5:13–6:10. In effect, with 4:21-31 Paul brings the argument of 3:1–4:7 to a final conclusion by picking up two essential threads that up to now have been left hanging: the issue of "freedom," first broached in 2:4 and implied in 4:1-7 ("so you are no longer slaves"); and the issue of the agitators themselves, as to what the Galatians are to do about them.

Paul's primary concern in this new section is to show once more that the true children of Abraham are not under confinement to Torah, and thus are "free." So in one sense the former concerns remain: (*a*) the immediate focus is again on *Abraham*; (*b*) the ultimate question is who are *the true "sons"* of Abraham, since (*c*) the "true sons" are sons *according to the promise*, who (*d*) are thus destined to *inherit the promise*; and (*e*) the Spirit once again plays the primary role, this time as the key to both the promise and the inheritance.

However, Paul now returns to these matters by way of the theme of slavery that emerged in 4:1-7. This theme is picked up through Hagar, who in the Septuagint is regularly called "the slave woman" (ἡ παιδίσκη). But the issue remains the same: "enslavement to the law," with perhaps a hint of their being "enslaved" by the agitators. The theme of "freedom" is then picked up through Sarah and her son Isaac, who, Paul asserts, was "born according to the Spirit" (κατὰ πνεῦμα).[1] Paul thus concludes the argument by making the same point he made in 3:29 and 4:1-7, that "we are children of freedom (= Christ), not of slavery (= the law)." Near the end (4:29) he brings

---

[1] One should note in fact that the present passage is not really about the two mothers – their role is purely analogical – but about the two sons. Note how it both begins (v. 22; "Abraham had two sons") and ends (vv. 28-31) with this focus.

in the agitators again, as those "sons according to the flesh," who are persecuting those born "according to the Spirit," and who must be "thrown out." Thus to recapitulate the point of these three "concluding" paragraphs:

a. 3:23-29: By faith in Christ, Gentiles belong to the true "seed" of Abraham; and the law was a temporary measure until this should happen.
b. 4:1-7: By faith in Christ, Gentiles are true "sons of God"; the law meant slavery, but they are now free through Christ and the Spirit.
c. 4:21-31: By faith in Christ, Gentiles are true "sons of Sarah" (born into freedom); since the law means to be born into slavery, they must cast out the persecutors.

The present argument comes in three observable parts: the *presentation* of the Scriptural data (vv. 21-23); the analogical *"interpretation"* of the data (vv. 24-27); and the *application* of the data to the Galatians (vv. 28-31). One should note that the reader could go directly to the application from the presentation without missing a beat. So one of the questions the reader-interpreter of the passage must ask has to do with the role of the "interpretation," which at one level seems quite unnecessary to the argument as a whole. But this recognition of the structure of the passage should also lead one to recognize its primary concerns, which are not found in the interpretation, but in the application (vv. 24-27).

In the first two paragraphs of chapter 5 Paul wraps up this argument with a twofold appeal, by far the strongest in the letter to this point. The first appeal (5:1-6) picks up the theme of "freedom" from the preceding argument. Here Paul goes straight for the jugular, pointing out the disastrous results if the Galatian men submit to Jewish circumcision rites: they will be alienated from Christ and thus will have fallen from grace. But even here Paul cannot end on such a note, so he concludes in vv. 5-6 with the divine alternative. The second appeal (5:7-12) is full of pathos and perplexity; Paul simply cannot understand how the Galatian believers can have been so completely duped by those who in reality are their enemies. So he ends on the strongest note yet; instead of applying the knife to other men's flesh, the agitators should rather emasculate themselves. And with that Paul turns to his final argument, setting forth how the Spirit functions as the fully adequate divine replacement of Torah, thus eliminating altogether any need to be "observant" (5:13–6:10).

Galatians 4:21-23 – The Scriptural Data Presented

> [21] *Tell me, you who want to be under the law, are you not aware of what the law says?* [22] *For it is written that Abraham had two sons, one by the slave woman and the other by the free woman.* [23] *His son by the slave woman was born as the result of human effort;ᵃ but his son by the free woman was born as the result of a divine promise.*

> ᵃ23 Or *born according to the flesh*

In this opening paragraph Paul first (v. 21) sets forth *the challenge* to those who want to come under Torah; vv. 22-23 then offer the *data* from Genesis that will eventually be interpreted in vv. 27-31.

Verse 21. With this sentence Paul throws down the gauntlet, as it were, challenging his Galatian friends who are seriously contemplating circumcision. The "tell me" with which it begins follows directly from the "I am perplexed about you" in v. 20. He now describes their condition directly: they are "those who want to be under the law." So the challenge is, "then let's look for a moment at what the law itself says." This latter use of "the law" offers clear evidence for its twofold use in first-century Judaism: as the "law" that is binding on those who wish to belong to Yahweh; and as the "*book* of the law" that contains both the laws and their narrative setting. It is the narrative setting that Paul now wishes to interpret in light of Christ and the Spirit.

Verses 22-23. With an explanatory "for" (γάρ) Paul in these two sentences offers the basic biblical data that he will go on to expound by way of analogy. The presentation of the data has some unique features that need to be noted. First, when Paul elsewhere uses the formula "for it is written," he invariably *cites* some portion of the biblical text itself, usually from the Septuagint. But here by way of contrast he does not cite a text at all, but simply offers key information from the narrative of Genesis 16. Second, this is one of only two instances in Paul where the formula "it is written" is followed by a "that" (ὅτι);[2] in this case it functions not to introduce direct discourse (as the Greek equivalent to quotation marks) but rather to reflect on some basic content from the Genesis passage. Third, the only actual language from Genesis 16 that Paul picks up is that used by the Septuagint translator to refer to Hagar as a "slave woman" (ἡ παιδίσκη); and Paul's entire interest in the passage focuses here.

---

[2] The only other instance in Paul's letters is in Gal 3:16 above, where it functions as a ὅτι-*recitativum* (the technical term for its introducing direct discourse). For a discussion see Wallace, *Grammar*, 454-55.

Thus the first sentence (v. 22) sets forth the biblical data themselves: that "Abraham had two sons." Abraham, of course, had more than two sons; but Paul's interest lies with only two of them: Ishmael, who is never named in the narrative, and Isaac, who is named but once (in v. 28). He begins by picking up the key term regarding Hagar, that she was a "slave woman," which is the primary reason for alluding to the Genesis 16 narrative. In the next clause Paul describes Sarah as the "free woman," his own description based on what the text says about Hagar; by so doing he sets in motion the "slavery/freedom" contrast that will dominate the passage.

The crucial point for Paul in the Genesis narrative is to be found in his interpretation (v. 23) of the action of Sarah and Abraham that led to the birth of Ishmael. Returning to the language of "flesh" that he had used earlier to contrast life in the Spirit and life under law (3:3), Paul says that "the son of the slave woman was born according to the flesh" – which, in keeping with 3:3, the TNIV has interpreted as "by human effort," but which elsewhere has been rendered "sinful nature." Thus when Sarah and Abraham preempted God's purposes and took things into their own hands, they were acting "in keeping with the flesh," that is, basic human fallenness, and thereby failing to put their trust wholly in God.[3] The Galatians themselves could hardly have missed Paul's point, given the argument in 3:1–4:7: living under the law is to live "in the flesh" (3:3) and thus to live under slavery and not as genuine children of God (3:22–4:7). The irony here is that Abraham, the man of faith, himself acted in this case "according to the flesh" and not "by faith" in God's promise.

The Isaac-clause of v. 23 is set in deliberate contrast to the Ishmael-clause, with language used earlier regarding the status of believers in Christ. This happens in two ways. First, Isaac was born "of the free woman," rather than "of Sarah," or "of Abraham's wife." The language of "freedom" first appeared in 2:4, and will be used again to begin the application in 5:1, as well as to begin the final argument in 5:13. In each case "freedom" means to be free from the obligation to keep, and thus to be enslaved to, Torah. Second, in sharp contrast to Ishmael's being born "in keeping with the flesh," Isaac was born "through promise." This latter phrase functions both to pick up the theme of promise from the preceding argument (3:14-29) and to indicate the divine instrumentality of Isaac's birth – and both words

<hr/>

[3] It is therefore especially unfortunate that the NIV and NAB translate this as "in the ordinary way" and "naturally." It is hard to imagine the Galatians' having heard this phrase in such a non-pejorative way!

(freedom and promise) have obvious implications for the Galatians themselves.

So with these words Paul offers the biblical data for his interpretation and application that follow, which in the "interpretation" portion (vv. 24-27) focuses on the two mothers and in the "application" portion (vv. 28-31) focuses on the two sons, without further regard to the "interpretation" itself.

Galatians 4:24-27 – An Interpretation of the Scriptural Data

> [24]*I am taking these things figuratively, for the women represent two covenants. One covenant is from Mount Sinai and bears children who are to be slaves: This is Hagar.* [25]*Now Hagar stands for Mount Sinai in Arabia and corresponds to the present city of Jerusalem, because she is in slavery with her children.* [26]*But the Jerusalem that is above is free, and she is our mother.* [27]*For it is written:*
>
>> *"Be glad, barren woman,*
>>> *you who never bore a child;*
>> *shout for joy and cry aloud,*
>>> *you who were never in labor;*
>> *because more are the children of the desolate woman*
>>> *than of her who has a husband."*[b]

[b]27 Isa 54:1

By any reading of Galatians to this point, nothing quite prepares one for this unique moment in Paul's letters. The closest he comes to it elsewhere is his "interpretation" of Exodus 33 in 2 Cor 3:16-18. While someone reading Galatians for the first time might wonder where Paul was going with the biblical data in vv. 22-23, they would be little prepared for this.

This is not Paul's regular use of Scripture, to be sure, but he was a student of the rabbis after all, and here he shows himself adept at one of their special ways of dealing with texts. As pointed out above, the most striking thing about the "interpretation" itself is that nothing that is said here appears in any noticeable way in the application that follows in vv. 27-31. Nonetheless it is not irrelevant; the crucial matters appear, first, in v. 25 with its mention of "the below Jerusalem" and its connection with Mount Sinai, and, second, with the contrast to Sarah in vv. 26-27, so that those in the community of faith are a part of the fulfillment of Isa 54:1.

Verse 24a. Although one can only guess at the reasons for it, Paul himself is up front about what he is now setting out to do: "these things are to be [now] taken allegorically." Such an "interpretation" does not take the place of standard historical understanding of the narrative, as the application that follows makes clear; rather, there are some further things from these biblical realities on which one can reflect when they are taken "figuratively." Thus he begins, "these mothers represent two covenants." And with this language we are taken back to the argument in 3:15-19, where the term "covenant" first occurred. Now the two covenants will be illustrated by way of the two mothers.

Verses 24b-25. What Paul is after by way of this analogy is what he has argued previously: that with the advent of Christ and the Spirit, continuing to live "under the law of Moses" means to be in slavery and thus *no true* "son," since true sonship has been effected for the Galatians (and us) through the Son and the Spirit of the Son (4:5-6). Thus Paul begins with Hagar; but his interest is not in Hagar as such, but in "the covenant (of law that came) from Mount Sinai that gives birth to slavery." There is nothing new here, except for the specifics themselves. That is, Paul has already said that the law functioned as a "slave-pedagogue" that "enslaved" people until God's appointed time. Now he specifies the law as "from Mount Sinai"; the surprise element comes in the application to Hagar, who is said to represent the former covenant. In a kind of "shorthand" where several images are in view at once, the slave woman, who will bear children destined for slavery, represents the former covenant of law that "enslaves"; thus she represents "Mount Sinai."

That much seems easy enough; the surprise comes in the next clause, that she also "corresponds to the present Jerusalem." With the verb "corresponds"[4] Paul makes a sudden shift from the giving of the law on Sinai to the keepers of the law in Jerusalem. While this latter might seem to condemn the Jerusalem apostles as well, that is not what Paul has in mind; rather this is another (now indirect) confrontation with the agitators, who have presented themselves as having come from Jerusalem. Those in the present city of Jerusalem, the "capital" of Judaism whatever else, who insist on Torah observance whether they be Christian or non-Christian, are still in slavery to the former covenant from which Christ and the Spirit have come to release them.

---

[4] Gk. συστοιχέω, a word that occurs only here in the NT. It has to do with things "standing in the same line," thus "corresponding" to present-day Jerusalem.

Thus, keeping the Hagar/Sinai analogy intact, but with his present-day Jerusalem in view, Paul concludes with an explanatory clause: "for she remains in slavery with her children."

Verse 26. By way of contrast, and with a clause full of still more surprises, Paul brings the comparison to a conclusion with the brief clause, "but the Jerusalem above is free, and she is our mother." What one must not do with this clause is to try to interpret it out of context, a context which alone has determined this unusual moment for Paul. First, one must be mindful of the limitations Paul has in order to effect the necessary contrast. Although the "she" should refer to Sarah, for the moment Sarah is no longer in purview – but will be picked up again in vv. 30-31. That means, second, that having put the primary geographical places on the Hagar/Torah/slavery side of the analogy, Paul has nowhere to place the Sarah/Christ/freedom contrast. So he does the only logical thing if he is to keep the "geographical" analogy alive, and that is to place them in heaven, where Christ is now enthroned. The key to our understanding lies with the phrase, "the 'Jerusalem' that is above," and our putting "Jerusalem" in quotation marks, indicating a play on terms. Thus with this brief, considerably condensed, phrase Paul intends his readers to see a side reference to Sarah, as the "free woman" who bears children for freedom, but especially a reference to Christ and the Spirit, who are responsible for the Galatians' being God's children under the new covenant.

Verse 27. That this is Paul's intent is further indicated by his supporting citation of Isa 54:1, as the introductory "for it is written" makes certain. Although Paul has sometimes been accused of citing this passage out of context in order to support his own argument, such a judgment seems unnecessary and pejorative. Isaiah's sudden call for rejoicing on the part of a people in exile is best understood as his own inspired response to (*a*) the "desolation" that Judah has experienced in Babylonian exile, which lies behind all of Isa 40–52:12, and (*b*) the atoning sacrifice of Yahweh's Suffering Servant in 52:13–53:12. Here the prophet deliberately recalls the story of Sarah and Isaac, while at the same time he echoes language from Hannah's prayer in 1 Samuel 2, especially vv. 1 and 5.

Paul now applies this Isaiah passage, with its echo of Sarah's barrenness, to the "Jerusalem above," that is, to the work of Christ and the Spirit. The call of lines 1 and 2 are to be understood as referring directly to Sarah's anguish over being childless; the cause for rejoicing in line 3a is Paul's own prophetic application of Sarah's giving birth to

Isaac – and thus eventually to a multitude – as pointing to the inclusion of the Gentiles into the newly constituted people of God.

Thus historically Sarah was barren, but rejoiced at the birth of Isaac; but Isaiah prophesies that after exile the formerly barren woman will have many children. Paul now applies this to the present situation, which takes "Sarah" in a new sense, as the mother of the "children of promise," both Jew and Gentile alike.[5]

What is of interest for our present purposes is that with this citation Paul now abandons the "allegorical" interpretation of the Sarah-Hagar story, while keeping with the historical realities of that narrative. So in the application that follows he returns to the storyline of Genesis 16 presented in vv. 22-23, and shows how it applies to the present situation in Galatia; and with this twofold application everything that has preceded falls into place and makes perfectly good sense. Here he gives the two specific reasons for his using this second argument from Scripture: to establish once more that the Galatian believers are free from Torah observance, and to urge them to "cast out" the agitators.

Galatians 4:28-31 – The Application of the Scriptural Data

> [28]*Now you, brothers and sisters, like Isaac, are children of promise.* [29]*At that time the son born by human effort[a] persecuted the son born by the power of the Spirit. It is the same now.* [30]*But what does Scripture say? "Get rid of the slave woman and her son, for the slave woman's son will never share in the inheritance with the free woman's son."[b]* [31]*Therefore, brothers and sisters, we are not children of the slave woman, but of the free woman.*

> [a]29 Or *born according to the flesh*   [b]27 Gen 21:10

Although at first reading this application is not especially easy to follow, the function of the paragraph in fact seems quite clear: to set up the entire appeal and argument that follow, first in 5:1-12 and then in 5:13–6:10. Its two themes are readily apparent. First, Paul applies the analogy to the Galatians themselves, that as children[6] of the

---

[5] Thus the only clause in the Isaiah oracle that does not fit the present situation is line 3b. But that is something of an irrelevancy, because Paul's point is clearly supported by lines 1-3a, and he often includes the whole passage in a supporting citation where his interest is limited only to part of it.

[6] One should note here that a subtle shift of language takes place here, from "sons" (υἱοί) to "children" (τέκνα), apparently as the direct result of the citation of Isa 54:1. This shift to more inclusive language most likely happens in this instance because the emphasis is no longer on the relationship of the "sons of God" to the "Son of God,"

promise they are therefore the true heirs of the free woman; second, he uses the analogy to set up his repeated urgency that they "get rid of the slave woman and her son," now as applied to the agitators who are currently "persecuting" the Galatians by insisting on the circumcision of the men. This twofold application is what will be spelled out in further detail in the two applicational paragraphs that follow – although the second matter is picked up in a slightly different way. Thus the two sentences that serve to "enclose" the paragraph (vv. 28, 31) are the basis of the first application in 5:1-6, while the three middle sentences (vv. 29-30) are the basis for the application in 5:7-12.

Verse 28. The content of this sentence can be readily grasped, since the reader has known right along that the son of the "free woman" (v. 22), who is therefore the "son of promise" (v. 23), is ultimately going to be applied to the Gentile Galatian believers.[7] Thus, "you, brothers and sisters, like Isaac, are children of promise." And even though the way Paul got here was through the apparently more circuitous route of vv. 24-27, the latter is not irrelevant to Paul's urgencies. The crisis in Galatia has been engendered by some men sent out from "law-keeping" believers *in Jerusalem*, who insist on a minimal degree of "law-keeping" on the part of the Gentiles. And this has obviously set up the further application in vv. 29-30.

Verse 29. Since its content was not in fact an expressed part of the analogy, the reader is momentarily caught off guard by this follow-on application: "At that time the son born by *means of the flesh* [TNIV, human effort] persecuted the son born by the power of the Spirit. It is the same now." Nonetheless, given the content of the whole letter, this is hardly a great surprise. With a "then" and "now" contrast Paul spells it out plainly, but without naming names on either side, neither in the biblical account itself nor in the present situation in Galatia. On the one hand, Paul assumes his readers will know the essential elements of the biblical story; on the other hand, one would have to be especially dull to miss his point of present application.

---

but on Isaac's later descendants (now Jew and Gentile alike) as the rightful heirs of Abraham, thus Abraham's (and thus God's) "children" (cf. Rom 8:14-17).

[7] The unfortunate scribal history of this passage was to change Paul's "you are" (found in the earliest and best evidence both East and West [𝔓[46] B D F G 1739 1881 b sa]) to "we are," which made its way into the Textus Receptus and thus the KJV. While this is understandable in light of v. 31, it unfortunately misses Paul's habit of beginning with "you" Galatians before including himself and other believers, as in 4:6 above.

So Paul makes his point the more strongly by this "nameless" application, in which he does two things at once. First, he picks up the contrasting language of "flesh" and "Spirit" with which the first argument from Scripture began (3:3-5). Nothing in the analogy itself prepared us for this, but it hardly comes as a surprise; for this is Paul's own way of tying the two arguments from Scripture together, beginning the first one this way and applying the second. At the same time this language obviously anticipates the final applicational argument in 5:13–6:10, which is dominated by these two phrases' being constantly kept in contrast.

Second, by returning to Spirit-flesh language in this way, Paul also instinctively returns to the issue of the agitators themselves, who have never been totally out of sight, and were most recently mentioned in vv. 17-18. In the present sentence Paul offers a kind of "midrash"[8] of Gen 21:9, which is ambiguous in both the Hebrew and Greek texts as to how Ishmael "made sport of" the younger Isaac. Paul interprets Ishmael's actions as something that was ongoing: "he used to[9] persecute the son 'born in keeping with the Spirit.'" Thus Paul's own contrast between the two sons is that one was "born in keeping with the flesh," the other "in keeping with the Spirit." Although this is something of a midrash on the Old Testament text, Paul's language is nonetheless in keeping with the concerns of the Genesis text; at the same time it offers him a proper lead-in to the applications that follow.

Verse 30. Having thus used v. 9 in the Genesis account as a lead-in, Paul now cites v. 10, whose twofold purpose can hardly be missed, and almost certainly is the ultimate reason for this analogy from Scripture in the first place. The first part of the sentence describes the action Sarah wants Abraham to take regarding Ishmael: "Cast out the slave woman and her son." Since this follows so poorly on the twofold application of the Genesis narrative in vv. 28 and 29, one may be sure that its primary intent is to indicate by implication how the Galatians are to treat their present persecutors – even though that is not expressly said in any of the charges against them that follow (5:7-12; 6:11-16). Its significance for Paul is that these are the exact words of Sarah in Gen 21:10, following v. 9, which Paul has interpreted in

---

[8] This term, often used loosely by NT scholars, refers primarily to a kind of interpretation that offers a second, often "deeper," meaning to the words of a biblical text.

[9] Paul's Greek verb is imperfect (ἐδίωκεν), which has the force of an ongoing reality, rather than one specific event; thus "he was regularly persecuting," or as here, "he used to persecute."

terms of the agitators' "persecuting" the Galatian believers. They must now be "cast out."

The second part of the sentence from the Genesis passage quoted by Paul gives the *reason* for the command in the first part: "for the son of the slave woman (= those who live by law, thus the agitators themselves) will not inherit with the son of the free woman (= those who are born 'in keeping with the Spirit,' thus the Galatian believers)." Here again, in this indirect way, we are faced once more with Paul's unyielding "either-or" regarding Torah observance. One simply cannot have it both ways; it is either Christ or the law, faith or observance. Faith in Christ plus Torah observance is an unworkable equation, since the latter totally subverts the former. And it is this larger concern, not the actual citation of Gen 21:10, that leads Paul to his concluding application of the analogy to the Galatians.

Verse 31. With a final "therefore," which skips past the citation of Gen 21:10 in v. 30, Paul makes direct application of what began in v. 28 to the Galatians themselves. In so doing he abandons the "you" of v. 28 for the inclusive "we," thus affirming Jew and Gentile together as on equal footing. Picking up the emphases in vv. 28-30 in reverse order, he begins, "we are *not* children of the slave woman." This self-evident application first of all intentionally divorces the Galatians from their present "tormentors." The latter are to be cast out from their midst, precisely because they have themselves chosen to make the gospel that saves a matter of human effort (= doing works of law); but "we" are not like them, children of slavery to law who have missed the point of the gospel and the Spirit. Rather, he concludes, "*we* are children of the free woman," and thus those who have experienced God's saving grace through Christ and the Spirit. And with that Paul launches into his most direct, and telling, application of the entire preceding argument to the situation in Galatia.

Galatians 5:1-6 – Application and Appeal: The Danger of Capitulating

> [1]*It is for freedom that Christ has set us free. Stand firm, then, and do not let yourselves be burdened again by a yoke of slavery.*
>
> [2]*Mark my words! I, Paul, tell you that if you let yourselves be circumcised, Christ will be of no value to you at all.* [3]*Again I declare to every man who lets himself be circumcised that he is obligated to obey the whole law.* [4]*You who are trying to be justified by the law have been alienated from Christ; you have fallen away from grace.* [5]*But by faith we eagerly await through the Spirit the righteousness for which we hope.*

> [6]*For in Christ Jesus neither circumcision nor uncircumcision has any value. The only thing that counts is faith expressing itself through love.*

This paragraph and the next function in relation to the preceding argument from Scripture similarly to how 4:8-11 and 4:12-20 did for the former one (3:1–4:7). Thus the present paragraph serves as application/appeal to the Galatians' situation (cf. 4:8-11), while the next one (5:7-12) functions as personal appeal from Paul himself (cf. 4:12-20).[10] The paragraph begins with a janus sentence (a sentence that looks two ways at once): an imperative that applies the preceding analogy directly to the Galatians also serves as the heading for the rest of the paragraph. This is followed by three sentences (vv. 2-4) that spell out the fearful consequences of yielding to circumcision. But, typically for Paul, he cannot bring himself to conclude on such a note, so he adds two further sentences: one that affirms the divine (eschatological) reality, which "by faith we eagerly await" (v. 5); the other which once more negates circumcision as a meaningful option of any kind, while also pointing toward the final resolution to be spelled out in 5:13–6:10.

Two further observations about the paragraph as a whole are in order. First, one should note that the paragraph is dominated by what Christ has done (vv. 1, 2, 4, 6), and in each case the mention of Christ stands in sharp contrast to the law, especially circumcision. Second, one needs to be alert to Paul's alternating use of the first and second person plural pronouns. As in preceding instances in the letter, Paul uses "we" when referring to the work of Christ that includes both him and the Galatians; thus in v. 1, "Christ has set *us* free," and in v. 5, "*we* eagerly await [the future])." But elsewhere, focusing in particular on the men in the communities, he refers to "*you* who let yourselves be circumcised" (v. 2) and "*you* are alienated from Christ; . . . *you* have fallen from grace" (v. 4). These matters pretty well tell the story of the paragraph as a whole.

Verse 1. With a remarkable, and undoubtedly purposeful, redundancy, Paul begins his application of the preceding argument with the affirmation, "It is for freedom that Christ has set us free." That is, through his

---

[10] In a serious misreading of this passage, historically it was considered the beginning of a third major section in the letter, which was divided into three major parts (historical/apologetic [chs. 1-2], theological [chs. 3-4], and practical/hortatory [chs. 5-6]). Calling chs. 5-6 "hortatory" is especially misleading since that word implies the presence of imperatives; but v. 1 contains the only imperative in this entire section (5:1-12), and it serves a purpose of its own.

death and resurrection Christ has purchased the Galatians' freedom
from the double yoke of both sin and the law, and Paul is here focused
on this second freedom in particular. Freedom from the yoke of sin is
marked indirectly by the word "again" in the second clause. Since
Christ has freed them from their former bondage to the "powers"
(4:3, 8), Paul now urges them to "stand firm" in their freedom and
not "return again" to bondage, this time to Torah observance. The
next three sentences then spell out the consequences of doing the
latter.

Verse 2. This sentence is the first of three consecutive assertions, all
focused on the dire consequences for the Galatian men if they actually
capitulate to being circumcised as a way of "completing" their
salvation. This sentence and the third (v. 4) speak to their losing their
relationship with Christ, while the middle sentence (v. 3) reminds
them that they cannot be selective regarding the law. Indeed, so
concerned is Paul for their welfare in Christ that he begins with the
imperatival "behold" (KJV, NASB/U; "look," ESV), which is intended
as an ear-catcher and thus rendered in more idiomatic English by other
translations ("Mark my words," T/NIV, REB; "Listen!" NRSV, GNB,
NLT). This is then followed with the further attention-getting, "I,
Paul," a phenomenon that occurs five other times in his letters,[11] all
designed to put special emphasis either on himself as the writer or, as
here, on what he is about to say. While it is possible that this is an
indirect reassertion of his apostolic authority,[12] it more likely picks up
the relational matters spoken of in 4:9-20, a passage which has only a
tinge of "authority" in it. Here "father Paul," the one responsible for
their coming to faith in the first place, is now calling attention to that
relationship as a way of emphasizing what he is about to say.

The conditional clause that follows suggests that Paul still has hope,
since it implies a future event that has not yet happened: "if ever you
are circumcised."[13] At issue, it should be noted, is not circumcision
itself; on this matter Paul is adamant – neither condition counts for a
thing with God (v. 6). What is at stake, therefore, in the present
situation is that the Galatians are being pressured to give it value in
terms of their relationship with God, when in fact it has none.
Furthermore, if they were to yield to circumcision under pressure,
they would in effect be saying that Christ's death and resurrection are

---

[11] See 2 Cor 10:1; Eph 3:1; Col 1:23; 1 Thess 2:18; Phlm 19.

[12] Which has obviously come under fire in Galatia; see on 1:1 and 10 above, plus
the entire "defense" of 1:10–2:13.

[13] Gk. ἐὰν περιτέμνησθε, on which matter see Burton (273).

not sufficient for one to be in right relationship with God. And this is what Paul recognizes clearly: it is either "Christ + nothing"[14] or they *miss out on Christ altogether.*

The consequences of such action on their part would therefore be of the severest nature: that "Christ will be of no value to you at all." With this very direct assertion Paul is picking up what he had said earlier, but by implication only, in 3:10-14. What is here spelled out plainly is the "either-or" nature of what they are about to do. One can be related to God only by trusting in Christ and his life-giving death, and not at all by bearing the identity marks of the first covenant, especially circumcision. The Galatians simply cannot have it both ways; there can be no "plus-factor" to grace. It is either Christ alone, or nothing at all in terms of one's relationship with God; indeed, he had argued earlier, "If righteousness (δικαιοσύνη) is through Torah, then Christ died to no avail" (2:21).

Verse 3. But that is not all. Added to this, and now returning to the argument of 3:10-12, Paul reminds them that to receive circumcision is to put themselves under obligation to do the whole law. Thus they had better be prepared for the consequences. One simply cannot be selective about the law: to accept one part as binding is to accept the requirements of the whole. And as he has argued earlier, this is the curse; they must now live by Torah, the whole of Torah, which by its very nature excludes living by faith. Paul's "again I declare" that begins this sentence is what makes certain that this is in fact Paul's intent in 3:10-12 (which see).

Verse 4. With this sentence Paul returns to the first matter (from v. 2), spelling out in specific detail the twin results of their yielding to circumcision. The reason Christ will be of no value (v. 2) is related to the either-or nature of salvation spelled out in v. 3. It is either Christ or Torah, and if it is Torah then it is the *whole* of Torah. So with a perfect chiasm Paul affirms the final results of going the way of Torah:

> You have been estranged   from Christ
> [you who by Torah are being righteous]
>   from grace   you have fallen.

This is to put the matters in vv. 2-3 theologically. We begin with the vocative (the middle line). To submit to circumcision in effect becomes an attempt on your part to "be righteous by Torah" (ἐν νόμῳ δικαιοῦσθε); and that, of course, is precisely what cannot be done – primarily because the law was never intended to make one righteous.

---

[14] On this matter see the comments on 2:18 above (pp. 89-90).

The reason for the law was to establish boundaries for conduct within the already-established covenant God had made with Israel on the basis of grace alone. Failure to keep covenant meant to experience the "curses" of the law, to be sure; but the law itself was never given as a *means* of righteousness.

Thus in attempting to be righteous by the law, one is also thereby "alienated from Christ" (line 1), since righteousness as rightstanding with God is God's gift through Christ, not our achievement through obedience to the law. The irony, of course, is that this is the same fate as will happen to those who make no pretense of righteousness, who not only do not trust Christ, but have no intent to do so. So those who attempt to be *over*-righteous and those who do not attempt to be righteous at all share the same fate of exclusion from Christ. And as harsh as that may sound, Paul is both clear and adamant on this point.

Finally, therefore, "to be righteous by Torah" means to have "fallen from grace" (line 3), which is simply a more theological way of putting the first clause. The reason for this should be obvious to all, although it seems seldom to be so: One can add nothing to grace and still experience grace. It is like doing a special favor for someone (on the basis of "grace" alone) and then watch them try to "pay you back," which has the effect of negating the gift of grace. Grace is grace; and adding law-keeping to grace as a means of righteousness is to insult grace and thus to nullify it altogether.

What all of this means, of course, is that for Paul the language of "falling from grace" does not have to do with falling into sin, but "falling into law-keeping" – as a means of gaining God's favor, whose favor simply cannot be realized this way. Whether this also has to do with "eternal salvation" is a more moot point, since this is the language of rhetoric, not theological precision. On the one hand, the "for" with which the next sentence (v. 5) begins, with its emphasis on eschatological realization, seems to suggest that the one attempting to be righteous by means of the law really has abandoned Christ and thus, having fallen from grace, does not have eschatological hope. On the other hand, Paul speaks so strongly elsewhere of Christ's "keeping" those who are his (e.g., Rom 8:32-39), that one should probably keep this within its immediate context (that of being "super-righteous" by "doing law") and not use it as a means of threat for those who have fallen into sin.

Verse 5. The "for" with which this sentence begins is almost certainly intended to be explanatory; but explanatory of what is the question. Since the sentence stands in obvious contrast to the fate of those who would be "righteous by law," the NIV translators simply turned it into a "but," which was kept in the TNIV. Unfortunately, such an adversative misses the fine nuance of *explanation* that is intended by this sentence, which the Good News Bible catches by rendering it "as for us."

The key to the contrast lies both with the language, where Paul once again brings together the three key terms – Spirit, faith, righteousness – and with their order in Paul's Greek sentence: "for by the Spirit, based on faith, the hope of righteousness we await." This word order catches all of Paul's emphases. He begins with the divine means of our realizing this righteousness, "by the Spirit," thus picking up the emphasis with which the first argument from Scripture both began and concluded (3:3-5; 4:6) and with which the second argument concluded ("born by the power of the Spirit," 4:29). Here is the divine alternative to every form of law-keeping, which Paul will spell out in considerable detail in the next major section of argument (5:13–6:10).

He follows that with "by faith," which is our response to the work of Christ, whose death and resurrection secured our standing with God and thus eliminated all forms of law-keeping, especially in this case, the ultimate boundary marker of the former covenant, circumcision.

This in turn is followed by the eschatological goal of the divine work of Christ and the Spirit in our behalf: the sure hope regarding the future that God's righteousness has provided by Christ and the Spirit. Unfortunately, the turning of this phrase into literal English ("the hope of righteousness") has given rise to unnecessary theological discussion. In ordinary English this latter phrase would mean "having hope to obtain righteousness in the eschaton." And while there may be some measure of truth to putting it that way (i.e., we thereby realize the final expression of "righteousness" that has been our sure hope), Paul surely intends "righteousness" to be the grammatical subject of our hope, meaning the "righteousness that Christ and the Spirit" have provided is the sure guarantee of our hope's being fully realized at the Eschaton. This in turn stands in direct contrast to v. 4: Thus "we who are by the Spirit and faith (vis-à-vis by doing Torah) await as our sure hope the outcome of present righteousness," which those based on doing Torah cannot have since they have been alienated from Christ and thus fallen from grace. And such sure hope is something "we await eagerly," the standard New Testament verb for the believers' awaiting what is certain to come to pass.

Verse 6. The "for" with which this sentence begins offers a second explanatory contrast between those attempting righteousness through Torah and those receiving it through Christ and the Spirit. But whereas the former sentence began with the Spirit, and "Christ" came by way of allusion through the phrase, "based on faith," here the sentence begins, "in Christ Jesus," a phrase that last occurred in 3:26 and 28. Without further qualifiers this phrase is ambiguous enough to be understood either as a locative (we exist *in* Christ Jesus) or as means (through the work of Christ Jesus).[15] But since the sentence is notable for its absence of a personal pronoun – either the "you" of vv. 2-4 or the "we" of v. 5 – it is almost certainly positional (locative).

Thus for those who now exist "in Christ Jesus" here are the essential realities in terms of wrapping up the present discussion. First, picking up a theological truism first articulated in 1 Cor 7:19, Paul asserts that neither circumcision nor uncircumcision count for anything. And while, in the course of the present argument, that is easy to see with regard to circumcision, Paul is equally adamant about uncircumcision. This is most likely intended to undercut the possibility that the uncircumcised Gentile who has put his faith in Christ will try to make something of his being accepted by Christ while bypassing circumcision. Paul's point – surely to the dismay of the Jewish community that he dearly loves (see Rom 9:3) – is that Christ has superseded the law in such a way that neither one or the other counts for anything with God. The only thing that counts now is faith, putting one's full trust in Christ.

But Paul is equally loath to leave it there, since there is in fact something that does indeed count with God: that God's children (4:6-7) bear God's image in their relationships with one another and with the world. Thus what "counts" is "faith that works itself out in love." Moreover, there is very likely a touch of irony in Paul's use of the verb "to work" in this clause after the steady diet of pejorative uses of this noun earlier in the letter. "Work" there is to be done, to be sure, but it is "the work of God," not "works of law." So with this last phrase Paul anticipates the final argument of the letter that begins in 5:13 and carries through 6:10. But before he follows up on it, and in light of what he has argued right along, especially in vv. 5-6, he makes yet one more direct appeal to the Galatians to come to their senses, while at the same time offering yet one more biting condemnation of their "persecutors."

---

[15] For the latter, see NLT, "when we place our faith in Christ Jesus."

Galatians 5:7-12 – Second Appeal: Condemnation of the Agitators

> [7]*You were running a good race. Who cut in on you to keep you from obeying the truth?* [8]*That kind of persuasion does not come from the one who calls you.* [9]*"A little yeast works through the whole batch of dough."* [10]*I am confident in the Lord that you will take no other view. The one who is throwing you into confusion will have to pay the penalty, whoever that may be.* [11]*Brothers and sisters, if I am still preaching circumcision, why am I still being persecuted? In that case the offense of the cross has been abolished.* [12]*As for those agitators, I wish they would go the whole way and emasculate themselves!*

Paul could very easily have gone from the preceding paragraph, with its final word about "faith working through love," straight to the admonition in v. 13, which picks up the two key words, "freedom" and "love." But that must wait until he has made a final appeal based on the preceding argument from Scripture (4:21-31). What is left unfinished is a final application of the Genesis 21 passage, which Paul had interpreted in 4:29 in terms of the son born "according to the flesh" as persecuting "the son born by the power of the Spirit," which was followed by the single citation from the Genesis passage: "Get rid of the slave woman and her son." To this matter Paul now turns.

The paragraph is basically a singular, but two-sided, appeal that ends up finally in three parts. The primary appeal is directed toward the Galatians themselves (vv. 7-10), in light of the clear possibility that they might capitulate with regard to circumcision. The second appeal has to do with the agitators (vv. 7, 9, 10b, 12), who by implication from 4:29 should now be "cast out" of Galatia. The third issue has to do with Paul himself and a scandalous accusation brought against him by the agitators (v. 11). Thus, while the paragraph is still directed toward the Galatians, it deals primarily with these troublemakers, whom we have met heretofore in 1:7; 3:1; and 4:17 – although their unmentioned presence lies heavily across the entire letter. Because of this, the paragraph is in many ways the least easy in the letter in which to trace a careful flow of thought. Rather, Paul's concern for the Galatians and his desire that they rid themselves of the agitators tumble over each other in his attempt to affirm the Galatians and to see them rid of their problem. Added to our difficulty are the sudden changes of metaphors in vv. 7-10: from a race, to baking (leaven in dough), to a law court (pay the penalty). But despite all this, Paul's concerns themselves are quite clear.

Verses 7-8. Paul begins his appeal with a metaphor, common to him,[16] that he had already used of himself in 2:2 – of the Christian life as running a race. His various uses of the metaphor make it certain that Paul was well acquainted with the games. In this case it is the problem of another runner cutting someone off by moving in front of them without adequate space. Paul's point is clear: these men are not only not helping you reach the heavenly goal, but are in effect cutting you off so that you do not reach the goal at all (as argued in v. 4 above). "Who has done this?" he asks rhetorically, knowing full well the kind of men they were, even if he did not know them personally. So with this metaphor he simply repeats what he has stated in plain Greek in vv. 2-4 above.

With a probable play on words, Paul accuses these intruders of "cutting in on them," which has resulted in the Galatians' no longer being "persuaded by the truth." Although the verb for "persuade" (πείθω) in the passive tends to move toward "obey," it is less "obedience" that concerns Paul here as it is "persuasion," the primary meaning of the verb. After all, "obedience" in this context would imply commands; what is at stake in Galatia are not commands, but "persuasion" regarding the truth, which in this letter has altogether to do with "the truth of the gospel" itself (2:5, 14) – in each case a matter of trusting Christ and not going the way of circumcision. So at stake ultimately is whether the Galatians will stay with the gospel or believe a lie, which says that God requires obedience to the Jewish law as well as putting their trust in Christ.

That this is Paul's concern is made clear by the next sentence (v. 8): "That kind of persuasion does not come from the one who calls you." This is the second time in the letter (see 1:6) that Paul has referred to the Galatians' relationship to God in terms of God's calling them to himself, language Paul also used in referring to his own conversion (1:15). The shift to the present tense in this case is especially noteworthy; the One who first called them to himself is now through this letter calling them again – not to "conversion" in this case but to come back to their senses regarding "the truth of the gospel." At least this letter can be an instrument of calling them back, which ultimately must be the work of the Spirit.

Verse 9. In reading Galatians through, one comes on this saying ("a little yeast works through the whole batch of dough") as a rather

---

[16] For Paul's various uses of this metaphor see 2 Thess 3:1; 1 Cor 9:24-26; Rom 9:16; Phil 2:16; 3:13-14.

abrupt moment. Since Paul had previously used it to refer to the incestuous man in 1 Cor 5:7, it is almost certainly a proverbial saying whose point is that a very small amount of an otherwise unseen substance can be so pervasive as to infect the whole. But whereas Paul clearly commands the Corinthians to remove the old leaven from the community in the earlier instance, that is not said directly here, so one is left a bit up in the air as to its primary intent.

At the very least it refers to the teaching of the agitators, especially their insistence on circumcision for these Gentile followers of Christ. While it may very likely, as in the former case, also refer to the agitators themselves, and their negative influence on the community, in this letter Paul never directly tells the Galatians to "expel them" from their community. The closest he comes to it is by way of implication in 4:30, in his citing Gen 21:10 that they should "get rid of the slave woman and her son." In any case the emphasis here seems to be on the pervasive, and in this case evil, influence these outsiders are having on the community; Paul's concern is that the Galatian believers not be infected further by the false teaching.

Verse 10a. Picking up the word "persuasion" from vv. 7 and 8, Paul now speaks more confidently than at any other point in the letter that his Galatian friends will come back to their senses: "I am persuaded (thus, confident) in the Lord." This expression occurs often enough in Paul's letters, and over a considerable time span,[17] to recognize it as a common idiom for him, as a way of expressing not just his confidence, but especially the source of his confidence – the Lord himself.

What Paul is confident about is that "you will have no other mindset." The verb in this instance (φρονέω), which occurs only here in Galatians,[18] has to do with setting one's mind toward something, or giving it careful consideration. Hence the TNIV has captured its basic sense by here rendering it, "that you will take no other point of view." In view of what has been said up to this point in the letter, one is not quite prepared for this vote of confidence; but again, Paul's

---

[17] Although the phrase "in the Lord" (ἐν κυρίῳ) occurs throughout his letters in a variety of ways, as a modifier of the verb "persuade" (πείθω), it occurs elsewhere in 2 Thess 3:3; Rom 14:14; Phil 1:14; 2:24. Since this covers a long range of time (2 Thessalonians to Philippians), one can be sure it functioned as a standard idiom, as to where Paul's confidence comes from.

[18] The verb occurs 24 times in all, 9 in Romans and 10 in Philippians. Unfortunately often translated "think," it has very little to do with "thinking" as that word is most often used in English; rather it has to do with the set of one's mind toward a certain thing, or one's disposition toward anything.

confidence in this case is ultimately "in the Lord," that the Galatians
will see things from Christ's own point of view.

Verse 10b. In contrast to what he expects of the Lord with regard to
the Galatians, and to alleviate any sense of guilt on their part, Paul
places the ultimate condemnation on "the one who is troubling you."
With this verb he picks up the initial language used of these outsiders
in 1:7; they are creating trouble for you. The surprising element is the
sudden shift from the plural regarding these outsiders to the singular,
which occurs only here in the letter. This is also the evidence that all
of the troublemakers are not equally responsible for the trouble. That
is, just as Paul had colleagues who traveled with him and might be
referred to by others as "them," they in fact are led by one person,
Paul himself. So also with these trouble-making agitators, they are
probably led by the one person who, though unknown to Paul, is the
ringleader of the invaders. So "whoever he is," he will in fact "bear
the judgment," which the TNIV, following the Bauer-Danker
lexicon, has correctly rendered, "pay the penalty." Thus Paul clearly
expects that those who have been "troubling" the Galatians by insisting on circumcision will come under divine judgment for doing so.

Verse 11. Given all that has been said to this point, this next
sentence is one of the most puzzling moments in this letter – or in any
other of Paul's letters. Quite abruptly we discover here for the first
time, that one of the tactics used by the trouble-makers was to argue
that Paul himself "still preaches circumcision." This seems to mean, by
implication, that Paul has been known to do so elsewhere, but has not
done so in Galatia, so as to curry the Galatians' favor. This in turn
helps to make some sense of the accusation against which Paul was
defending himself in 1:10 – that his aim right along has been to win
human approval.

Since it is hard to imagine anything more absurd than this, one has
to wonder where such an idea could have sprung from. The best
answer to this is found in the narrative in Acts 16:1-3, where Paul had
Timothy circumcised so as not to offend the Jewish community
among whom he always began his mission. Indeed, Paul has been
severely criticized among modern scholars for the action taken in Acts
16. But all of this is precisely in keeping with Paul's own missionary
strategy, based on two absolute principles.

First is the affirmation in v. 6, that neither circumcision nor uncircumcision counts for a thing with God. Paul is only upset on this issue
when people like the present agitators make it count for something;
and then he comes out fighting for the truth of the gospel. Second,

and quite in keeping with the first, is the principle articulated most clearly in 1 Cor 9:19-23, that "though I am free and belong to no one, I have made myself a slave to everyone, to win as many as possible. To the Jews I became like a Jew, to win the Jews. To those under the law I became like one under the law (though I myself am not under the law), so as to win those under the law" (vv. 19-20). This is precisely the kind of freedom in Christ that those who live by law simply find intolerable; and their way to fight it is to argue for "inconsistency" on the part of the apostle.

But Paul's consistency is to be found in his very gospel-oriented view of life, in which the law ceases to exist as law and has been replaced by God's own empowering presence, the Holy Spirit himself – as will be argued in the final section of the letter. For now his defense rests solely on the other well-known reality, that he is in fact still being persecuted, mostly by the very ones – or their ilk – who are also accusing him of being two-faced with regard to circumcision.

The final clause in this verse is easily discerned in terms of its content and its relationship to what Paul says in 1 Cor 1:18-25. But its immediate relationship to the preceding question is not quite as clear. The word that the TNIV has translated "in that case" (ἄρα) has the nuance of a result, and can only refer back to the protasis ("if-clause") of that sentence. Thus, "if I am still preaching circumcision, ... then the scandal of the cross has been removed." The scandal, of course, is the proclamation of a "crucified Messiah" (1 Cor 1:22). It was simply unthinkable for Jew and Gentile alike that a deity would die by crucifixion, an execution reserved by the Romans for only insurrectionists and recalcitrant slaves. Nobody, but nobody, could have dreamed up this heart of the Christian gospel, since it would have been so scandalous as to be scorned or laughed at. Paul's point is that anyone who preaches such a message is not going to preach circumcision at the same time in order to curry favor with any particular group!

Verse 12. Finally, in a moment of considerable frustration and in direct response to the accusations of v. 11, Paul wonders – in the form of a wish – if the agitators are so keen to use the knife on male genitals, why not rather castrate themselves. There is, of course, a double irony here, since castrated males could not serve in the temple. One should note the similar play on this idea in Paul's equally scorching condemnation of such "agitators" in Phil 3:1-3.

Paul has often been criticized for this moment; but his critics seem also to miss the fact that had Paul lost this battle they themselves would not exist as Christians. For the plain fact is that Christianity among Gentiles would not have lasted a generation had these agitators won the day. Furthermore, this letter as a whole and Paul's equally strong response to them much later in Philippians makes it clear that they did no evangelism at all, but rather went from Pauline church to Pauline church trying to make observant Jews out of Gentiles who have believed in Christ and received the Spirit. So the language is strong, to be sure, but the issue is an ultimate one; and all of this is said for the sake of his Galatian friends, so that they might stay with "the truth of the gospel."

Reflection and Response – Part Four

Reflection

Since this passage is primarily a second stage of the argument presented in 3:1–4:7, one might wish to begin reflection by reviewing what was said there. Nonetheless, this passage has its own moments that call for reflection and response on our part.

One of the difficulties with the present passage is Paul's allegorical use of an Old Testament narrative in 4:24-27 to further his point. At issue for us in the twenty-first century is whether it is legitimate to emulate Paul's example and do the same thing with biblical texts. My first response to such an idea is that Paul was inspired of the Spirit in ways that we are not; and this passage was not written to give us an example of "how to do Scripture." But two further observations are needed. First, there is no evidence of any kind in the text that Paul is offering us an example of how to use Scripture in argumentation. Furthermore, we simply do not know enough about their situation to know how much, if any, of this paragraph is in direct response to what was being argued by the agitators themselves.

Second, the most striking thing about the paragraph is how unnecessary it is to the present passage itself. As was pointed out in the commentary, one could very easily go from v. 23 to v. 28 without missing a beat, which suggests that nothing in this brief "interpretive" moment is actually crucial to Paul's point. What it does, rather, is to give Paul further leverage against his opponents by making clear that they come from "unbelieving" Jerusalem, even though they would consider themselves followers of Christ. By insisting on observance of the Torah for Gentile followers of Christ, they are in fact a "throwback" to the law-observant Judaism of which Paul himself was a part and from which Christ had redeemed him. So this should probably be considered a unique moment in this letter and therefore does not offer a kind of interpretive model for us to emulate.

Much more significant for us is to reflect on what Paul meant by "falling from grace" in 5:4, which most later Christians have tended to turn on its head and make it refer to someone who has fallen into sin. But here it is the *law-keeper* who has fallen from grace not the sinner. We need to take much more seriously than we do how much many of us really do rely on our own righteousness (= our obedience to our own form of "law") as the ultimate guarantor of heaven! Not only so, but because it is easy for us to think our form of "law" is so important, we tend to make it a rule for all others, and thus "teach" them that to be "completed" in Christ people must become obedient to our own "standards."

I have often reflected on the fact that hardly any of my own companions from my teenage years in the Pentecostal church in which I grew up are now followers of Christ. And I am convinced it was because they could see through the "smoke screen" too easily. The people most insistent on "the law" (= matters of behavior having to do with food, drink, dress and entertainment) were very often the least gracious and most critical people in the community. From Paul's perspective such people had "fallen from grace" and were determined to make us young people into the hypocrites that we clearly saw they were, but that they were unable to see for themselves.

Thus, what does one do with the various forms of "law keeping" that abound in present-day Pentecostal and evangelical churches? How does one handle those people who believe in grace but are ready to impose their "law" on Spirit-gifted women so that they are excluded from functioning with their gifts in the community of faith? I want to say to my Pentecostal brothers and sisters, "You were running well" regarding this matter; who has cut in on you so as to exclude women from using their grace-given gifting for the sake of the church?

The real problem with such "law-keeping" is that it gives people a false sense of security, so that they never really learn to trust Christ. The "law" functions like a fence to keep people inside and safe; and if the fence is ever torn down then they go wild after their desires. Whereas "grace" demands a constant leaning on Christ and enabling of the Holy Spirit, so that one would scarcely notice if the "fence" were torn down.

Finally, what does one do with the concluding paragraph (vv. 7-12)? This is especially acute for us since there are so few settings in which a situation similar to Paul's could ever occur. The great danger is that one might use this passage as an excuse for treating with disrespect brothers or sisters in the local church who might disagree with one on some important issue. But whatever else, these people are in fact outsiders altogether, whom Paul never blesses by calling them "brothers." So it would seem to take a most unusual circumstance for the passage to apply in a day like ours.

Response

So in light of such reflection, I need to ask some of the same questions again. Am I really ready to trust Christ alone and rely on his grace, or am I also a "pocket" Judaizer, who secretly thinks that unless people live up to certain standards of the law, they are not really "good Christians"? What form of "law" do I hold so dear that I am ready to go to the wall for it, and especially so for others, fearing that if they do not share my convictions they must be displeasing to God? In what ways might I have "fallen from grace" into law-keeping? Or worse yet, in what ways might I have imposed my own "falling from grace" onto others? Am I as much concerned over any of God's people having "fallen from grace" into law-keeping, as Paul under inspiration of the Spirit was? Indeed, am I as concerned about this as I am about someone's having been ensnared by a besetting sin? In what ways might I monitor myself on this matter, since relating to God by keeping the law is an ever-present problem?

1. Examine your life in the light of the foregoing questions focusing on moments or periods of time when you have tended to rely upon your own form of law-keeping in order to please God.
2. Assess the reasons for such actions in the light of Paul's argument in Galatians.
3. In a specific time of prayer confess this temptation for self reliance and allow the Lord to remind you cognitively and affectively of his all-sufficiency to keep you alive in the Spirit.
4. Seek out a brother or sister who is struggling with similar tendencies for the purpose of sharing your testimony and mutual edification.

Galatians 5:13–6:10

The Text

The Spirit Supersedes the Law

Historically this passage has been understood to reflect a major shift in the letter, from the argument proper to a concluding section of paraenesis[1] (exhortation). Thus all of chs. 5 and 6 together have most often been viewed as "ethical instruction" following "right thinking about the Christian gospel" set forth in chs. 3–4.[2] But despite the popularity of this view, not to mention that the passage does indeed begin with two significant imperatives, this section as a whole is much better understood as bringing the *argument* of Galatians to its proper conclusion. It functions, in fact, as Paul's own response to his question in 3:3: "Having *begun* by the Spirit, do you now *come to completion* by the flesh?" His answer is, "No, you come to completion by the same Spirit with whom you began."

In his transitional "speech" in 2:15-21 Paul had set forth both of the basic theological propositions of the argument that followed (that righteousness is "not by works of Torah" but "by faith in Christ Jesus"). He has now twice argued the case for these two propositions (in 3:1–4:7 and 4:21-31). But Paul had concluded his "speech" by pointing to the indwelling Christ (by his Spirit, is implied) as the effective agent for living out true righteousness (v. 20). With the present passage Paul picks up that concluding concern, expressed now in terms of the sufficiency of the Spirit over against both Torah and the flesh. The indwelling Spirit brings about the true righteousness that Torah called for but could not produce, and thus stands effectively over against the "flesh" – that inherent human fallenness which had characterized their former life as Gentiles and had made Torah ineffective for Jews.

---

[1] This technical term will be used throughout this chapter, since it is more precise than "exhortation" or "imperatives." By definition it is "a technical term referring to various kinds of exhortations or admonitions" (A.G. Patzia & A.J. Petrotta, *Pocket Dictionary of Biblical Studies* [Downers Grove: InterVarsity Press, 2002], 89).

[2] For an especially helpful overview of this historic understanding, see John M.G. Barclay, *Obeying the Truth: A Study of Paul's Ethics in Galatians* (Edinburgh: T & T Clark, 1988), 9-26.

As noted throughout, at stake in this letter is the inclusion of Gentiles as full and equal members of the people of God – whether having believed in Christ, they must also accept the "identity markers" of Jewishness in order to be genuine "children (thus 'heirs') of Abraham." The issue raised by the agitators is thus not how one *enters* life in Christ (they would have agreed that this was through the death and resurrection of Christ), but how such life is brought to *completion* (3:3) – especially for Gentiles.

We have also noted throughout how crucial to the argument as a whole is the role of the Spirit in the life of the believer – both at the beginning and throughout one's entire life in Christ. Thus the key element of Christian *conversion* is the Spirit, dynamically experienced (3:2-5; 4:6), as the fulfillment of the promise to Abraham (3:14). So too with the whole of Christian life. The Christian experience of the Spirit sets off the believer in Christ from all other existences, which are alternatively seen either as "under law" (5:18) or as "carrying out the desire of the flesh" (5:16). The Galatians had previously lived the latter; the agitators had turned up to place them under the former. Paul will have none of it. The Spirit alone is the antidote to the "works of the flesh"; Torah not only does not help, but rather leads to bondage. Set free from that bondage through Christ, the person who walks, lives, is led by the Spirit is not only not under law, but by the Spirit produces the very fruit to which the law pointed forward but could not produce.

But for Paul all is not automatic. One must sow to the Spirit (6:8), and be led by the Spirit (5:18); indeed, "if we have been brought to life by the Spirit" (v. 24), we must therefore also "by the Spirit behave accordingly" (v. 25). This final argument in the letter thus becomes one of the most significant in the Pauline corpus for our understanding of Pauline ethics, as Spirit-empowered Christ-likeness, lived out in Christian community in loving servanthood. At issue is *not* a Spirit-flesh struggle within the believer's heart, but *the sufficiency of the Spirit* for life in the believing community – over against both the law and the flesh, as God's replacement of the former and antidote to the latter.

This concluding argument of the letter comes in three basic parts, set out by Paul's own structural signals: (*a*) The opening paragraph (5:13-15) is signalled by the vocative "brothers and sisters" (ἀδελφοί) and is tied to what precedes with a "for." Here Paul sets forth the basic issues ("flesh" and "love") that will be spelled out in greater detail in what follows; v. 15 (and later, v. 26) indicates that the real ethical concern is about interpersonal conflict in the community. (*b*) The second section (5:16-26) is signalled by the contrasting phrase, "but I say." Here he presents life in the Spirit as superseding the law precisely because such life does what the law could not do – serve as an adequate antidote to the "flesh." (c) The final section (6:1-10) is signalled by the second vocative ("brothers and sisters"). Here Paul offers some practical examples of life in the Spirit (vv. 1-6), while vv. 7-10 serve to bring the whole to a fitting conclusion.

Before looking at the argument in its specifics, some general observations are in order. First, from beginning to end the concern is with *Christian life in community*, not with the interior life of the individual believer. This material, therefore, has to do with the individual as he or she is part of the community of faith. This point must be stressed again and again, since failure here has resulted in a considerable misreading of much of this material, especially vv. 16-23. Second, the general lack of imperatives[3] before the practical application in 6:1-10 suggests that this is not simply a series of commands based on the preceding argument, but rather is in itself a fitting *conclusion to the argument* of the letter as a whole. Third, the (otherwise surprising) mentions of Torah in 5:14, 18, and 23 and of the "law of Christ" in 6:2 indicate that this is still part of the concern of this material. The argument moves forward to be sure, but not without concern for what has been argued till now. And fourth, while the relationship of the Spirit to flesh and Torah seems easy enough to discern, what is more tenuous is the relationship between flesh and Torah that is implied, a relationship that is only hinted at here, but spelled out in some detail later in Romans 6–8. Nonetheless, it is clear in this earlier letter that the law and the flesh are on the same side of things, as dealing in death not life, as Paul will make abundantly clear in Rom 7:4-6.

Galatians 5:13-15 – The Argument from Scripture

[13]*You, my brothers and sisters, were called to be free. But do not use your freedom to indulge the sinful nature;[a] rather, serve one another humbly in*

---

[3] In fact the only imperatives in vv. 13-26 are in vv. 13 and 16 ("perform the duties of a slave"; "walk by the Spirit"). As vv. 25-26 move the argument back to application, Paul shifts to "hortatory" imperatives ("let us ..."). The number of imperatives does increase in the practical application of 6:1-10 (3 second plural imperatives; 2 hortatory subjunctives; and 2 third singular imperatives). The whole is thus framed by imperatives; and the argument is carried forward at crucial places by an imperative (e.g., 5:16; 5:25; 6:1, 7). But by and large the imperatives are regularly explained or elaborated by material that is consistently in the indicative.

love. *For the entire law is fulfilled in keeping this one command: "Love your neighbor as yourself."* ^b ¹⁵*If you keep on biting and devouring each other, watch out or you will be destroyed by each other.*

ᵃ13 Or *the flesh*; also in vv. 16,17,19 and 24   ᵇLev. 19:18

As noted above, this opening paragraph picks up several matters from what has just been said, while serving at the same time to introduce the final argument of the letter. Verse 13, whose love command is the only imperative in the paragraph, picks up the two crucial matters from vv. 1-6: the call to "freedom" from v. 1 and the call to love from v. 6. Verse 14 then ties the love command to the earlier theme of "doing the whole law," but does so in terms of "the entire Torah" as *fulfilled*, thus indicating why the time of the Torah itself is now past. Verse 15 then presents the surprising element. While we might have expected the "love command" to appear for purely theological reasons, what we discover is the existence of strong discord within the communities themselves. Thus the argument that *freedom* is not for *flesh* but for *love* (v.13), which in turns brings an end to *Torah* as its "fulfillment" (v. 14), indicates that *flesh* and *community strife* belong together (v. 15), while true *freedom* moves in exactly the opposite direction through *love*.

Verse 13. This paragraph is related to what has preceded by means of the conjunction "for" (γάρ), which usually functions as an explanatory marker, but here serves simply to express continuation of the narrative (so BDAG). It was therefore (rightly) left untranslated in the TNIV. What it obviously continues is the application that was dropped at v. 6, since it picks up the key words "freedom" and "love" from that paragraph. Thus, using one of his key terms for conversion, Paul reminds them that when "you were called"⁴ to become a part of God's people, that call was explicitly to "freedom" – the key word in the preceding biblical argument.

With a strong "not-but" contrast Paul immediately defines "freedom," first negatively and then positively, in both cases in terms of what freedom is all about. First, "freedom" has nothing to do with selfishness, meaning freedom to do whatever one wants, whenever one wants to. Using a word having to do with a "base of operations" for further activity, Paul indicates what "freedom in Christ" does *not* mean; it is not

---

⁴ On the use of this word in Galatians (and elsewhere) see on 1:6 (and n. 24).

to serve as a "base of operations" for "the flesh."[5] The word "flesh," which first appeared in 3:13 in this letter, will finally be defined – in terms of its actions – in vv. 19-21, selfish actions all.

Alternatively, as one of the paradoxes of Christian faith, true freedom means servanthood; it means following in the steps of Christ, who not only in love "gave himself up" for others (2:20), but who also insisted that the only discipleship worthy of the name is to be a servant to others: "Whoever wants to become great among you must be your servant, and whoever wants to be first must be slave of all" (Mark 10:43-44). Thus, picking up on the love command that permeates his understanding of Christian discipleship,[6] Paul urges that with love as the motivation, they "perform the duties of a slave for one another."[7] It is not by accident, therefore, that "love" will appear first in the list of virtues in vv. 22-23.

Verse 14. With an explanatory "for," Paul now gives evidence from the law itself as to this understanding of the proper use of "freedom" in Christ. In doing so, he offers his basic understanding as to why the law is no longer active for those who follow Christ, and thus he gives his second reason for its no longer having a role in Christian life. Earlier he had declared that God had sent his Son "to redeem those under the law, so that we might receive adoption to sonship" (4:5). Thus the first reason that the law no longer functions for the believer has to do with the redemption that brought us out of "slavery" into a familial relationship with the Father and Son. Now he offers the second reason: the whole law is summed up, and thus "fulfilled" (in the sense of being brought to its full expression) in "one word," meaning "in carrying out this one command."

The command is that found in Lev 19:18 ("Love your neighbor as yourself"), and at this point Paul is once more indicating that he knows the teaching of Jesus, who himself had pointed to this "command" as the fulfillment of the whole law.[8] The command itself should be easy enough to understand; it is the doing of it that creates

[5] On the meaning of this crucial word ("flesh" [σάρξ]) for Paul, here translated "sinful nature" by the TNIV see the discussion on 3:3 above, where it was rendered "by human effort"; cf. also 4:23 and 29 above.

[6] In letters preceding this one, see 1Thess 3:12; 5:8; 1 Cor 13; 16:14; in letters that follow, see Rom 12:9-10; 13:9-10 (the companion to the present one); Col 3:14; Eph 4:2; 5:2; Phil 2:2.

[7] For this rendering of the verb (δουλεύω), see BDAG, entry 2, who offer this as its first meaning when used metaphorically.

[8] See Matt 19:19; 23:39; Mark 12:31-33; Luke 10:27-36; for Paul's later use of this teaching see Rom 13:9-10.

the difficulty for many of God's people.[9] But in our present
therapeutic culture something more needs to be said, since this text is
often seen now as evidence that one should first of all have love for
oneself, and then love for one's neighbor in the same way. Such an
understanding, of course, could not possibly have been available
culturally either to Moses, Jesus, or Paul.[10] The command is not that
one should first care for oneself and then one's neighbor in the same
way; rather the point is that in the same way that a person instinctively
"looks out for number one," that same kind of instinct should be
carried over to one's "neighbor," where "neighbor" is now defined
not as the person next door, but as referring to any and all with whom
one comes into personal contact. Or to put all this in the terms
intended by Moses and Jesus, "giving priority to neighbor" is not
intended to demean oneself, but to "fulfill" the whole law, "whole"
having to do with that large portion of Torah that has to do with
human relationships. To love neighbor as self means not just "not
stealing," but "giving oneself for" the other even at personal cost.

Verse 15. This final sentence in the introductory paragraph catches
one by total surprise. One rather assumes that people who are adamant
about "doing the law" are equally concerned about caring for one's
neighbor. But the exact opposite prevailed in Galatia. They apparently
were concerned about "doing (certain aspects of) the law" so as to
secure their eternal relationship with God. In so doing they were
missing the point of the law altogether, which did not primarily have
to do with "getting it right" regarding some *external* matters that gave
people identity as belonging to Israel's God, but "getting it right" as
God's own people by bearing his image in their relationships with
others. Thus, quite in contrast to how Paul, following Jesus, encap-
sulates the entire law in terms of one's relationship to neighbor, they
were apparently quite ready to go to the wall over purely "religious"
matters (circumcision, sabbath, food laws), while treating some fellow
believers as enemies to be defeated.

Thus in this sentence the "flesh" reveals itself in the form of
community strife, in which believers "bite and devour" one another.
It is precisely at this point, the "life of the flesh," that Torah had

[9] As was already in evidence for the rabbi who gave the right response to Jesus'
question on this matter, but then had the temerity to ask the follow-up question:
"Who is my neighbor?" To which Jesus responded by telling the parable of the "Good
Samaritan" (Luke 10:25-37).

[10] This view is the direct result of North America's becoming a predominantly
therapeutic culture in the second half of the twentieth century.

demonstrated itself to be inadequate. Torah obviously "laid down the law" against such behavior; but by deflecting Torah toward "works of law" in the form of Jewish identity symbols, one could be "religious" without being "righteous." Christ brought an end to Torah observance in part for that very reason; the Spirit replaced Torah, so that God's people, Jew and Gentile alike, would have a new "identity" – the indwelling Spirit of the living God himself – who would at the same time be sufficient to accomplish what Torah could not: effectively stand in opposition to the flesh.

The point to be made is that Paul's conditional sentence is neither hypothetical nor suppositional, suggesting that "if you were ever to do this, this would be the result." Rather it is expressed as a "present particular condition," meaning as the TNIV (and NAB) has it, that "if you keep on (with your present conduct of) biting and devouring one another." As is unfortunately all too often the case with "the religious," they continue to care about external things that God has put aside altogether through Christ and the Spirit, while the things that God truly cares about – relationships within and without the community of faith – are easily put aside in the interest of getting the religious stuff right. The result is that circumcision and food laws and the observance of Sabbath carry primary importance, while caring for one's neighbors becomes more optional, especially so if the "neighbor" does not share my same passion for being religious.

So Paul warns them, not in terms of their relationship with God, but in terms of their capacity to self-destruct as a community of faith. "Watch out," he warns, "or your biting and devouring" will result in your being "destroyed by each other." Paul's point seems to be that self-destruction as a people of God is the way God will judge those who claim to be his but behave like those who are not. Here is the first evidence in this section that what is at stake in this argument is not the "interior life" of the individual believer, but the "behavioral life" of believers in relationship to one another and the world.

Galatians 5:16-26 – The Application: The Sufficiency of the Spirit

> [16] *So I say, walk by the Spirit, and you will not gratify the desires of the sinful nature.* [a] [17] *For the sinful nature desires what is contrary to the Spirit, and the Spirit what is contrary to the sinful nature. They are in conflict with each other, so that you are not to do whatever[b] you want.* [18] *But if you are led by the Spirit, you are not under the law.*
>
> [19] *The acts of the sinful nature are obvious: sexual immorality, impurity and debauchery;* [20] *idolatry and witchcraft; hatred, discord, jealousy, fits of*

rage, selfish ambition, dissensions, factions [21] *and envy; drunkenness, orgies, and the like. I warn you, as I did before, that those who live like this will not inherit the kingdom of God.*

[22] *But the fruit of the Spirit is love, joy, peace, patience, kindness, goodness, faithfulness,* [23] *gentleness and self-control. Against such things there is no law.* [24] *Those who belong to Christ Jesus have crucified the sinful nature with its passions and desires.* [25] *Since we live by the Spirit, let us keep in step with the Spirit.* [26] *Let us not become conceited, provoking and envying each other.*

[a] 16 Or *the flesh*, also in vv. 17, 19 and 24   [b] 17 Or *you do not do what*

With these several paragraphs Paul offers not only a direct response to the problem that surfaced in v. 15, but also a considerable argument that the Spirit effectively replaces Torah and is therefore sufficient for the much larger problem of "the flesh" (TNIV "sinful nature"). Although the passage begins in a hortatory way, "walk by the Spirit," and thus suggests that there is indeed a "practical" element involved, it nonetheless functions primarily as a concluding argument to the issues that have been raised throughout the letter. The opening paragraph (vv. 16-18) in turn offers the primary imperative that controls the entire passage (v. 16), followed by an explanation of the Spirit's sufficiency over against the flesh (v. 17), while also pointing out that the Spirit thus eliminates the need of Torah (v. 18). Whatever else, for Paul flesh and Spirit and Torah and Spirit are mutually exclusive options: walking by the Spirit is the antidote to making provision for "flesh"; and for such a person, the law is an irrelevancy.

This opening paragraph is then followed by contrasting *descriptions* of the "deeds" of the flesh (vv. 19-21) and the "fruit" of the Spirit (vv. 22-23), apparently designed to explicate vv. 16-17, as to how it is that they stand in such unrelieved opposition. Both conclude with an indication of the outcome of living each way: eternal loss on the one hand; without need of law on the other. The argument is then brought to a threefold conclusion (vv. 24-26) in which Paul brings Christ back into the picture. In turn (*a*) Christ's people are those who have through his crucifixion experienced death to the old way of life (v. 24) and (*b*) who now live a resurrected life by the Spirit (v. 25); therefore (*c*) they must stop the infighting that brought on this whole argument (v. 26).

Verses 16-18. Paul begins his response to the internal conflict noted in v. 15 by asserting the sufficiency of the Spirit over against the flesh. When this is recognized, Paul's otherwise difficult flow of thought in this first paragraph is easily accounted for. The solemn asseveration with which it begins, "but I say," stands in direct contrast to v. 15 with its warning that their kinds of "deeds of the flesh" (v. 13) lead eventually to their being "consumed" by one another. Thus in the present verse the prescription against using freedom from Torah as a "base of operations for the flesh" resides in the primary Pauline ethical imperative, "walk by the Spirit." By so doing, one will thereby "not carry out the desire of [= make provision for] the flesh." Verse 17 in turn offers an explanation as to *how* the assertion in v. 16 is true, namely that the Spirit stands in unrelieved opposition to the flesh, so that doing whatever the flesh desires is no longer a viable option. So also, the sudden, seemingly disjointed, mention of Torah in v. 18 is accounted for at this point as a response to v. 14. That is, the Spirit who empowers love thereby "fulfills" Torah, so that the one led by the Spirit is "not under law." Its mention at this point in the argument suggests that Paul's concern is to put forth the Spirit as God's response to *both* the flesh and Torah, because the latter could *not* counteract the desire of the flesh, but the Spirit can and does.

In *verse 16* Paul thus sets forth the basic imperative for all of Christian life: "Walk by the Spirit." In so doing he picks up a primary metaphor for obedience to the law in the Pentateuch. Israel was to be instructed in the law so that they could be shown "the way in which they are to walk" (Exod 18:20); indeed they were to "walk in obedience to all … the Lord has commanded" (Deut 5:33). Since the Spirit is God's own sufficiency for "obedience" among the new covenant people of God, the primary new covenant imperative is "walk by Spirit." With this imperative Paul has shifted the emphases from the *arena* of obedience (the law) to the *means* of obedience (the Spirit). It is through the enabling of the Spirit that one will fulfill the entire law in loving one's neighbor as oneself (v. 14).

And since we may rightly assume that Paul still has vv. 14 and 15 in view, he attaches to the imperative the divine promissory note,[11] that by such "walking" the Spirit empowers one not to carry out the desire of the flesh, namely to "eat and devour each other." This is how the "one command" is to be fulfilled; and for Paul it is an unassailable proposition. The flesh (sinful nature) is always concerned about the "rights" of number one; but such desires are quite antithetical to the ways of God, as they have been revealed in Christ, "who loved [us]

---

[11] Contrary to the NRSV, the apodosis of this sentence must be taken as a promise, not an imperative. That is, Paul is hereby indicating the *result* of "walking by the Spirit," not *commanding* them "not to fulfill the desire of the flesh" (NRSV).

and *gave himself up* for [us]" (2:20). The way of the flesh is to fight back in order to get even, or to oppose someone who sees things differently. The way of the Spirit is to love one's neighbor in any and all such circumstances, and only the Spirit can enable fallen people like ourselves so to live – which is what Paul then sets out to explain in the next sentence.

Our *verse 17* has had a long and unfortunate history of interpretation within the Protestant tradition, where it has been understood as having to do with the interior life of the believer and has thus been interpreted (very badly as it turns out) in light of Rom 7:13-25 – where the Spirit is not so much as mentioned! Paul is setting out to explain two matters simultaneously: the *sufficiency* and the *necessity* of the Spirit, so that one may walk obediently regarding the imperative in the preceding sentence (v. 16). Despite some convolutions in the order of clauses in his sentence (which is the cause of much of our difficulty), Paul's *point* seems clear enough: that the Spirit and the flesh are absolutely antithetical to each other; and *the Spirit opposes the flesh* precisely so that, even though Torah is gone, *one may not do* whatever one wishes. Rather, one will carry out the purposes of the Spirit who opposes those of the flesh.[12]

Perhaps the easiest way to "see" the sentence in terms of Paul's own emphasis is to offer a structural diagram, in which the indented clauses indicate where they fit and how they modify the main clause(s).

(*a*) For the flesh has desires against the Spirit;
(*b*) but (δέ) the Spirit [is] against the flesh
(*c*)   (for these two stand in opposition to each other)
(*d*)   so that you may *not* do whatever you wish to do

Line *a* follows naturally out of v. 16, with its phrase "desires of the flesh." Paul's point is one of simple explanation (indicated by the "for" [γάρ]). At issue is the affirmation that the newly formed people of God, God's "Spirit people," who walk by means of the Spirit will thus not "fulfill" the desires of the "flesh." After all, he reminds them, "the flesh has desires that stand over against the Spirit." But that is clearly

---

[12] This way of looking at the text can be found as early as Chrysostom (late 4th c.), which points out that the common interpretation is very much the result of reading the text through the lens of "the introspective conscience of the West" (to use K. Stendahl's indicting language). The present view stands over against the many who see v. 17 as "explaining" an implied assumption of "warfare" found in v. 16 – which might be possible if in fact it fitted at all with Paul's clear point: the sufficiency of the Spirit vis-à-vis life under law and against the flesh.

not his *main* point, which rests with the immediately contrasting second clause ("but the Spirit [is] against the flesh"). The awkwardness (for us) of the sentence lies in the two follow-on points Paul wants to make with regard to the antithesis. The first (line *c*) is an explanatory clause regarding the second clause of the antithesis (line *b*), whose emphasis, although put in the plural, lies altogether with the fact that the Spirit, in whose power they are now to "walk" (= "live"), stands over against[13] the flesh in every way. That is, Paul's concern lies not with line *a*, the "lusts" of the flesh; that is merely the setup sentence for his ultimate concern, which is found in the final purpose clause (line *d*). Thus by momentarily setting aside the intervening explanation in line *c*, one can easily see that this purpose clause is not intended to explain that line (*c*), but rather line *b*, and thus it makes perfectly good sense in context: The Spirit stands over against the flesh precisely "so that whatever things you might desire to do, these you do not do." The last clause, therefore, assumes that people's *desires* can still reflect the flesh; that is, even in Christian community some are "biting and devouring" others. But that is no longer a valid option for people who live in and walk by the Spirit. The Spirit stands in unrelieved opposition to such internecine contention.

Having made that point, Paul's instincts immediately take over, since v. 17 could easily be read in a kind of legalistic way. So in *verse 18*, he quickly points out that "if you [plural] are being led by the Spirit (as you walk by the Spirit), you (also) are not under the law." That is, with regard to the kinds of desires that make conflict within the Galatian communities possible, the law has absolutely no power whatever. Therefore, the Spirit is sufficient for life over against the flesh, precisely because of who he is: the Spirit of the Father and the Son (4:6). Thus the Spirit can bring about what the law could not, namely, the right "desires" regarding others in the believing community.

So this final clause (v. 18) does two things at once as a way of wrapping up the paragraph. First, it offers the needed verb in order to make sense of the imperative in v. 16. Those commanded to "*walk* by the Spirit" are now told that they can do so because they are in fact

---

[13] It is of some interest, therefore, that Paul deliberately avoids repeating the verb in this second clause – almost certainly because for him this verb is ordinarily pejorative (very often meaning "have lusts"). So Paul can keep the contrasting parallel alive by simply leaving out the verb. Under no circumstances would Paul in isolation ever say that "the Spirit has desires against the flesh"; and he keeps from saying it here by simply omitting the verb, while at the same time keeping the concept of the Spirit's standing in unremitting opposition to the "flesh."

"*led* by the (self same) Spirit." Second, it picks up the theme of "the law" from v. 14, especially as that theme has had a dominant place in both of the preceding arguments from Scripture (3:1–4:7; 4:21-31), and substantiates why the ineffective law is no longer in effect. The law, which included aspects of religious observance on which so many in Israel had come to rely for their relationship with God, was powerless to effect the real thing – attitudes and behavior that cause God's people to bear his image in their interpersonal relationships. This is what the Spirit can do and does. At issue, therefore, in this paragraph is not some internal tension in the life of the individual believer,[14] but the sufficiency of the Spirit for life without Torah – a sufficiency that enables them to live so as not to *revert* to their former life as pagans (i.e., in the flesh), as what follows in vv. 19-21 makes clear.

Verses 19-21. The contrasting lists of fifteen vices and nine virtues that follow are so well known that it is difficult for the modern reader to keep them in context, to listen to them as if in a Galatian assembly and for the first time. After the momentary "digression" in v. 18, Paul now returns to the theme of v. 17, spelling out with specifics why flesh and Spirit stand in such unrelieved opposition to each other. The one describes the world in which they once lived, and in which their pagan neighbors still live. These are the "evident deeds" of those who live according to "the desire of the flesh," and thus offer a vivid illustration of the kind of life that those who "walk by the Spirit" shall no longer be party to. The second describes what people will look like who walk by following the leading of the Spirit. It is difficult to imagine two more utterly contradictory ways of life.

Vice and virtue lists such as these occur elsewhere in the Greco-Roman world,[15] and are found throughout the Pauline corpus;[16] many

---

[14] It should be pointed out here that those who take this (decidedly majority) view of vv. 16-17 to a person fail to show how it fits into the overall argument of the letter, which to this point has singularly had to do with Gentiles' not needing to come under (now passé) Torah observance. How, one wonders, would this sudden shift to Christian existence as primarily one of (basically unsuccessful) *internal* conflict which ultimately immobilizes the believer fit into this argument at all? No wonder it has been so popular among scholars to see this section (5:13–6:10) as generally unconnected "practical" exhortation!

[15] For a helpful overview see Longenecker, 249-52.

[16] Vice lists occur in 1 Cor 5:10-11; 6:9-10; 2 Cor 12:20; Rom 1:29-31; 13:13; Col 3:5, 8; Eph 4:31–5:5; 1 Tim 1:9-10; Titus 3:3; 2 Tim 3:2-4. Elsewhere in the NT see Mark 7:21-22 (//Matt 15:19-20); 1 Pet 4:3; Rev 9:21; 21:8; 22:15. Virtue lists are

of the same vices and virtues are repeated in several of them, although no two lists are alike either in content, order, or kinds of items listed. As in other cases, both of the present lists are adapted to the situation in Galatia as that emerges in v. 15. The lists, therefore, are intended to be neither delimiting nor exhaustive. Rather, by his use of "such things as these" (v. 21; cf. v. 23), Paul specifically indicates that the lists are merely representative. Furthermore, even though the two lists describe unbelievers and believers as such, Paul also intends by them to describe the "before" and "after" of the Galatians themselves.[17] These "deeds of the flesh," and others like them, are the very things that "those who belong to Christ Jesus have crucified" (v. 24) and therefore are no longer an option for those who "walk by the Spirit" (vv. 13, 16).

This is now the fourth such vice list in Paul's letters (cf. 1 Cor 5:10-11; 6:9-10; 2 Cor 12:20[21]), which he here entitles "the *works* (ἔργα) of the flesh." In so doing he is most likely making a deliberate word association with the repeated "by *works* of Torah" in the earlier part of the letter (2:16 [3x]; 3:2, 5, 11). This is not to suggest that Paul saw similarity between these two kinds of "works." Rather, by means of word association, this is his way of reminding the Galatians that *both categories of "work"* (religious observance and sins of the flesh) *belong to the past* for those who are in Christ and thus walk by the Spirit. These "works (or 'acts,' 'deeds')" express the "desire of the flesh" against which the Spirit stands in such unrelieved opposition – to which reality God's people should joyfully respond, "Praise God."

The fifteen items in this case fall into four clear categories,[18] signalled in the TNIV by the use of semi-colons and the insertion of an "and" before the final item in each category: thus, illicit sex (3 items), illicit worship (2), breakdowns in relationships (8), and excesses (2). Two preliminary observations about the list as such are in order before looking at the various sins themselves. First, this list has an interesting relationship to the three in the preceding two letters. For example, the three words that stand in first place in the first, second,

---

far less common, since in the Pauline corpus the items that make this list occur in the context of Pauline paraenesis; but see Col 3:12.

[17] As vv. 24-26 make clear, and in keeping with other such listings. See esp. in this regard the vice lists in 1 Cor. 6:9-11 ("but such *were* some of you") and Col. 3:5-8 ("in which things *you also once walked*, when you lived in such things; but now ...").

[18] An observation frequently made in the commentaries. For reasons that are not at all clear, Betz (283), followed by Longenecker (254), thinks the opposite – that this list is "chaotic" and the next "orderly."

and fourth groups ("sexual immorality, idolatry, drunkenness") occur as the first, second and eighth items on the second (and longer) list in 1 Cor 6:9-10,[19] in a letter where sexual immorality and idolatry are major issues. Of greater interest, however, is that the first four words in the third group are identical to the second through fifth in 2 Cor 12:20,[20] while the three items in the first group are identical (except for the word order of the first two) with the additional list in 2 Cor 12:21. Thus in part of this list Paul follows his immediately preceding letter quite closely.

Second, what is striking in this case are the missing items, especially covetousness or greed, which appear on most of the other lists, and the related sins of theft and robbery, as well as sins of violence (murder, etc.) and the various sins of the tongue, which is the category with the largest number of words when all the lists are collated. This suggests that whatever "eating and devouring one another" meant in v. 15, it most likely did not include various forms of verbal abuse.

Together these observations suggest that Paul is basically building on the two lists in 2 Corinthians 12, but ordering them in a way that highlights the long central group, and thus focuses on community disorders. Some brief words are in order about each of the groups and their individual words.

(1) *Sexual sins* occur at the top of the catalogue, just as they did in the two lists in 1 Corinthians, whose first one (5:11) came into existence in the context of such sin. Repeating the three words used of such sins in 2 Cor 12:21, Paul here highlights a group of "sins" that were not necessarily considered so by the pagan world. The first word, which is the general noun derived from the word for "prostitute," is the catch-all word for various kinds of "unsanctioned sexual intercourse" (BDAG), while the second word ("uncleanness," thus "impurity") is regularly used by Paul in connection with sexual impurity. The third word ("debauchery") is that used by pagan Greeks for sexual conduct that exceeded all bounds of decency, or at least what a given group considered socially unacceptable. It is very likely that the Galatian believers, though Gentiles, had earlier been associated with the Jewish synagogue – as was common in the Pauline churches – and would therefore already have adopted a "Jewish-Christian"

[19] They are first, third, and fifth in the earlier list (1 Cor 5:11).
[20] Interestingly enough, the NIV translating teams who did 2 Corinthians and Galatians apparently did not consult with each other, since three of these four items (no. 1, 3, 4) are translated quite differently ("quarreling, outbursts of anger, factions" in 2 Cor; "discord, fits of rage, selfish ambition" in Galatians).

attitude toward these sins. Thus Paul begins with sins wherein he knows many of them will already be on his side, probably having abandoned such sins even before becoming followers of Christ.

(2) *Idolatry* and *witchcraft* again highlight "sins" that are so only from Paul's Jewish–Christian perspective. Indeed, pagan Greeks would never have used the word "idol" for their deities, a matter which Paul himself recognized when in 1 Cor 10:28 he puts into the mouth of such a person the word "sacred (or temple) food," which Jews and Christians consistently referred to as "idol food," hence "food offered to idols." Idolatry, therefore, is consistently understood to be a breaking of the second commandment, which goes beyond the first ("no other deities") to the creation of "images" that represent these deities. This is forbidden by the eternal God because he had created human beings to be his image-bearers on earth. But while primarily a breaking of the second commandment, "idolatry" by the time of Paul also included devotion to any deity other than God and Christ. The addition of "witchcraft" (or "sorcery") occurs only here in the Pauline vice lists, where its use in conjunction with "idolatry" reflects the fascination with "magic" that was pervasive in the Greco-Roman world.

(3) As noted above, the common denominator of the eight words that make up this larger section of the current vice list have in common various forms of *breakdowns in interpersonal relationships*. This section of the list is also noticeable for the sudden shift to the plural for all but the second and third of these words,[21] a phenomenon that will carry over to the final set as well. Thus, while the first two sets described a phenomenon as such, the final two sets put emphasis on the individual recurring acts.

Paul begins with "hatreds" (plural), referring to individual acts of hatred or enmity toward another, a word that properly heads the distressing list that follows, which spells out the variety of ways such hatred can manifest itself. The next four ("discord, jealousy, fits of rage," and expressions of "selfish ambition") can be easily recognized as flowing directly out of hatred. But two of them need special notice. The word "discord" (ἔρις), which was rendered "quarreling" in 2 Cor 12:20 by the NIV translators, has to do with "engagement in rivalry, especially with reference to positions taken in a matter" (BDAG), an issue that tends to be a universal ill in human relationships. The word

[21] Although, typical of later scribal habits, these were both changed to plurals by various scribes, so that by the sixth century the plurals had become the dominant text.

"selfish ambition(s)" (ἐριθεῖαι) is a noun derived from the former, but one which has a broader range of possible meanings, so that the NIV translators rendered it "factions" in 2 Cor 12:20 and "selfish ambition" here. In light of its unambiguous use in Philippians (1:17 and 2:3) to mean "selfish ambition," this is probably its sense here as well, thus referring to expressions of selfish ambition (note the plural) that lead to community in-fighting. This is especially so in this case where it is followed by two words that explicitly refer to selfish ambition gone awry: "dissensions" and "factions," which latter word can mean only this in its present context. The last word of the eight is also plural, referring to specific instances of "envy."

So while this large list of words that deal with community discord may be merely random, they also can be shown to have a modicum of order to them. But what must be especially noted about them is how overbearing this part of the list actually is. A point that could have been made with any two or three of these words is made by eight of them, some of them near synonyms. In light of v. 15 above and v. 26 that follows, one suspects that this list is especially tailored for the Galatians themselves.

(4) The final two items on the list, both being *excesses* and both plural ("drunkennesses" and "orgies"), are probably intended to help the Galatians to see how their own sins fit into the bigger picture of the "deeds of the flesh." For here again, these would be easily recognized as evil by the Galatian believers. Thus the shock would be to have them follow such a long list of breakdowns in human relationships. Experience would suggest that this difficulty is not peculiar to the Galatian churches alone. But sin is sin, and what some of us might be willing to brush off with a "nobody's perfect" attitude, Paul is quite prepared to see as "deeds of the flesh" that stand in utter contradiction to those whose lives are led by the Spirit.

It should also be noted, finally, that this is not a list of sins of the *flesh* per se, that is, having to do with the physical body or bodily appetites. The only items that fit this category are the three sexual aberrations which appear first and the two excesses which appear at the end; these indeed are "cravings of the flesh = human body." Indeed, for the most part the various sins are not the kind associated with internal warfare within the human breast. Noticeably missing are "lust" or "covetousness," matters over which the individual often struggles in the face of temptation. Rather, this list basically describes human *behavior,* which is essentially very visible and identifiable –

"works" that people do who live in keeping with their basic fallenness and that of the world around them.

But having said all of that, a list is still a list; and one that concludes with "such things" is to be taken seriously by believers of all generations and geography. God is against such "deeds." Christ has died to deliver us from their grip (v. 24); and the Spirit has come to empower us not to cave in to their "desire."

This first list then concludes on an eschatological note: "those who practice such things as these will not inherit the kingdom of God." For Paul "inheriting" or "not inheriting" the final eschatological glory is predicated on whether or not one is a Spirit person, having become so through faith in Christ Jesus. The "works of the flesh," therefore, do not describe the behavior of believers, but of unbelievers.[22] It is not that believers cannot or do not indulge in such sins; after all, Paul's emphasis on his having warned them before and now again in v. 21 makes that point plain enough. Paul's concern rather is with "people who *practice* such sins," and who thus have no inheritance with God's people. His emphasis here, as in 1 Cor 6:9-10 and Eph 5:5, is to warn believers not to live as unbelievers, those who are destined to experience the wrath of God (Col. 3:6).

Even though Paul is here speaking negatively about the destiny of the ungodly, the positive implication of believers' inheriting the kingdom should not be missed – especially since the question of "inheritance" played such a major role in the argument of 3:6–4:7 (cf. 4:30). As earlier (4:6-7), "inheritance" belongs to those who, by the Spirit, give evidence that they are God's rightful "heirs." Because such an inheritance is here *implied* for those who live by the Spirit, Paul concludes the next list by taking it in another direction altogether, namely to come back to the issue of the Spirit and Torah observance.

Verses 22-23a. By describing the list of virtues as "fruit of the Spirit," Paul once more sets the Spirit in sharp contrast to the flesh: the vices are "works" (cf. "works of the law"); the virtues are "fruit." But "fruit" does not mean passivity on the part of the believer. To be sure, "works" puts emphasis on human endeavor, "fruit" on divine empowerment.[23] But the emphasis in this argument is on the Spirit's

---

[22] A point too often missed in the commentaries, apparently because of the way they handle v. 17. See, e.g., Calvin, Meyer, Fung, Betz, Longenecker.

[23] It should be noted, however, that when "human endeavor" is Paul's emphasis for the Spirit side of things, "works" is also the word that Paul will use, as at the end of the present argument (6:10, "let us work what is good," which becomes the "good works" of Eph. 2:10). Anyone who thinks that Paul is not keen on good works has

effective replacement of Torah. Not only do people who walk by the Spirit *not* walk in the ways of the flesh just described, but also the Spirit effectively produces in them the very character of God himself. Thus, the activities and attitudes of those who are "led by the Spirit" are designated as the "product" of life in the Spirit. Paul's point in context, of course, is that when the Galatians properly use their freedom to serve one another through love, they are empowered to do so by the Spirit who produces such "fruit" in/among them. But they themselves must walk, live, conform to the Spirit. After all, in almost every case these various "fruit" appear elsewhere in Paul as imperatives!

It has been unfortunately common to make more of the singular "fruit," in contrast to the plural "works," than the language itself will allow. Paul himself probably had no such contrast in mind, nor does he think of the "works" as many and individual but the "fruit" as one cluster with several kinds on it. The fact is that "fruit" (καρπός) in Greek functions as a collective singular, very much as "fruit" does in English. In both Greek and English one would refer to "the fruit in the bowl," whether "they" are all of one kind or of several; no native English speaker would refer to the "fruits" in the bowl.

As with the preceding list, this one is also representative, not exhaustive. That love appears in first place reflects the Pauline perspective (cf. v. 14); the rest of the list appears to be much more random, where one word, for reasons not fully clear, calls for the next. For the most part the virtues chosen stand in marked contrast to many of the preceding "works of the flesh." Again, what is surprising is the "omission" of items that Paul elsewhere includes in his paraenesis.[24] What results, therefore, and this does become significant for Pauline theology, is a list of virtues which tends to cover a broad range of Christian life and which thereby helps to broaden our own perspective as to the breadth, and all-encompassing nature, of the activity of the Spirit in Paul's understanding.

As noted, the decided majority of these items have to do with the corporate life of the community, not with the internal life of the individual believer. To be sure, individual believers must love, work toward peace, express forbearance, kindness, and goodness, or be

---

either not read Paul carefully or has come to the subject with emotional resistance to this language, usually predicated on the theological agenda of the Reformation.

[24] Missing, for example, are thankfulness, forgiveness, humility, gracious talk, and endurance. In this regard see esp. 2 Cor. 8:7; Rom. 12:9-21; Col. 3:12-17; Eph 4:32-3; 5:2; the only other real "list" of this kind occurs in Col. 3:12, where three of the five items in that list appear here as well.

characterized by gentleness. However, since these virtues characterize God[25] and motivate his conduct toward, and his relationship to, his own people, they must therefore do the same within the believing community. Again, lying behind much of this is the situation of the Galatian churches as we get some insight into that from 5:15 and 26. So here is what life in the Spirit, both in Galatia and beyond, is intended to look like.

(1) That *love* should assume pride of place is no surprise. Paul has already accorded it such a place in this argument (5:6, 13-14), a place it always holds in his ethics. The reason for this is that in Paul's theology, resulting from his long life in the Old Testament (by way of the Septuagint [LXX]), this word captures the essence of the character of God as that is seen in his relationship to his people. Thus in the Trinitarian benediction of 2 Cor 13:14, in which the primary characteristics of the divine Persons are expressed, Paul prays for the Corinthians to know "the love of God." God's love for his people is what has been poured out into their hearts by the Spirit (Rom 5:5). For Paul this love has been expressed most powerfully in God's sending his Son, and in the Son's death on the cross (Rom 5:6-8). God's love is full of "forbearance" and "kindness" (see below) toward his people, and finally expresses itself to the full in the self-sacrificial death of Christ on behalf of his enemies.

For Paul this is not simply theory or abstract reality; the Spirit had poured this love into his heart. In the present letter he has already described the indwelling Christ as the one "who loved me and gave himself for me" (2:20). This is surely what he intends by the "law of Christ" in 6:2 (q.v.), which lies behind the imperative by which all of this began in v. 13 ("through love perform the duties of a slave for one another"). Such love is the direct result of being loved by the God whose love has been lavished on us in his Son, who likewise loved us and gave himself for us, and by whose indwelling presence we now live. In Pauline theology, therefore, love is the result of a personal encounter with the living God, who above everything else loves his people.

Love, therefore, is not something one can do or feel on one's own. Nor is it to be distorted into its current North American version of

---

[25] This reality, plus the fact that this language is so deeply embedded in Paul through his lifelong association with the OT and the Jesus traditions, seems to negate Betz's bold comment that "the individual concepts are not in any way specifically 'Christian,' but represent the conventional morality of the time" (p. 282). This would fit Phil 4:8 very nicely, but hardly this list.

"good feelings" toward someone, so that love is turned on its head: instead of self-sacrificial giving of oneself for others, it has become identified with what I do or feel for another for the sake of my own self-fulfillment. Love heads this list of virtues over against the "works of the flesh" precisely because it stands as the stark opposite of the self-centeredness of most of the items on the former list. As the fruit of the Spirit, love spells the end to "hostilities, strife, jealousy, outbursts of rage, selfish ambitions, dissensions, factions, envies," and the like. This can only be lived out in the context of other people, especially other believers. Thus it is Paul's own solution in vv. 13 and 14 to their internecine strife in v. 15.

(2) *Joy* is one of the primary characteristics of genuinely Christian, and therefore genuinely Spirit, piety. What is remarkable is its appearance in this list of virtues that are primarily ethical in character. As with love and peace that stand on either side of it, Paul is probably not thinking so much of the personal, individual experience of joy – although as with this whole list, that can scarcely be excluded – but of the joy that characterizes life together in Christ. Life in Christ, and therefore life by the Spirit, is a life of joy; such joy is to characterize the Christian community above all else (1 Thess 5:16). In this regard the two other texts (Rom 14:17; 15:13) where joy, peace, and the Holy Spirit stand in collocation may be instructive. There joy and peace occur together, first as resolution and secondly as prayer, in a section (14:1–15:13) that is written specifically as an appeal for Jewish and Gentile believers to "accept one another" (15:7), rather than to judge or look down on each other (14:1-4). A righteousness that includes joy and peace in the Holy Spirit will have little room for internecine strife (Gal 5:15) or disdain of others (5:26–6:5).

For Paul, as for the rest of the New Testament in general, the presence or absence of joy is quite unrelated to one's circumstances, as Philippians makes plain. It is related in its entirety to what God has done for us in Christ through the Spirit. The Pauline imperative, stemming from joy as the *fruit* of the Spirit, is not simply, "rejoice" – although it often comes in that simple form as well – but "rejoice *in the Lord*." This focus is the key to our understanding the joy of the Spirit. A community that is "rejoicing *in the Lord* always" is not a community easily given to "eating and devouring one another" (v. 15), in which people think much too highly of themselves (6:4).

God has brought us eschatological salvation. The future has already made its appearance in the present. God's people have already tasted the life that is to be. Already they have received full pardon, full forgiveness. By the Spirit they cry out *Abba* to the God who has loved them and given his Son for them. This is cause for joy, untrammeled, uninhibited joy, as "by the Spirit we eagerly await the hope of righteousness" (v. 5). The fruit of the Spirit is *joy*, joy in the Lord. What must begin at the individual level must also therefore characterize the believing community, among whom God still generously supplies the Holy Spirit.

(3) As with love, *peace* for Paul is especially associated with God and his relationship to his people. And as with love and joy, peace is especially a community matter. That is, Paul's first concern with "peace" is not "the well-arranged heart" – although again, it is difficult to have "peace" in a community where God's people know little peace individually. But here peace occurs in a list of virtues that deliberately stand over against the "works of the flesh," eight of which describe the causes or results of human discord.

First of all then, as with love, God himself is often described as "the God of peace," the God who dwells in total *shalom* (wholeness, well-being) and who gives such *shalom* to his people in their life together. What is striking is that in every instance this divine ascription occurs in contexts where there is strife or unrest close at hand. Thus the final response to unruly *charismata* in the believing community is the theological note that God himself is a "God of peace" (1 Cor 14:33); or in a community where the unruly-idle live off the largess of others, Paul prays that the God of peace will give them peace at all times (2 Thess 3:16); or in a context where believers are warned against those who "cause divisions and put obstacles in your way," he assures them that the God of peace will bruise Satan under their feet shortly (Rom 16:20).

Not only so, but in Paul the mention of peace in his letters (apart from the standard salutation) most often occurs in community or relational settings. Thus Christ is "our peace" who has made Jew and Gentile one people, one body (Eph 2:14-17), who are thus urged to "keep the unity of the Spirit through the bond of peace" (4:3). Similarly in the argument of Rom 14:1–15:13, Jew and Gentile together are urged to "make every effort to do what leads to peace" (14:19); and in the community paraenesis of Col 3:12–4:6, they are urged to "let the peace of Christ rule in your hearts, *since as members of one body you were called to peace*." The present context, both 5:15 and the fact that these fruit of the Spirit stand in sharp contrast to the works of the flesh just described, would suggest that this is the first setting for this fruit of the Spirit as well – not the only one, to be sure, since lists by their very nature can carry a kind of independent existence apart from their first context.

(4) *Patience* is the now common way to translate Paul's Greek word (μακροθυμία), which actually means "forbearance" (KJV "longsuffering"). To be sure, in some cases it may very well carry the meaning "patience," but in English, this latter word tends to be individualistic; i.e., one is "patient" about all kinds of very non-personal matters pertaining to life in general (computers that go haywire, for instance). But in Paul this noun and its corresponding verb are always used in contexts involving one's *forbearance toward others.* As such it often occurs, as it does here, as the passive side of love, of which its companion "kindness" is the active side. Thus Paul describes God's attitude toward human arrogance as one of forbearance and kindness (Rom 2:4); these are the first two words that describe (God's) love in 1 Cor 13:4, and they occur together in Col 3:12 as part of Christian dress when one "puts on Christ."

"Longsuffering," therefore, has to do with long forbearance toward those who stand over against one in some way. Nowhere else does Paul attribute such forbearance to the direct working of the Spirit; but its appearance here makes it clear that Spirit-empowering is not simply for joy and miracles, but for this much-needed quality of persistent caring for those who need long-term, patient love and kindness (cf. Col 1:11). This is the divine answer to "outbursts of rage" (v. 20) or "provoking one another" (v. 26).

(5) The word *kindness* and the next one ("goodness"), which are close synonyms, are strictly Pauline words in the New Testament. Both words are difficult to pin down with precision, because they occur most often in lists like this or in contexts where the general sense is easy enough to ascertain but where nuanced differences are not at all easy to capture. The clues come most often from associations with other words. As with the "forbearance" with which it is frequently allied, the key to understanding "kindness" is to be found in the instances where it describes God's character or activity toward people. Thus it occurs as a verb in 1 Cor 13:4 to express the active side of love, for which the preceding word ("forbearance") expresses its passive side. In such a context it thus refers to God's active goodness, lavished upon those whom he loves. God's kindness, therefore, is to be found in his thousandfold acts of mercy toward people like ourselves who deserve his wrath. This is especially borne out by its usage in Eph 2:7, where the lavish expression of God's grace is demonstrated in his "kindness" toward us in Christ.

In this list, of course, where it occurs again in conjunction with forbearance, it has to do with the active expression of grace toward others. As such it fits the larger context as another opposite to the "works of the flesh," with their self-centered, basically hostile-toward-others way of life. The Spirit not only empowers one to endure the hostility or unkindness of another; he also enables one to show kindness to such and actively to pursue their good. If "longsuffering" means not to respond in kind to someone else's ill-will (see 5:15), "kindness" means to find ways actively to benefit them.

(6) *Goodness*, as noted above, is very closely allied with "kindness." If there is a difference, "goodness" is the more all-embracing quality, describing one's character. Although it does not occur often in the Septuagint (LXX), the adjective ("good") from which it is formed is a primary word to describe God's character in the Old Testament. Goodness, therefore, is something that believers may be described as "full of" (Rom 15:14). When put into practice it takes the form of "doing good." Indeed, goodness does not exist apart from its active, concrete expression. Thus, this is the quality of Christian grace, produced in the life of the believer by the Spirit, that Paul picks up on at the end to bring conclusion to the present argument (6:9-10). Again, as with the preceding words, its appearance here presupposes the present context. Those who "sow to the Spirit" are those who "do good to all;" obviously this stands as yet another antonym to those "works of the flesh" which have found a measure of existence among the Galatians.

(7) The word here translated *faithfulness* (πίστις) is Paul's primary word for "faith," having to do with one's basic stance toward God of utter trust in his trustworthiness. But in the Septuagint (LXX) it was the basic Greek word available to translate the concept of God's faithfulness. This is the sense that Paul himself picks up in Rom 3:3, that the "unfaithfulness" of God's people does not call into question God's own "faithfulness" (πίστις). Thus, even though one would have no theological objection to "faith" as the meaning of the word even here – that one of the fruit of the Spirit is one's trust in God – it is more likely, given the other virtues, and especially those that immediately surround it, that Paul is referring to faithfulness, that is, one's faithful living out one's trust in God over the long haul.

The more difficult question, given the context, is whether it also carries a nuance of faithfulness in relationship to others. Since there are no other New Testament examples of such usage, it seems unlikely, despite the context, that this is what Paul had in mind here. More likely the sense is that of faithful devotion to God, which in turn will express itself toward others by means of the various other fruit in this list. True "faith" for Paul always includes the element of "faithfulness;" and thus true "faith" for him in this sense, as a fruit of the Spirit, expresses itself in love (5:6).

(8) *Gentleness* (πραΰτης) is the word that in earlier versions was translated "meekness." For Paul it derives its Christian meaning from its relationship with Christ. In Matt 11:25-30, this is one of the two words used to describe the character of Jesus, which he, as the only Son of the Father, revealed about the character of the Father to the "infants" as over against the wise and understanding. That Paul knew this tradition, or one like it, seems certain from his appeal to the "gentleness (πραΰτης) and graciousness of Christ" in 2 Cor 10:1.

As a Christian grace, reflecting the character of Christ himself, it occurs eight times in Paul. This is the one fruit, more than the others, for which one has difficulty in finding an adequate English word. Whatever else, it carries the sense both of humility toward oneself (i.e. a proper estimation of oneself over against God) – hence the historic rendition "meekness" – and considerateness toward others, the dimension lacking in the English word "meekness." Thus it is to this fruit that Paul will appeal in 6:1, when he urges those who walk by the Spirit to restore a brother or sister overtaken in a fault. One needs to do so with the Spirit's "gentleness" both because the life of the other person is at stake, but also because one thereby remembers one's own frailties and susceptibility to temptation. In this list it stands as the exact antonym to the "work of the flesh" called "selfish ambition" (ἐριθεία). It is the fruit of the Spirit at work in those who do not think too highly of themselves (6:3), but who "in humility consider others better than themselves" (Phil 2:3) – in the sense that they look after others' needs and concerns before their own.

(9) The last word on this list, *self-control*, is unique in several ways. It is the one word on the list that does not appear elsewhere in Scripture with reference to the character of God. Indeed, the noun occurs only here in the Pauline corpus, although the verb occurs in 1 Cor 7:9 with reference to sexual continence and in 1 Cor 9:25 with regard to the self-discipline of the athlete. Furthermore, it is the one virtue in the list that is clearly aimed at the individual believer. This is not something one does in community; it is a general stance toward excesses of various kinds.

Therefore, in contrast to the rest of the list which takes aim at those eight "works of the flesh" that have primarily to do with relational matters, this one takes aim at either – or both – the sexual indulgences that appear as the first three "works of the flesh" or/and the excesses with which that list concludes. This, too, is the effective working of the Spirit in the life of the believer.

But in terms of Pauline ethics, what one may not do is to turn "self-control" into abstinence as such. It is clear from such passages as 1 Cor 10:31-33, Rom 14:1-23, Col 2:16-23, and 1 Tim 4:1-5 that Paul is death on anything that even smacks of abstinence itself as a Christian virtue. Therefore, because of this fruit of the Spirit, one is free to abstain from any and everything for the sake of others; but one may never turn such free giving up of food or drink or whatever into some kind of virtue on its own. These are merely "human traditions," Paul calls them in Col 2:22, the "teachings of demons," in 1 Tim 4:2.

Verse 23b. Similarly to the vice list that has preceded it, but in contrast to how that one was expressed, Paul appends a concluding word to this list of virtues. That Paul has not done what we so often do with this passage – namely to lose sight of the argument in context – becomes especially clear by this concluding clause. Significantly, he does not conclude as before with an eschatological word, in this case a word of promise, probably because such a promise is already inherent in the previous concluding word. That former word, after all, speaks not about the "wrath of God coming upon those in the flesh," but about such people's "*not* inheriting the *kingdom*." Implied in that is the opposite reality, that Spirit people *will* inherit the kingdom. But the lack of an eschatological word in the present case, one would guess, is also because Paul simply cannot bring himself to say that "those who exhibit these virtues will inherit the kingdom." That inheritance, after all, is predicated altogether on their being God's children through Christ and the Spirit, not on the kind of life they exhibit as his children. Paul will indeed finally speak to the believer's involvement in making that calling sure – in the final wrap-up of this argument in 6:7-10, where he both warns and exhorts them to "sow to the Spirit" with the eschatological goal in mind. But for now the concern is quite different.

Paul's present interest lies once more with the main point of the argument of the entire letter, that the work of Christ and the coming of the Spirit have eliminated Torah altogether from the agenda of God's people. Hence he concludes, "against such things as these there is no law." Paul's point seems clear enough, although this is stated a bit awkwardly to our thinking. After all, the law exists because people are evil, not because they are good; it exists therefore "against" sin, not "against" virtue. He almost certainly intends, therefore, that "when these virtues are evident in one's life because of the presence of the Spirit, Torah is an irrelevancy." There is no need of Torah to say, "you shall not kill," to people who by the Spirit are loving one another, nor to say, "do not covet," to those who are actively pursuing the good of others out of kindness. This does not mean, of course, that such *reminders* are irrelevant – Paul himself regularly does so – but that the need for Torah to "hem in human conduct because of the transgressions" (3:19, 22) has come to an end with the advent of the Spirit, God's own way of fulfilling the promised new covenant. This is Torah being etched on the heart, so that God's people will obey him (Jer 31:33; Ezek 36:27). Here also is the clear evidence that for Paul the elimination of Torah does not mean the end of righteousness. To the contrary, the Spirit produces the real thing, the righteousness of God himself, as his children reflect his likeness in their lives together and in the world.

Verses 24-26. With these three sentences Paul brings the present argument full circle. He does this, first, by drawing the work of Christ back into the picture (v. 24), but now over against the flesh rather than Torah. In v. 25 he then offers something of an inclusio by restating the basic imperative from v. 16. In doing so, these first two sentences thus appeal to the death and resurrection of Christ as the basis for "keeping in step" with the Spirit. Verse 26 in turn concludes the whole section by restating the reasons for these admonitions as they were first expressed in v. 15. These sentences, therefore, belong integrally to what has preceded, but at the same time they lead directly into the specific applications that follow in 6:1-6.

With a rather abrupt turn in the argument, Paul in *verse 24* begins the application of the argument that began in v. 16 by returning to the work of Christ, which serves always as the foundation of the Galatian believers' now being people of the Spirit. Thus he here offers the theological basis for the imperative and promise in v. 16, that those who walk by the Spirit will not carry out the desire of the flesh, as that is spelled out in the dreadful picture in vv. 19-22. He does this by picking up language he used to describe his own testimony in 2:19-20, as that must now be understood in light of the argument in 3:6–4:7. Those who have put their trust in Christ, he maintained earlier, have also been "crucified with Christ," so that current life in the (literal) flesh is not predicated on the perspective of the (fallen) flesh. Through their association with Christ in his death, they have themselves been crucified with regard to life in the "flesh." Now he puts that in the active voice, purposely recalling their union with Christ in his death, but now with the bold new metaphor as to what they have done with their past way of life: they have nailed the flesh, with its passions and desires, to the cross.

Just as in the argument of 3:1–4:7, where Paul seemed intent to tie the life of the Spirit to the work of Christ (3:14; 4:6), so now by these words he seems equally intent to link the life of the Spirit to the earlier argument in which Christ played the leading role. The reason seems obvious: In Pauline theology everything that God has done in the new covenant to create a people for his name God has done through Christ. Here is the first reason for Paul's confidence that those who walk by the Spirit will not fulfill the desires of the flesh. The "flesh" itself, with its passions and desires, has experienced death in Christ's crucifixion ("I have been crucified with Christ," 2:20). Thus Spirit people have experienced a more radical way of dealing with the flesh than merely subjecting it to Torah (v. 23), which failed in any case. In Christ Jesus they have crucified it. Thus under the new covenant living according to the flesh is no more an option than is living under the law. Christ's death has brought an effective conclusion to the reign of both.

This is not wishfulness on Paul's part, but a declaration of eschatological realities. Having been crucified with Christ, the believer now lives by faith in Christ, who by his own Spirit has taken up residence within (2:20). At the same time this is not to be understood as some form of triumphalism, as the exhortation that follows in v. 25 makes clear. Rather this is to be understood within Paul's eschatological framework. Here is the "already" of eschatological salvation; the death of the "flesh" – the former way of life – has "already" taken place through Christ's death and resurrection. But at the same time vv. 25-26 bring one back to the reality that there currently remains a "not yet" to this same salvation. Indeed, the possibility for obedience regarding the exhortations in vv. 25-26 rests on the twin facts (*a*) that the "flesh," which belongs essentially to the old order, has been crucified in Christ Jesus, and (*b*) that present life this side of that crucifixion is empowered by the Spirit.

In typical fashion Paul in *verse 25* responds to the theme of death (to the flesh) in v. 24 by appealing to the resurrection and the gift of the Spirit. He thus rounds off the argument with an exhortation that harks back to the opening imperative in v. 16, where he had urged that walking by the Spirit is God's antidote to life in the flesh. Now, he urges, since Christ's crucifixion has spelled death for the flesh, believers are to behave in keeping with the Spirit, by whom they "live" and whose fruit they are to evidence. Thus the conjunction "if" (εἰ) is in this case introducing a reality, and is correctly rendered "since" in the TNIV. So just as v. 16 responded directly to their "fleshly" behavior described in v. 15, Paul now follows this summary exhortation by indicating in v. 26 the kind of community life against which the Spirit stands in strong opposition.

But v. 25 is also the sentence which shows that triumphalism is not what vv. 16, 22-23 and 24 are all about. Along with the preceding sentence (v. 24), here one catches another glimpse of the "already/not yet" of Paul's understanding of salvation in Christ, in which the (necessary) imperative follows hard on the heels of the divine indicative. The preceding sentence has put it boldly – death to the flesh through Christ. The first clause in this sentence (the protasis) follows that up in terms of life empowered by the Spirit that issues from that death, while the follow-up clause (the apodosis) calls for action based on the protasis. The reality lies with the protasis, which expresses not supposition but presupposition: God's new covenant people have in fact come to life – and thus live – by the Spirit. But precisely because this is so, one must heed the exhortation of the apodosis. Thus: "since we [have died with Christ and have been raised by him so as to] live by the Spirit, then let us also conform our lives to behave in keeping with[26] the Spirit [as that has been spelled out in vv. 22-23]."

Verse 26 now brings the argument that began in v. 13 full circle. Whereas what we might have expected following vv. 24 and 25 would have been something positive expressed in terms of the fruit of the Spirit, what we get in fact are negatives, how people who conform to the Spirit do *not* behave. Thus Paul's concern is unlikely to be with life in the Spirit in general, as it is often suggested, but rather with certain forms of life in the flesh that Paul is hoping to counteract. Thus, even though not expressed in the same language as v. 15, these are the kinds of attitudes ("empty conceit"[27] and "envy") and actions ("provocation")

---

[26] The Gk. verb here, στοιχέω, literally means "to be in line with [something] one considers to be a standard for one's conduct" (BDAG); it will appear again at the end of the letter (6:16), and elsewhere in Paul only in Rom 4:12 and Phil 3:16. Hence the TNIV's "keep in step with," which is an excellent rendering of the basic meaning of the idiom, but which would not work well in 6:16.

[27] This is a stronger rendering of Paul's Gk adjective (κενόδοξος, lit. "empty glory") than the TNIV's "conceited." Paul uses the cognate noun (κενοδοξία) in Phil 2:3, where similar community problems appear to exist. One might note other similarities between this passage (through 6:5) and Phil 2:1-4, where the Philippian believers are

that lead to their "eating and devouring" one another. As the following exhortations seem to make clear, Paul's concern regarding their "life in the Spirit" that precludes "life in the flesh" is expressed specifically in terms of conflict in community relationships.

These three sentences thus serve both as a conclusion to the argument that began in v. 13 and as a transition from the more general imperatives and descriptions of life in the Spirit in vv. 13-23 to the specific applications of all this in 6:1-6 to their situation. In all of this the Spirit, following the work of Christ, is the prime mover. The Spirit is God's own response to the problem of the flesh, whose reign was brought to an effective end through Christ and whose effect in the life of the believer is negated by the empowering of the Spirit. But what Christ and the Spirit have thus brought about, the believing community must actively participate in; they must walk by, and behave in keeping with, the Spirit.

Galatians 6:1-6 – Some Specific Examples of Application

> [1]*Brothers and sisters, if someone is caught in a sin, you who live by the Spirit should restore that person gently. But watch yourselves, or you also may be tempted.* [2]*Carry each other's burdens, and in this way you will fulfill the law of Christ.* [3]*If any of you think you are something when you are nothing, you deceive yourselves.* [4]*Each of you should test your own actions. Then you can take pride in yourself, without comparing yourself to somebody else,* [5]*for each of you should carry your own load.* [6]*Nevertheless those who receive instruction in the word should share all good things with their instructor.*

Paul begins his direct application of what has preceded to their corporate life with a series of imperatives which illustrate how people who live and walk by the Spirit should behave in their everyday relationships. Because a sequential flow to these various imperatives and their elaborations is not immediately apparent, it has been common to look upon all of 6:1-10 as a series of "gnomic sentences," somewhat randomly strung together. But if one assumes, as one should, that 5:15 and 26 refer specifically to matters within the Galatian congregations, then most of the material can to be shown to have an inner logic to it. The context is obviously that of the

---

urged on the basis of their "participation in the Spirit" and "mutual love" to do nothing out of "empty conceit" but rather with "humility" to "look out for" the interests of others, considering others as having precedence over themselves.

community, not that of the private life of the believer, which only reinforces the points just made about the community aspect of "walking" and "living" by the Spirit – that "love" has not to do with how one "feels" toward someone or others, but how one cares for them.

On this view vv. 1-3 form something of a unit in response to vv. 25-26. "Let us behave in keeping with the Spirit," Paul has urged in v. 25, meaning, let us *not* be full of empty conceit and provocation (v. 26). People of the Spirit should, for example, restore a fallen brother or sister, remembering one's own susceptibility to temptation (v. 1). Indeed, they ought, on the one hand, to bear any and all of one another's burdens, and so fulfill the law of Christ (v. 2); those who think themselves to be something when in fact they are nothing (who are thus full of empty conceit and thereby provoke rather than restore and assist others) are merely deceiving themselves (v. 3). On the other hand, Paul goes on in vv. 4-5, each one should put their own work to the test, and then alone will there be grounds for "boasting." In that sense, each person must mind their own affairs, carry their own load, and thus not envy or challenge one another.

If this is the "flow" of thought, even if it takes the form of "stream of consciousness," the two parts to the first paragraph (vv. 1-3, 4-5) are thus a double-sided response to the "empty conceit" and "provocation/envy" of 5:26. And it at least assumes what we knew all along, that Spirit people are not perfected; they may in fact be overtaken by a fault, and others may be less than gracious with such "failure." In any case, the Galatians are now about to see how, for example, love, peace, gentleness, self-denial, and goodness work out in everyday life. The whole package thus illustrates 5:13-14, what it means to "fulfill the law" through loving service toward one another.

The role of v. 6 in all of this is a singular mystery; but whatever else, it serves in a transitional way between vv. 1-5 and 7-10, and seems to fit more easily with the former than the latter, even though it uses language that anticipates the latter.

Verse 1. Both the grammar and the language of this verse indicate that Paul is not starting something new, but rather is applying to their own situation what he has just been arguing. Thus he begins with the vocative, "brothers and sisters," which marks a turn in the argument; but his first clause is a present general conditional sentence, which in other cases in Paul always carries on some matter from the preceding sentence. People of the Spirit are to live by the Spirit, he has just urged (v. 25); and that means no envy, conceit, or provocation of others (v. 26). To the contrary, he now urges on them an expression of life in the Spirit that is quite the opposite.

The example offered describes a believer in the most vulnerable kind of situation – a person who is guilty of a transgression known by others. Paul's verb in this case (προλημφθῇ), when used in the passive as here, can mean either "to be detected in" or "to be overtaken, surprised by" something. At issue is whether the man himself is "overtaken by" some transgression which is known by others, or whether the others have "detected" the man in his transgression. While the latter is the more common view, the former seems to fit the context better. Here is a brother who has not gone seeking sin, but who found himself in a situation where he easily fell into some form of "wrongdoing" (παραπτώματι, for which the English word "sin" is probably much too strong). And in any case, there is not a hint that we are here dealing with ongoing behavior. But in either case his transgression has become known to others in the believing community.

The surprise comes in how Paul urges the community to handle the brother's "transgression." Rather than with "provocation" or "empty conceit," those who live by the Spirit should see to it that the fallen one is fully restored to his former condition. This means, of course, that they not act as "normal human beings" (= people without the Spirit) do under such circumstances and either neglect or disgrace the fallen one. Here is the touch of realism, both the fallenness of the one and the susceptibility of all others, that should keep one from ever reading 5:16-25 in a triumphalistic way. God's newly formed people, through Christ's death and resurrection and the gift of the Spirit, are not thereby instantly perfected. When God's people receive the Spirit, it is not "divine perfection" that sets in, but "divine infection," an "infection" that is to work its way into every bone and sinew, as it were. But in the process, such people are sometimes "overtaken by a transgression," and such people (that is, "we") are not to be scorned, but are to be "restored."

Those who are to do the "restoring work" of grace are designated by Paul as "you who live by the Spirit" (οἱ πνευμάτικοι), that is, "you who, in keeping with v. 25, live by and in conformity to the Spirit." The context simply demands this understanding. Indeed, to render this phrase with the lower case, "you who are spiritual," as in most English translations, not only undermines it in terms of meaning for a contemporary English-speaking person, but also leads to connotations that are precisely the opposite of Paul's intent. With this word he is not, as some would have it, addressing a special group within the community who are, or think they are, "spiritual," who must restore the fallen one because both he and others in the community are (presumably) not "spiritual." In such a case, Paul would surely have said, "*those* who are spiritual." Rather, Paul is addressing the entire community ("*you* [plural] who are Spiritual" = "you who live by the Spirit"), just as he has with all the second person plurals that have immediately preceded this sentence.

Paul's point is to remind them of who indeed they are in Christ – people of the Spirit, who walk by the Spirit and live in keeping with the Spirit, and thus do not carry out the desire of the flesh to "eat and devour one another" (v. 15). If a distinction is to be made at all, it would be between those who are in fact already living by the *imperatives* in vv. 16, 18, 22–23, and 25, as over against those who are responsible for the works of the flesh that are disrupting the life of the community – which "doing [certain aspects of] the law" does nothing at all to impede. But in fact Paul himself does not make even that distinction.

Paul's concern, therefore, by using this form of direct address, is to tie together everything that has just been said about the life of the Spirit vis-à-vis the flesh as it relates to the specific behavioral ills that have crept into this community. That this is his intent is ensured by the final clause, "looking out for your own selves,[28] lest you also be tempted." To be a person of the Spirit does not make one an elitist or "pneumatic" in the midst of others who are not so. As all the preceding imperatives imply, a Spirit person is not a perfect person, but one who by the Spirit's empowering lives in keeping with the life the Spirit produces (the fruit of the Spirit). But such people are also always susceptible to temptation – the more so if they think not! And Paul's point is that it is exactly our common vulnerability that causes people of the Spirit to restore the fallen, rather than to kick them while they are down, as many of us are so prone to do.

That this is Paul's concern is further corroborated by his description of the means whereby Spirit people are to restore the vulnerable one. They are to do so "by the Spirit's gentleness," one of the fruit of the Spirit listed in v. 23. Historically this phrase has been interpreted to refer to the *attitude* of the restoring one, that is, "with a gentle spirit," which the TNIV reduces to "gently"! But that seems to run roughshod over the context itself, where Paul has referred to

---

[28] For the purist, Paul's grammar breaks down a bit here, in that this participle is singular, while the verb it modifies is plural. But here is the plain evidence that even though this is a community concern, one is tempted and overtaken by sin individually.

"gentleness" as a fruit of the Spirit. Furthermore, this is the *only* meaning this word has had both in the immediate context and throughout the whole of Galatians; indeed, it is difficult to imagine that this connection would have been lost on the Galatians themselves. Thus, it is with this fruit in evidence that one is to restore the fallen brother or sister. "Gentleness" (πραΰτης) is what is called for – humility toward oneself and considerateness regarding others – and that as the fruit of the Spirit, not some merely human disposition.

The net result, therefore, is that the entire sentence is a direct application of the point of the argument (from 5:13) to a specific congregational matter. This is how "freedom from Torah" manifests itself. This is how as servants they love one another and so fulfill Torah. And this is what it means to walk by the Spirit so as not to carry out the desire of the flesh.

Verse 2. Although the matter just spoken to is probably to be included under the rubric "bear one another's burdens," the lack of a nuancing connective ("so," "therefore," etc.) in this sentence suggests that this verse is a somewhat independent exhortation, but one which the preceding imperative has brought to mind. The connection therefore probably lies with the vulnerability of the erring one. Not only must the Spirit-led Galatians care for such people, but they must go beyond that by "bearing one another's burdens," lifting the load of the weak and needy, as it were. Since such "burden bearing" is further described as "filling to the full the law of Christ," one can be sure that with this sentence the Galatians are being brought back in a practical way to 5:13-15, especially v. 13. This is how one through love performs the task of a slave for one and for all.

But what does "the law of Christ" mean? Is Paul now suggesting, despite what he has just said in 5:23, that life in the Spirit is actually some new form of Torah, requiring observance or obedience? Hardly. The clue to this usage lies in three directions. First, regarding Pauline ethics, God's glory is their *purpose* (1 Cor 10:31), the Spirit is their *power*, love is the *principle*, and Christ is the *pattern*. As suggested above on v. 22, Christ serves as the pattern for the principle, love itself. Thus, the "law of Christ" is first of all an appeal not to some new set of laws or even to some ethical standards that the gospel imposes on believers, but to Christ himself, who in this letter has been deliberately described as "the one who gave himself for our sins" (1:4) and who "loved me and gave himself for me" (2:20). Thus he has already served as the paradigm for the argument in 5:13-14. In Horatius Bonar's

words, "It is the way the Master went, should not the servant tread it
still?"

Second, the combination of language – "fulfill" and "law of Christ"
– points back to 5:14, where similar language is used of love as
"fulfilling Torah." But at the same time, the choice of different verbs
is probably deliberate. In the one case Torah has been fulfilled
(πεπλήρωται) = brought to its full expression, so as no longer to be in
effect; in this case "the law of Christ" is "fulfilled" (ἀναπληρώσετε) =
"carry out its obligations," in every situation where in love believers
bear each others' burdens. Thus the "bringing-to-an-end fulfillment"
in the first instance (5:14) is to be understood in light of its obligations
now being carried out fully by those who, empowered by the Spirit,
live as Christ himself did.

Third, this turn of phrase in itself is one more gentle reminder that
life free from Torah and flesh, empowered by the Spirit, does not lead
to "lawlessness." Rather it leads to patterning one's life after the
ultimate expression of the law, namely, Christ, who through his death
and resurrection "bore the burdens" of one and all. Above all, Christ is
the one "who loved us and gave himself for us." This is the "law of
Christ" which people of the Spirit are called to reproduce by means of
the Spirit.

Verse 3. Paul follows this appeal to the "law of Christ" with a
sentence that has caused interpreters no end of difficulty: "If any of
you think you are something when you are nothing, you deceive
yourselves." The difficulty that many have had here can be seen in the
several English translations that offer no rendering of the (apparently)
explanatory "for" (γάρ) with which the sentence begins.[29] But Paul is
rarely – if ever – careless with his use of this conjunction, so the
sentence must be taken seriously as having some form of explanatory
value to what has preceded. Most likely, therefore, in light of the new
"law" as just articulated, this sentence brings the Galatians back to
5:26. Those who are conceited, thinking too highly of themselves, are
both self-deceived and unable to carry out the law of Christ; such
people are *not* living in conformity to the Spirit.

Thus this sentence picks up the theme of "pride" from 5:26, but
now in light of its opposites spelled out in vv. 1-2. The person who is
too full of self-interest to show loving concern for a brother or sister
who stumbles, who instead is quite ready to gossip such failure all over

---

[29] Besides the T/NIV, see the REB (who actually begin an new paragraph here!),
NJB, NLT, GNB.

the community – often under the guise of concern(!) – by that very action suggests that they "think they are something" when in fact they "are nothing." These are the kind of "pious saints" who would never consciously think of themselves as "something," yet they stand self-deceived before God, because their gossip is a form of exalting themselves ("I wouldn't think of doing such a thing") in light of another's failure. Such "saints" are not keeping in step with the Spirit at all.

Verses 4-5. In immediate response to the self-deception just described, Paul urges that such people who are unwilling to bear the burden of another by way of restoration, should turn their "examination" of others into "self-examination." But in making this point, Paul seems to offer advice that contradicts what has just been said. If we assume, however, as we should, that Paul does not intend such self-contradiction, and if we further assume, as we also should, that these sentences are part of the present package, then Paul's point seems manageable. Unwillingness to restore someone overtaken by a sin indicates "pride" and "self-deceit" for which these sentences offer a twofold remedy. First, in v. 4a he attacks the problem of "self-deceit": "each of you should test your own actions." Second, in v. 5 he offers the workable alternative: "each of you should carry your own load."

Our difficulties lie with the intervening explanation (of the first remedy), that by "testing one's own actions," then [literally] "each one has the boast with reference to oneself only and not with reference to the other." Part of the solution to this difficult clause lies with Paul's ambiguous use of the word "boast" (καύχημα). In 1 Cor 1:26-31, where he picks up this language from Jer 9:23-24 (LXX), it has to do with "putting one's confidence in" either one's own strengths or in the Lord. In other cases Paul uses it quite negatively, either with regard to the object of one's "boasting" (Rom 4:2) or of the Corinthians' "boasting" about their stance with God while tolerating gross immorality in their midst (1 Cor 5:6). In still other instances he uses it quite positively with regard to his being in the presence of God and Christ at the end (2 Cor 1:14; Phil 2:16). Here, unless it is a form of mild irony, the usage is probably intended to be generally positive. When one carries out the imperative of v. 4a, "putting one's own 'work' to the test," then one may have confidence in that "work" alone.[30] The negative side of that, "not with regard to 'the other person'," is then simply a way of indicating that people should first of

---

[30] The word "alone" (μόνον) was unfortunately omitted from the NIV/TNIV; but it seems necessary to the sense of the passage.

all "mind their own business" – in a good sense. For when they mind someone else's "business" without proper self-assessment, they end up condemning the one "caught in a sin," rather than restoring such a person with the Spirit's gentleness.

Paul recognizes clearly that what allows a person to think of themselves as better than the person who has fallen into sin is a form of pride that is in fact self-deception (v. 3). The remedy for such is a kind of healthy self-examination that allows each person "to boast" regarding oneself *only*, and thus not fall into the odious comparisons that are merely expressions of self-deception. In that sense, each person "will carry[31] his or her own load."[32]

Verse 6. If one were to make a list of puzzling sentences in Paul's letters, this one would come very near the top, not so much in terms of what it says, but as to what it is doing at this point in the letter. So much is this so that both the editors of our Greek texts and English translators show considerable ambivalence as to what to do with it. Usually it is placed at the beginning of the next paragraph, where it appears to make almost no sense at all, unless one actually wants to argue that it somehow introduces the final wrap-up regarding the Spirit and the "flesh" in vv. 7-8 and the concluding exhortations in vv. 9-10. A better option would be to make no decision on this matter at all and make it a paragraph of its own, as in the NIV, NRSV, and NASB; but that solves nothing in terms of context. The TNIV, on the other hand, has chosen to place it as the concluding word in the present paragraph. In any case, the reason for its appearance at this point in the letter remains a singular mystery, although a case can be made for its placement in the TNIV, as an immediate response to v. 5 – that carrying one's own load should not be taken so far as to neglect the needs of the one who teaches.

The sentence itself is straightforward and does not need a great deal of comment. In keeping with both the prevailing rabbinic tradition and that of some Greco-Roman philosophers, where the student or disciple was expected to provide for the teacher, Paul urges the Galatian believers to share their "good things" with the one who instructs them in "the word." Examples of this can be seen, for

---

[31] The verb in this case is not subjunctive, as the TNIV, but future indicative. This is what one *will* do when proper self-examination has taken place.

[32] In a most remarkable turning of Paul's sentence on its head, the Amplified Bible "amplifies" by suggesting that this final clause means, "For every person will have to bear (be equal to understanding and calmly receive) his own [little] load [of oppressive faults]."

example, in the Gospel accounts, where in John 4:8 we are told in passing that Jesus' disciples "had gone into the town to buy food." Even more to the moment is the reminder in Luke 8:1-3 that Jesus had many women among his itinerant disciples, some of whom provided for all of them "out of their own means." The present passage could serve as another bit of evidence of this phenomenon.

While this sentence is often seen as the earliest evidence of "paid ministry," that can hardly be substantiated from what is actually said. First of all, there is no evidence that the language "share in all good things" had to do with "money" or "payment"; in fact it occurs in several contexts in Luke's Gospel to refer to an abundance of food or other temporal blessings (Luke 1:53; 12:18-19). Moreover in Paul's own letters there are several passing references to the fact that he and his companions have been "cared for" by the largess of others (2 Cor 11:8-9; Phil 4:10, 14-16); and when in a later letter he speaks of "workers receiving their 'wages'" (1 Tim 5:17-18), he is simply quoting Jesus, where "wages" is used in a context of being cared for by "eating and drinking whatever they give you" (Luke 10:17).

One must also be careful not to equate "the word" in this sentence with Scripture as such. For Paul it simply refers to the substance of what is being taught, and most often has to do with the gospel message itself. Thus in its first occurrence in his letters, where Paul speaks of the Thessalonians as welcoming "the word," the TNIV appropriately renders it "the message," meaning the gospel that he preached (cf. 1 Thess 1:6; Col 4:3). All of this to say, then, that the sentence fits well within Paul's own understanding both of Jesus and of other such itinerant teachers, even though in this case he is almost certainly not referring to himself, but to the more permanent "teachers of the gospel" in Galatia itself. After all, the last thing he would need in this instance would be an accusation from them that he was after their money or supplies.

Galatians 6:7-10 – The Wrap-up: Doing Good to All

> [7] *Do not be deceived: God cannot be mocked. People reap what they sow.* [8] *Those who sow to please their sinful nature, from that nature^a will reap destruction; those who sow to please the Spirit, from the Spirit will reap eternal life.* [9] *Let us not become weary in doing good, for at the proper time we will reap a harvest if we do not give up.* [10] *Therefore, as we have opportunity, let us do good to all people, especially to those who belong to the family of believers.*
>
> ^a8 Or *their flesh, from the flesh*

Despite occasional suggestions to the contrary, these words are best understood as Paul's bringing to conclusion the argument that began at 5:13. Several matters of structure and content not only indicate such a view, but also seem to verify the basic correctness of the point of view here presented regarding this whole section.

First, all four verses clearly hold together as a unit. The opening warning and citing of what appears to be a common proverb in v. 7 leads directly into the application of the proverb in v. 8 in terms of the argument to this point. This in turn becomes the basis for the final exhortation and promise in v. 9, now in terms of "doing what is good." Finally, v. 10, picking up the motif of "doing good," brings both this paragraph and the argument from 5:13 to conclusion with a final application in the form of exhortation. This holds together too nicely to be either accidental or random.

Second, in his application of the harvest metaphor in v. 8 Paul brings together one more time the twin motifs that have dominated the entire argument from 5:13 – life in the Spirit over against life in the flesh – and does so by way of warning and encouragement in light of the eschatological outcome of each kind of life, thus reflecting the conclusion to the vice list in 5:21 To "sow unto the Spirit" is but another way of pressing the imperatives, expressed and implied, that dominate vv. 16-26 ("walk by the Spirit," "being led by the Spirit," bearing the "fruit of the Spirit," "conforming one's life to the Spirit").[33] The harvest of such "sowing" is eternal life. Likewise, to "sow to the flesh" reflects the various opposites: "eating and devouring one another," doing the "works of the flesh," being "conceited, provoking one another, envying one another," "thinking oneself to be something when in fact one is nothing." Such sowing, as Paul has already asserted in 5:21, reaps non-inheritance, now expressed in terms of "corruption" (φθορά), pointing to the total dissolution of such things in the last days.

Third, the obvious point of the whole is a combination of warning and exhortation based on the harvest metaphor, with its clearly eschatological orientation. That the penultimate word of this whole section should be one of warning is particularly noteworthy. Such warning, we have noted above, lay just below the surface at several points (especially 5:21), and on the surface in 5:15 in the language

---

[33] Some (e.g. Burton, 342-43) have argued for the human spirit here, but everything stands against such an option: the context, Pauline usage, and especially the contrast between "one's *own* flesh" and "*the* Spirit" (a point understood as early as Jerome).

"beware lest you consume one another." Here is the final warning that they desist in such "works of the flesh," for such sowing reaps destruction. Why else such a warning, one wonders, if the whole section has not been tailored to the conflict setting within the Galatian communities.

Fourth, that the final word of the whole should be one of encouragement toward "working at what is good for all, especially for those of the household of faith" is also noteworthy. This is what everything has been about. Those who are Christ's, who live by the Spirit, are thus no longer under Torah; its day has gone. But Spirit people are not lawless; they live by "the law of Christ," meaning that in love they perform the duties of a slave for one another. The problem in Galatia has been that some believers appear to have been quite willing to come under Torah, to become observant so as to be identified as God's people. But Torah observance would have done them no good at the one crucial point of internal conflict within the communities. Thus they were willing to close the front door to their being "Gentile sinners" by becoming Torah observant; however, such "coming under Law" became a matter of self-deception. It allowed them to open the back door to every kind of internal strife. Or to change metaphors, it allowed them to paint the barn red, but leave the dung inside. Real righteousness, that which is expressed in the "law of Christ," means to live in love, serving one another rather than biting one another, bearing one another's burdens rather than provoking one another; it means to live by the power of the Spirit so as not to carry out the desire of the flesh, but rather to evidence the fruit of the Spirit. Thus the final word is that they sow to the Spirit, by working for the good of all, and especially for the good of those within their own communities – the point of the whole section and of this final warning and exhortation in particular.

Verse 7. With another second person plural imperative, the third and final one in this section (cf. vv. 1-2), Paul appears to pick up from what he has just urged in the preceding sentence, but does so as a way of introducing his final wrap-up of the applicational argument that began in 5:13. On the one hand, the metaphor of sowing and reaping fits well with the requirement that those who are taught should "share all good things with their instructor," and is thus very likely to be understood in this light as a general truism. On the other hand, Paul makes no special point of it in the sentence itself; and what follows in vv. 8 and 9 indicates that the primary intent of the verse is to introduce these final wrap-up sentences.

Two matters are of special interest. First, Paul puts the need for sharing "in all good things" into the larger context of the way God has arranged the world of agriculture. So he begins with the imperative, "Do not deceive[34] yourselves," because the truism is that "one reaps what one sows." That Paul's first interest is with the application that follows is made certain by the introductory "because" (ὅτι) that begins v. 8, which is intended as an explanatory follow-on to this opening truism. And what is explained in v. 8 goes far beyond the matter of sharing "good things" with one's teacher.

Second, by putting what follows in the context of "mocking God," Paul highlights the seriousness of the truism with regard to their walking by the Spirit and thus keeping in step with the Spirit (5:16, 25). Thus the context, and the specific application in v. 9 of "doing what is good" and doing so "to all," especially to fellow believers (v. 10), indicates that Paul is using this metaphor as a way of introducing his concluding remarks to all that has preceded, beginning at 5:13.

Verse 8. This double-edged sentence about "sowing" to the flesh or Spirit now applies the general metaphor stated in v. 7: the one who "sows" to the flesh reaps destruction; the one who "sows" to the Spirit reaps life eternal. What is "sown" is almost certainly to be understood in terms of all that has preceded since 5:13. The two prepositional phrases, to sow "into" the Spirit/flesh and to reap "from" the Spirit/flesh, which seem a bit strange to our ears, simply keep the metaphor alive. As in 5:16-17 the flesh comes close to being personified, standing in perfect parallel with the Spirit as it does. In terms of the metaphor, these are the two kinds of "soil" *into* which one puts the seed, and *from* which one reaps the harvest. Our difficulty is basically one of translation, since for us the two kinds of "soil" do not fit well with the metaphor of "planting"; thus, we may make the slight change "unto the flesh/Spirit."

But the point of the metaphor seems clear. To live out of selfish ambition, to give way to outbursts of rage, to sow discord and provoke hostility, to give way to sexual indulgence or excesses like drunkenness – this is to "sow unto *one's own* flesh." This is to give way to behavior that is just like that of those who do not belong to Christ. And as Paul has already said of them in 5:21, such "sowing" will reap

---

[34] Although translated the same way in English, this is not the same verb that Paul used in v. 3, although both verbs have the same sense. The verb φρεναπατᾷ in v. 3 occurs only there in the NT, and has the implication of "mislead concerning the truth" (BDAG), while here it is the more normal verb for "deception" as such (πλανάω).

destruction, for the flesh stands in utter and unyielding contradiction to the ways of God. Alternatively, to perform the tasks of a slave for one another, to restore the fallen, to bear the burdens of another, to have a proper estimation of one's own worth, to bear with those who are hostile or slow to come along – this is to "sow unto the Spirit." This is to walk by the Spirit, to conform one's behavior to the Spirit by whom one now lives on this side of the cross and resurrection. The final result of such eschatological salvation is its consummation, eternal life itself.

The difference between this final call to life in the Spirit and those that have preceded is the clear eschatological focus of this final one. The eschatological consummation of each kind of life has already been mentioned in 5:5 ("by the Spirit we await the hope of righteousness") and in 5:21 ("those who do the works of the flesh will not inherit the kingdom"). Now this motif is the direct and express concern. Paul's point is that the eschatological outcome is determined by whether one is living from the flesh or by the Spirit. In 5:21 the outcome of life in the flesh was expressed in terms of unbelievers, people who live like this as a way of life. At the same time, of course, it served as warning to people of the Spirit who would remain in such behavior themselves. Here that same point is made as an unmistakable warning. Those who would persist in living on the basis of the flesh have by that very fact opted out of life in the Spirit. Again, this has nothing to do with being "overtaken in a trespass"; it has to do with not coming under "obedience to the truth," resisting life in the Spirit for the indulgence of one's own sinfulness. Paul undoubtedly intends such warnings to be taken seriously.

Nonetheless, warning is never the final word for Paul. The outcome for God's people, who by definition are those who "sow unto the Spirit," is the final realization of the "hope of righteousness" – eternal life. But as before, Spirit life is not automatic; it means the making of choices. One must *sow* to the Spirit, that is, one must walk in the sphere of the Spirit by the Spirit's empowering; having been given life by the Spirit, one must live in conformity to what the Spirit wills, as illustrated in the fruit of the Spirit. Such fruitfulness is neither automatic nor optional. Hence, as before, all of this comes by way of imperative. The Spirit is sufficient; Torah never was. But the believer must go in the direction the Spirit leads. And such "sowing" has the promise of full harvest.

Lying being the final clause, "shall from the Spirit reap eternal life," is Paul's view of the Spirit as the primary reality of our eschatological existence as "already" and "not yet." The same Spirit who gives life (5:25; 2 Cor 3:6) is the same Spirit by whom we await our final hope (5:5) and because of whose presence within/among us we shall also enter into the final consummation of that life. This usage, therefore, reflects the same reality as one finds elsewhere in Paul with the metaphors "down payment," "seal," and "firstfruits." The Spirit is both the evidence of our having entered into life in the present and the ground and guarantee of our final, full realization of that life.

Verse 9. Paul now applies the truth of v. 8 with a penultimate hortatory word that re-emphasizes the eschatological conclusion of "sowing to the Spirit." He does so by focussing on one fruit of the Spirit – goodness. "Let us not grow weary in doing good," he urges, "for at the proper time we will reap a harvest," he promises by inspiration of the Spirit. Here is the clear evidence that "goodness" is not an abstract noun. Rather, as a fruit of the Spirit, goodness means to keep on doing good, continually, without flagging or growing weary at it. A singularly unfortunate part of the heritage of the Protestant Reformation has been to read Galatians in terms of salvation as either "by works (in general)" or "by faith" – unfortunate, because these final two sentences (vv. 9-10) put special emphasis on "good works," that is, "working at/doing [ποιοῦντες] what is good." The "works" that Paul has renounced throughout are singularly those "works of law" that gave Jews their unique identity in the Diaspora. But "good works" themselves have high priority in Pauline theology, as long as they are not understood in terms of religious duties or requirements. Indeed, in v. 10 they are identified as "working/doing *what is good* – what is life-giving – *to all people*"; it is the turning of this into religious duties that is as much an anathema to God as are the "works of law" Paul speaks so strongly against in this letter.

Paul concludes this sentence by returning to the theme of reaping from the preceding sentence. As we thus "sow to the Spirit," we shall accordingly reap "in due season" ("at the proper time" TNIV), provided of course that we continue to do so all of our lives long. Thus with two different verbs, full of metaphorical grist, Paul emphasizes for the Galatians that their "doing what is good" is neither to be spasmodic nor to come to an end. With one's "neighbor" still in focus, as v. 10 makes clear, and typically including himself in the process,[35] Paul urges first that "we" not "lose our enthusiasm" (BADG)

---

[35] For this phenomenon in Galatians, see the comment on 3:13-14 above; cf. 4:5, 31; 5:1, 25.

for doing what is good, and second, that "we" not be so overcome with weariness that we "lose heart" in the process. All of this to say that "doing what is good" for one and for all is the lifetime occupation of the person who "sows to the Spirit."

Verse 10. With a final "therefore,"[36] Paul brings the entire argument of Galatians, including these final exhortations, to its/their fitting conclusion. Again reflecting on the lifelong aspect of "doing what is good," this time with the metaphor of "having time" (= as long as "we" have life and strength), Paul now urges that, given opportunity to do so, "we do what is good unto all people." This concern should not be minimized by the final clause that focuses especially on the believing community. Changing verbs, he urges that we "work at [ἐργαζώμεθα] what is good," with other people as the recipients of such "good work."

Nonetheless, and quite in keeping with the thrust of the entire section, the final word focuses "especially" on "those who are members of the household of the faith" – "the faith" that has come with Christ (3:25-26), which expresses itself in love and "faith-fulness" within the believing community. This will be the certain evidence that "having begun by the Spirit," they are also "finishing by the Spirit" (3:3). It is of high interest, therefore, that in a letter where Paul comes down so hard on "doing works of law," he concludes with a repeated emphasis on "doing" (v. 9) and "working at" (v. 10) good works, that is, on doing what is for the good of one and all. One is not saved by so doing; but all truly saved people will give evidence of the Spirit's presence (without which there is no "salvation") by "doing good" through Christ-like actions.

The body of the letter thus concludes on the same note with which the argument proper began in 3:1-5. As was noted there, the ultimate contrast in Galatians is not between "works" and "faith," but between life under Torah and life by the Spirit. Life under Torah means to come under the very curse from which Christ has set us free; moreover life under Torah does not lead to righteousness, either in terms of relationship with God or in terms of godly behavior. Only the Spirit, who appropriates the righteousness secured through Christ's death and resurrection, can bring life and effect righteousness of the real kind. So having begun by the Spirit, the Galatians are urged to finish by the Spirit. And this, not only because here alone is the way of

---

[36] Paul's Greek here is the combined form ἄρα οὖν, which he tends to use when making final applications in his letters, either of a preceding argument or of the letter as a whole (cf. 1 Thess 5:6; 2 Thess 2:15; Rom 5:18; 7:25; 14:12, 19; Eph 2:19).

life in Christ, but also because here alone is God's own antidote to the life of the flesh. Christ's death provided both freedom from Torah observance and crucifixion with regard to the former way of life; the Spirit appropriates this freedom in such a way that the believer neither lives under the slavery of the law nor makes provision for the indulgence of the flesh. But to "finish" by the Spirit means to walk by the Spirit; it means, in the final words of the argument, to sow to the Spirit by doing (lit. "working"!) what is good to all people, especially those of one's own family in Christ.

Reflection and Response – Part Five

Reflection

This concluding argument to Paul's letter to the churches of Galatia turns out to be one of his finest moments. In effect it is the earliest Christian expression of the "two ways" phenomenon that flourished in the ancient world, although certainly not intentionally so on the part of Paul. In his argument the "two ways" are mutually exclusive, and whatever else, they are not two ways of being Christian. The key to everything is to be found in the One who eventually came to be known as the third person of the Trinity, the Holy Spirit.

At the same time, since the passage is eminently "practical" in the sense that it has to do with how Christian theology works its way out in everyday life, there would seem to be endless ways that one could reflect on this passage. The place to begin, it seems to me, is precisely where Paul himself begins – with the love command. For here is the divine disclosure as to what is absolutely paramount for life in the world. The problem sometimes lies with the second word in the phrase, "love *command*," since that language turns what should be fundamental in a person's character into a command that one must obey. But love does not function well as a command, since love flows out of one's rebirth into God's likeness, or it does not exist at all. After all, love begins when someone else's need is more important than my own. Love has to do with caring for "the other," not with my own feelings. It is the law of Christ, who "loved me/us and gave himself up for me/us."

Moreover, it is precisely because our fallenness has taught us to "look out for number one," that love is not natural to us. It is supernatural, and thus requires the infilling of the Holy Spirit. I think it is fair to say that the primary reason for breakdown in marriages lies with the fact that most of us get married because of deep "feelings of love" for our partner, but in time that turns into wanting the other person to "meet my needs." Indeed, it was a very wise man who many years ago observed that most of us love our spouses the way we ourselves want to be loved, rather than the way they wish – or more importantly, need – to be loved. And in the Christian community love means not simply "putting up with" some people whom we either don't really like or find ourselves uncomfortable to be with; rather, it means asking divine help, and then in the power of the Spirit to treat those people, to "bear their burdens" as it were, in ways that reflect the character of Christ.

But there is more. Love as the first fruit of the Spirit expresses itself in joyful fellowship with others, and especially as one seeks the "peace" (shalom) of not only individual believers but of the community as a whole. And it especially calls on us to care for each other with the two-sided fruit of "forbearance" and "kindness." How many petty differences would never surface in a Christian community, if we all as a community actively pursued love in this way.

That brings me to reflect on one of the real issues that is constantly raised with me when taking a class through Galatians. "But how do we get there?" someone asks; "how does this almost idealistic way of life get down to shoe-leather level?" Paul's answer is the only one: "walk by the Spirit." And immediately I am asked, but how does do that in everyday life? The only answer that one can give, which may sound facetious to some, is to return to the metaphor itself. How does one walk at all? Answer: one step at a time. Contrary to what most of us would hope to be true, with the infilling of the Spirit instant "perfection" does not set in; rather it is a case of instant "infection." And the infection must work its way out into every pore of our being. My experience is that most of us want "holiness" given to us in a more passive way. But "walking" does not mean "standing," it means to be active in pursuit of loving my neighbor as myself.

As one who has spent his entire lifetime within the Pentecostal tradition (born into a Pentecostal preacher's home in 1934), it would have been easy to become a bit jaundiced when reflecting on the biblical picture of life in the Spirit and watching it work out in the everyday life of the "saints." Indeed, only one of my several boyhood companions in the church is still following the Lord at all. While there are many reasons for this, the one that started many on a path of negligent skepticism was the all-too-frequent disparity between how some of the "saints" talked their faith and how they actually lived it at home or in the neighborhood. One of my own less-than-happy memories of growing up in the Pentecostal tradition is a somewhat jaundiced memory of "saints" who were big on the final virtue "self-control" – in the form of "abstinence"(!) – but all too short on many of the other virtues in Paul's list of "fruit."

Unfortunately that was also accompanied by a more deadening reality: the fact that, as has often happened historically with renewal movements, certain habits of lifestyle developed, which in time also served to give believers their identity. Thus, the list of things banned was long and important, while at the same time the actual "fruit of the Spirit" were at the short end of the stick. The irony was that what Paul claimed for the "strong," namely eating and drinking as one wishes, came to be identified as belonging to "the weak"! So without intent these "saints" were especially good at singling out the trans-gressors who did not toe the "holiness" line as they defined it, but they also frequently crossed the line with regard to the eight "deeds of the flesh" that dominate that list: "discord; selfish ambitions; factions; envy" and the like.

Fortunately, they were not the only "saints" I knew. Here the list is especially long; and what is true of almost every person on this list is that they were "saints" without especially trying to be so. The kingdom is full of such people, who without fanfare or public notice give evidence of the fruit of the Spirit by the way they live for the sake of others. And in many cases, the nice thing is that they are quite unaware of it. They have walked by the Spirit so long and so well that their first concern is with the needs of others; they are also the ones who by the Spirit's gentleness seek to restore the fallen one rather than to make the failure known to others – especially not piously in prayer! May their tribe increase.

A final word is in order here, especially for those of us who have a frequent sense that there is too much distance between what we read here and life as we live it day by day in the everyday world. I take courage that even concern over such distance between the ideal and the real is a work of the Spirit, without whose promptings and reminders one could very easily settle into a coasting toward mediocrity. And this is also why the basic assumption of this whole passage has to do with life in the community of faith, not life as an individual believer in isolation from the rest. It is as we learn to be loved and forgiven within the believing community that we also learn so to love and forgive.

Response

Perhaps the following questions may serve as helpful guides to walking in the Spirit, while avoiding the pitfalls of "standing" or "sitting" in the Spirit! Do I take time consciously to be reminded in prayer and meditation, prompted by the Spirit, to think in terms of "walking by the Spirit"? How would/does such conscious application of the text affect my life today in relation to others, including my family? What is my role in the community of faith when the kind of bickering and infighting takes place that Paul denounces in 5:15 and 26? Am I a part of the problem? Am I a peacemaker? Or am I the announcer of God's judgment on the guilty ones (!)? Have I learned well the difference between the need to be "right" and the need to be "good," when these two realities do not line up on the same side of a given failure in the church? And if I am in such a learning mode, how can I be a part of the solution and not part of the problem? Have I truly learned that this passage is not about me as an individual, but about us as a community of faith? And if so, how can I help to facilitate such an understanding within the community? Do I really believe, and demonstrate it by the way I act, that God the Holy Spirit is as concerned about my attitudes as such as he is about my actions? Am I truly ready to repent of my sins and failures in these matters? Or is my deeper concern to be "right" and win the day with those who might not as yet see it in a fully biblical way? Am I genuinely ready to repent regarding my failures here, and to seek forgiveness where necessary?

1. Focus on a time when you were especially carried along by the love of God manifested in the community, reflecting upon the circumstances and its effects on you.
2. If possible, find one or more members of the community through whom this love was expressed and remind them of how meaningful their love and support were at that time in your life.
3. Offer repentance to God in prayer for times when other concerns kept you from bearing this fruit of the Spirit in your life.
4. Reflecting upon the needs within your community of faith, become intentional about being an extension of God's love by being prepared to come along side a sister or brother in need, helping to support them in their time of need.

Galatians 6:11-18

The Text

Postscript: The Opponents One More Time

At the end of this letter, written with vigor and at times with great agitation, Paul takes the pen from his amanuensis (scribe) and brings it to conclusion with his own hand (v. 11). What we get is a genuine conclusion, in which he basically reiterates the significant matters of the letter. He begins with a final, especially strong, indictment of the agitators, who from his point of view are "compelling" the Galatians to be circumcised for two ignoble reasons: to avoid being persecuted because of the cross; and to "glory" in the "flesh" of the Galatians (vv. 12-13). As in 5:7-12, Paul sets this indictment in contrast to his own ministry: he will "glory" only in the cross they disdain (by their demanding circumcision); through that same cross he has died to the former way of life (the world; v. 14). The outcome: (in repetition of 5:6b) neither circumcision nor uncircumcision means a thing; the only thing that counts is the new creation that arises out of death through the cross. God's benediction, he concludes in v. 16, rests upon all who live by this rule (spelled out in v. 15); such people are God's true Israel. The net result is that the agitators should trouble him no further – either in Galatia or elsewhere – since he bears in his body the "marks of Christ," which thereby authenticate his ministry (v. 17).

Here, then, in conclusion are most of the great themes of the letter: (a) the genuineness of Paul's apostolic ministry, based strictly on the cross and Paul's continuation of the ministry of the cross in his own sufferings (cf. 1:10–2:14; 4:12-20; 5:10-11); (b) the cross has brought an end to Torah observance; any form of return to righteousness by law is to run roughshod over the cross and thus to glory in the flesh (cf. 2:15-21; 3:1, 10-29; 4:4-5; 5:2-6, 24); and (c) the cross which does away with circumcision does not thereby exalt the uncircumcised status of the Gentiles; rather both former states are irrelevant because of the work of Christ and the coming of the Spirit (5:5-6, 13-26). God's peace and mercy rest upon all who so believe and so live.

What is missing in all this is any mention of the Spirit; but that is simply assumed. The primary issue in the letter is the circumcision of Gentile men who have become followers of Christ. He had appealed to the work of the Spirit at the beginning of the major argument in the letter as the certain experienced evidence that they do not need to come under Torah (3:1-5); and at the end he appealed again to their life in the Spirit as God's provision for the practical outworking of righteousness at the behavioral level (5:16–6:10). But as he argued in 3:7–4:7, it was Christ himself, through his death and resurrection, who brought Torah observance to an end. Thus it is to this singular reality that he returns in this "wrap-up" paragraph.

Galatians 6:11-18

> [11] *See what large letters I use as I write to you with my own hand!*
>
> [12] *Those who want to impress others by means of the flesh are trying to compel you to be circumcised. The only reason they do this is to avoid being persecuted for the cross of Christ.* [13] *Not even those who are circumcised keep the law, yet they want you to be circumcised that they may boast about your circumcision in the flesh.* [14] *May I never boast except in the cross of our Lord Jesus Christ, through which the world has been crucified to me, and I to the world.* [15] *Neither circumcision nor uncircumcision means anything; what counts is the new creation.* [16] *Peace and mercy to all who follow this rule – to[a] the Israel of God.*
>
> [17] *From now on, let no one cause me trouble, for I bear on my body the marks of Jesus.*
>
> [18] *The grace of our Lord Jesus Christ be with your spirit, brothers and sisters. Amen.*

Verse 11. With this concluding word Paul is simply following a procedure for which there are hundreds of examples from the Greco-Roman world. The body of the letter would have been written from dictation by an amanuensis, who ordinarily would have had training both in penmanship and in taking dictation. Who among Paul's immediate companions would have had such training is simply unknown to us; the only one who also signed off on one of Paul's letters was Tertius in Rom 16:22, who in fact otherwise is unknown to us. Nonetheless, of his extant letters, only in this one does Paul expressly sign off the letter as he does here. Most likely he does so in this instance for the sake of the Galatians, so that no one could raise doubts as to its genuineness, as coming directly from the Apostle Paul himself.

Whether the mention of "large letters" has further significance also cannot be known, although it is certainly possible that it is related to the eye problems he mentions in 4:14-15. In any case, this is his way of calling attention to the fact that his "large letters" differ significantly from what one may assume to have been a smoother hand on the part of the amanuensis. Not only so, but since the majority of the recipients would not have been able to read, the reader himself would need to have shown the letter to them at this point; so Paul has simply called attention to the difference when he himself takes up the pen to draw the letter to its conclusion.

Verses 12-13. Given the cause and nature of this letter, it is no surprise that Paul's first concluding word is this fourfold indictment of the agitators. This is how the letter began – forcefully so, since an indictment of them has replaced the standard thanksgiving – and this is how the letter now concludes. Moreover, true to himself throughout the letter, Paul in vv. 14-15 sets their activity in striking contrast to his own; and the key issue for Paul is the cross. The absolute bottom line in all of this from Paul's perspective is that these agitators are not pressing the issue of circumcision for the Galatians' sakes but for their own. That is, they are not compelling you Galatian men to be circumcised because this will secure *your* salvation; they are doing so for their own sakes – to get "notches on their Bibles," as it were. To put this another way, Paul recognizes that these agitators know nothing about evangelism as such; they are not trying to win converts to Christ among pagan Gentiles. Rather they are deliberately going among Paul's converts, trying to persuade them to "complete" their salvation by being circumcised, and thus "truly" belonging to the ancient people of God. And so Paul blisters them, in four different ways, with the first and the fourth forming an inclusio to the whole indictment. Whether fully intentional on their part or not, here is what the agitators' trying to compel you Galatians to be circumcised amounts to.

First, Paul asserts that their primary goal is completely self-centered. With a nearly untranslatable word play, he asserts that they are trying "to impress others by means of the flesh." What they are trying to do, he tells the Galatians, does not have your interests as their primary focus; rather they are trying to "make a good showing"(BDAG) for themselves before others. And they are trying to do so "in the flesh," which first of all refers to the physical flesh cut off by circumcision, but which here also implies "before people," and thus "in the flesh" with all the negative implications that this word has had throughout the letter, having to do with "the sinful nature." Without putting it this way, Paul's point is that his Galatian brothers should not be deceived by these agitators, whose motives are altogether impure – although they most likely perceived of themselves as doing God, and thus the Galatians, a great favor.

Second, this desire to "make a good showing in the flesh" is accompanied by a desire to avoid persecution related to the cross of Christ. This is almost certainly an attributed motive on Paul's part, since it would be most unlikely deliberate on the part of the agitators. But what Paul sees clearly are the full implications of their desire to have the Galatians circumcised. This will put you Gentiles under the Jewish banner, and thus give you legitimacy in the eyes of Rome, whereas you are now suspect because as *Gentiles* you are followers of One whom the Romans crucified as a messianic pretender.

To appreciate what Paul is intending here, one needs to reflect momentarily on the scandal of the cross, as he articulates it in 1 Cor 1:18-25. The scandal rests in the fact of a "crucified Messiah," which stands at the very center of Christian faith, ultimate oxymoron that it is. "Messiah," after all, was the title for God's coming king who would subdue, and thus triumph, over all his enemies – including the terribly pagan, terribly self-exalting Roman Empire – while crucifixion was among the most heinous of all executions ever dreamed up by humankind. Only two kinds of people were crucified by the Romans, both non-citizens: runaway, or otherwise recalcitrant, slaves; and non-Roman insurrectionists. From the Roman point of view, Jesus of Nazareth died as a state criminal, guilty of insurrection, and proclaimed so by the wording attached to the cross: "Jesus of Nazareth: 'king' of the Jews." To worship Jesus as Lord was double jeopardy, since he had been executed by the Empire and the reigning Caesar (Nero in this case) was the only one to whom the attribution of "Lord" was to be made.

The way to avoid being "persecuted for the cross of Christ" would be to downplay the crucifixion in some way, while still maintaining active Christian faith. The way the agitators were doing so was by trying to bring these Gentile Christians under the banner of Judaism, which was a *religio licita*, a recognized and thus legitimized religion within the Roman Empire. Thus, whether intentional on their part or not, Paul recognizes the larger implications of their insisting on the circumcision of Gentiles: it would legitimize them with the Empire and thus "avoid being persecuted for the cross of Christ."

Third, and perhaps the most damning indictment of all, Paul charges that "not even those who are circumcised keep the law." In order to understand this charge, one must keep in mind the comments on 3:10-13 and 5:3. Paul's understanding of "keeping the law" meant that one was obliged to keep the *whole* law, not conveniently keep just selective parts of it. Thus it is not because the agitators do not keep the law at all that they are herewith condemned, but because they are arbitrarily selective in doing so; and from Paul's point of view that is precisely what one may not do and still be loyal to the law. It is the whole thing, or none; partial obedience is simply not an option.

Finally, fourth, and now back to the beginning, the agitators are ultimately judged by Paul because the only interest they have in the Galatians' being circumcised is for their own glory. From Paul's perspective they are merely in the "numbers" game, not truly concerned about the Gentiles' relationship to God as such. Picking up language from 6:4, Paul asserts that they simply wish (literally) to "boast about your in-the-flesh circumcision," with the emphasis again resting with the words "in the flesh." "Boasting," putting one's confidence in and glorying in something, is what drives the agitators. Thus, it is not the "circumcised heart" (Deut 30:6) that they care about, the point Paul himself will raise forcefully later in Rom 2:28-29, but only the (literal) circumcision of the flesh, which may make one a Jew outwardly, but will do nothing at all to curb the present infighting that is going on in the Galatian churches. Their goal is "boasting" in your flesh – a totally unworthy, basically anti-Christian motivation.

Verses 14-15. True to himself throughout the letter, Paul immediately sets his own ministry in the sharpest kind of contrast to that of the agitators – further evidence that they have consistently denigrated Paul in their pursuit of Galatian foreskins as trophies. Picking up on the accusation in v. 12 that they are trying to avoid being persecuted for the cross of Christ, Paul counters that the cross is his only "boast." On this word see the discussion in v. 4 above; here is a clear instance where it does not mean to "brag," but to put one's full confidence in something and thus to elevate it by "boasting" in it. While the agitators are intent on "boasting[in your flesh[ly circumcision]]," Paul's only "boast" is in the scandal they are trying to avoid, "the cross of our Lord Jesus Christ." And he says this with the strongest kind of negative asseveration, traditionally translated "God forbid" (μὴ γένοιτο). In its previous occurrence in this letter (2:17), in response to a rhetorical question, it was rendered by the TNIV, "Absolutely not!" The present rendering, "may I never boast," seems a bit weak for this idiom; the KJV had the better of it: "God forbid that I should boast except in the cross."

Returning to the theme of "the crucifixion of the flesh" in 5:24, Paul now puts that in very personal terms. The reason for Paul's "boast" is that the cross has been a place of twofold crucifixion for him. On the one hand, "the world has been crucified to me," meaning the world itself came under God's judgment on the cross, and therefore has no hold of any kind on him. And it is clear from this context that circumcision now belongs to "the world," and not to God. On the other hand, as he had earlier asserted in 2:20, he himself had died with Christ in his crucifixion, so that the only life now available to him is that of one "raised from the dead to live in newness of life" (Rom 6:4), lived now "by faith in the Son of God" (2:20). It is in this sense that "I have been crucified to the world." Sentences like this are best understood in light of Paul's own exposition of it earlier in 2 Cor 5:13–21, where he asserts that the whole world was brought under God's judgment when Christ died on the cross; and therefore the only people now truly "alive" are those raised to "newness of life" through Christ's resurrection.

That this is the right place to turn for an exposition of these tight sentences is made clear in v. 15. Picking up now for the third time in his letters,[1] Paul reasserts as his basic truism, that the death and resurrection of Christ have made circumcision totally irrelevant, so that *neither* state means a thing to God. One is not in God's favor by having been circumcised, nor is one out of his favor by not submitting to the Jewish identity rite. The only thing that now counts is "the new creation," brought about through Christ's bringing the old order to an end through his death and the new order into being through his resurrection. Thus, just as in 2 Cor 5:17, "if anyone is in Christ, the new creation has come: The old has gone, the new is here!" (TNIV). This is simply basic Pauline theology, which puts the whole letter into divine perspective and is stated at the very end for emphasis.

Verse 16. With that said, and with a deliberately joining "and,"[2] Paul concludes his brief encapsulation of the letter by announcing God's peace and mercy to rest with those who "live in keeping with"[3] this rule, the "rule," of course, referring to the content of v. 15. Paul's own emphases are borne out by his word order, which makes for nearly impossible English: "And as many as to this rule live in conformity, peace on them and mercy, even on the Israel of God." Both the introductory conjunction ("and") and the immediate reference to "this rule" indicate that he is here referring to the content of v. 15. The wish of "peace" on them picks up the traditional Jewish greeting ("shalom"), which has to do with full-orbed well-being, not just the cessation of hostility. Paul had already used it in its most Jewish form in 2 Thess 3:16 ("Now may the Lord of peace [= Christ himself] give you peace at all times and in every way"). For these Galatian believers,

---

[1] See on 5:6 above, and 1 Cor 7:19.
[2] For good reason left untranslated in most English versions.
[3] On Paul's verb here see the note on 5:25 above.

who obviously knew their Greek Bibles well, this is the final coup in the letter. God's shalom now rests on those who abide by the "rule" that "neither circumcision nor uncircumcision counts for anything" in terms of distinguishing people in their relationship with God. And not only so. Paul also desires for them to know God's mercy, a mercy that especially rests on those who abide by the new "rule" and thus do not need to earn God's favor by way of doing the law. Mercy, God's mercy, is what all people need, including (especially) the religious, who so often are without mercy to those who do not keep their form of law.

With a final kudo, Paul further distinguishes those who abide by this new "rule" and thus know God's shalom because they have experienced his mercy: they are in fact "God's Israel," a phrase that occurs only here in all of known Jewish literature. There have been some who would like to turn Paul's epexegetic "even" (signaled by the dash in the TNIV) into the conjunction "and," thereby suggesting that "God's Israel" refers to the Jewish people as such, even though they do not abide by this rule. But not only does that run counter to everything argued for in this letter, it throws a completely "red herring" into the mix – and that as the very last word in the letter proper. Indeed, it is hard to imagine a more self-defeating suggestion in the history of interpretation.

What Paul has done in fact is to make a final, deliberately "in your face," statement over against the agitators. They are trying to make Gentiles become a part of ancient Israel; Paul has spent the entire letter arguing vigorously against them. With this final coup he designates those who are truly Israel, God's Israel, as those who abide by the canon that the circumcision that the agitators are urging on these Gentiles counts for nothing. Christ is all and in all; and those who follow him are now designated by Paul with this neologism: they are "God's Israel," the real thing.

Verse 17. With what appears to be almost reluctance to let the letter go, Paul responds to what he has said in our verses 15 and 16 with a final personal note that echoes v. 14. "As for the rest," he says, meaning "from now on," let "no one cause me trouble." This is a fairly clear indication that the agitators were not just trying to make personal converts out of the believers in the Galatian churches, they were trying to do so at Paul's own expense, carrying on their crusade with very personal attacks against Paul himself. So at the end of the day, he has had enough. They can cease and desist, because Paul himself "bears on [his] body the marks of Jesus." Thus, not only has he fully identified with Christ in his crucifixion as such, so that he himself has experienced death and life through Christ, but he also has further identified with Christ in his sufferings themselves. Whatever these "marks" were in their actual expression, Paul sees them as identifying him as one who fully belongs to Christ. And every indication is that by implication these are exactly the identity marks, the true ones, that the agitators themselves lack.

Verse 18. In typical fashion Paul concludes the letter in the same way as it began, on a benedictory note of "grace," in this case following a benedictory note of "peace" (v. 16). Thus these two "benedictions" serve to enclose a letter that began with "grace to you and peace" (1:3). A similar grace-benediction has already concluded his earlier letters, either "with you" or "with you all" (1 & 2 Thess; 1 Cor; and, with elaboration, 2 Cor). This is the first instance where the "with you" comes in the form of "with your spirit"; it will occur three more times (Phil 4:23; Phlm 25; 2 Tim 4:22). One scarcely knows what to make of this phenomenon, especially since the later three letters in which it appears are full of affection for the recipients, which may also be true in this case, but seldom finds expression in the letter itself.

What is more striking is the fact that all of Paul's benedictions conclude with "the grace of our Lord Jesus" be with you, whereas the letters all begin with "grace to you and peace from God our Father and the Lord, Jesus Christ." But the wish of grace at the end in not grace that *comes from* Christ, but the grace that finds its greatest expression, and thus its ultimate meaning, in Christ. At the beginning of the letter their calling was expressed in terms of "in the grace of Christ;" and so the letter ends with "the grace of our Lord, Jesus Christ, be with you." That this is intentionally a benediction is made clear by the final "Amen."

But before the "amen," one final feature occurs here that is unique to Galatians in the entire corpus, namely his concluding with the vocative "brothers and sisters." It is as though Paul has a sixth sense that he has been a bit hard on his friends, so the last word is a reminder that whatever else, he and they are brothers and sisters in the same family of God. A good note on which to end such a forceful letter.

The "amen" as the very last word points to the presupposition that the letter was to be read aloud in the gathered assemblies, and was to be taken as a word from Christ himself, by his Spirit through his chosen servant, the Apostle Paul.

Reflection and Response – Part Six

Reflection

I toyed with not having a "reflection/response" section to this final wrap-up of the letter, since it is basically encapsulating what has been said throughout. But it occurred to me on further reflection that some such "reflection" might serve a useful purpose – even if only for myself as a good final reminder.

So while it is possible to reflect on this wrap-up material as yet one more bombast against the agitators who are playing havoc among the Galatian believers, one should perhaps reflect more closely on the single-mindedness that Paul demonstrates here. The great danger for those of us who have positions of leadership in the church is to assume at times that we also have the Apostle's authority when it comes to making sure that the church is "getting it right." And on this point I have considerable doubts! Whatever "authority" we might have in the church – and I doubt whether it is very much at all – it is totally derived, and it has nothing to do with position and everything to do with what has been earned by one's character, as that is in process of being shaped into Christ's own character by the indwelling Spirit.

And in any case, my experience with those keen on their own authority in the church is that to a person they are not very keen on being shaped by the cross. That is, they may preach the cross well as the means of salvation; but that is only part of Paul's concern in this passage. His greater concern has to do with living cruciform, to have his life "shaped" by, and in the likeness of, Christ's own crucifixion. If some of Paul's detractors think differently on this point, my guess is that they themselves have difficulty with the ultimate implications of this passage. And they surely have a warped sense of their own authority to speak judgmentally of one who, inspired by the Spirit, wrote such a letter to set us free from such judgments of others.

Finally, it was not until writing commentary on the final verse (18) that I realized this is the only letter where he concludes with the vocative, "brothers and sisters." Surely that is a telling moment. His disappointment over the Galatians' readiness to capitulate on the matter of law-keeping comes through in ever so many ways; and even in the tenderness of 4:12-20, his final metaphor is that of parent and child. On the other hand, he has addressed them as "brothers and sisters" (ἀδελφοί) no less that nine times in all in this letter; and given the nature of his scorching denunciation of the agitators in this closing passage, he reminds the Galatian communities that, apostle though he may be and is, his and their primary relationship is that of family.

Together they are God's children, who by the Spirit call out to him as *Abba*. This should serve as a helpful reminder to all who use this commentary who are also involved in Christian ministry. The people among whom we serve are not "my people"; they are Christ's people – and we and they are brothers and sisters.

Response
How does one respond to such a vivid affirmation of the cross as a way of life, except to pray, "Thy will be done"? And how does one respond to differences within the church community, except to be reminded by the Spirit, these are also my brothers and sisters? May it ever be so to every reader of Paul's letter to the Galatians.

1. Assess your relationship to the cross of Christ in terms of your identity and your sense of spiritual authority with regard to others within the Christian community by Paul's familial language of "brothers and sisters."
2. Identify those within the community you deem to be models of such a relationship to the cross.
3. Seek to integrate this theology of the cross into your daily life by being aware of the way in which identification with the cross informs your daily walk.
4. Be prepared in the next challenge brought about by differences within the community to pursue a course of action which is informed by the cross and reliant on the Spirit.

Bibliography

Barclay, John M.G. *Obeying the Truth*. Edinburgh: T & T Clark, 1988

Betz, Hans Dieter. *Galatians*. Hermeneia; Philadelphia: Fortress, 1979

Bruce, F.F. *Commentary on Galatians*. NIGTC; Grand Rapids: Eerdmans, 1982

Burton, E.D. *A Critical and Exegetical Commentary on the Epistle to the Galatians*. ICC; Edinburgh: T & T Clark, 1921

Dunn, James D.G. *The Epistle to the Galatians*. London: A. & C. Black, 1993

Hansen, G. Walter. *Galatians*. IVPNTC; Downers Grove: InterVarsity Press, 1994

Lightfoot, J.B. *The Epistle of St Paul to the Galatians*. Grand Rapids: Zondervan, 1957 (orig. 1865)

Longenecker, Richard N. *Galatians*. WBC 41; Dallas: Word, 1990

Martyn, Louis. *Galatians: A New Translation with Introduction and Commentary*. AB 33A; New York: Doubleday, 1997

Matera, Frank J. *Galatians*. SP 9; Collegeville, MN: Liturgical Press, 1992

Witherington, Ben III. *Grace in Galatia: A Commentary on Paul's Letter to the Galatians*. Grand Rapids: Eerdmans, 1998

Index of Names

Barclay, J.M.G.   200
Barr, J.   154
Betz, H.D.   6, 14, 15, 36, 85,
    110, 119, 149, 212, 216, 218
Bligh, J.   110
Bruce, F.F.   36, 110
Burkitt, F.C.   161
Burton, E.D.   36, 74, 110, 119,
    130, 133, 187, 237

Calvin, J.   110, 216
Chrysostom   209
Cole, R.A.   110

Danker, F.W.   32, 130, 138
Duncan, G.S.   61, 110
Dunn, J.D.G.   36, 46, 85, 92,
    140, 148

Erdman, C.R.   110

Fee, G.D.   24, 47, 50, 58, 82,
    107, 126, 141, 148
Fung, R.Y.K.   36, 110, 216

Grundmann, W.   154

Hannah, D.   165
Hansen, G.W.   36, 85
Hendriksen, W.   110

Jeremias, J.   154, 155
Jerome   237

Kasper, W.   148
Kern, P. H.   7

Lietzmann, H.   110
Lightfoot, J.B.   36, 46, 102, 106,
    110, 112, 119, 130, 137, 149
Longenecker, R.N.   36, 85, 110,
    211, 212, 216

MacDonald, W.G.   165
Martyn, J.L.   36, 65, 85
Matera, F.J.   14, 15, 36, 65, 85
Metzger, B.M.   44
Meyer, H.A.W.   110, 216
Michaelis, W.   110
Morris, L.   36
Mussner, F.   110

Ridderbos, H.   110

Sanders, E.P.   5
Schlier, H.   110
Stendahl, K.   209
Stowers, S.K.   11

Turner, N.   165

Wallace, D.B.   68, 74, 165, 177
Witherington, B.   14, 85

Index of Biblical References